**Explaining
Delinquency**

Explaining Delinquency

Construction, Test, and Reformulation of a
Sociological Theory

LaMar T. Empey
Steven G. Lubeck

with

Ronald L. LaPorte
University of Southern California

Heath Lexington Books
D.C. Heath and Company
Lexington, Massachusetts
Toronto   London

Second printing, October 1973

Published simultaneously in Canada.

Printed in the United States of America.

Standard Book Number: 669-74641-X.

Library of Congress Catalog Card Number: 70-158950

Table of Contents

vi

List of Figures

viii

List of Tables

xi

Preface

Some Suggestions for Review

The past twenty years have witnessed the flowering of a body of sociological theory whose most fundamental tenet is that official delinquency is a lower-class phenomenon. Class membership constitutes the precondition for a whole series of events which predispose lower-class young people to law-violating behavior and official condemnation.

This book is devoted to a test of that body of theory. Since the theoretical framework is highly complex, and since it poses some serious conceptual as well as research problems, the organization of the book will try to take them into account. The first chapter is devoted to an expanded narrative statement of the theory in which the pertinent literature is reviewed. Then, in the second chapter, the theory is stated in formal and operational terms so that precision can be applied to a test of it. In chapter 3, the research methodology is described—the samples on whom data were gathered, and the kinds of measurement that were used.

Following these introductory chapters, the remainder of the book is divided into three major sections. The first provides a test of the theory, proposition by proposition; the second tests the adequacy of the entire and complex sequence of events suggested by the theory, leading from membership in the lower-class, through poor achievement and strain, to identification with deviant groups and delinquency; finally, the last section is devoted to an assessment of implications and suggestions for theoretical reformulation in light of empirical findings.

A word is in order regarding the uses to which this book might be put. Since it is a research study, a great deal of attention has been paid to the problems of theory construction and research methodology, as well as to substantive findings. Consequently, the book might be reviewed in two ways.

For the person who is interested in the problems of logic and method, and in using the book as an aid to further inquiry, the entire work is recommended. For the person who is interested only in the substance and implications of the findings, a different review might be in order. After reading chapter 1, he may wish to review chapters 2 and 3 only briefly so that he might see how the theory was formalized and the study conducted. Then, rather than perusing all of the detailed findings in chapters 4 through 8, he may wish to read only the special summaries that have been provided at the introduction of each of these chapters. While some specifics will be missed, the main message will be obtained.

Finally, both readers will want to examine all of chapters 9-12. Chapter 9 is devoted to a reformulation of the original theory into several alternative models, and to a test of those models. The remaining chapters are then concerned with the implications of both these and other prior findings for future theory and research.

Acknowledgments

Like most research studies, this one is the result of contributions from many people and organizations. We would like to express our gratitude to:

the research staffs of the Provo and Silverlake Experiments whose dedicated service made the collection and preparation of data possible—Maynard L. Erickson, Max L. Scott, George E. Newland, William Yee, Jerome Rabow, and Mervin White;

the young men—some called "delinquent," some not—who patiently answered our questions and provided the substance for our investigation;

the Ford and Rosenberg Foundations, the Public Health Service (Research Grant No. 14397, National Institute of Mental Health), and the National Institute of Law Enforcement and Criminal Justice (Grant No. NI-050), all of whom supported parts of this investigation;

the Youth Studies Center and Public Systems Research Institute at USC, the Computer Sciences Laboratory at USC, and the Health Sciences Computing Facility at UCLA (sponsored by NIH Grant FR-3) for assistance and facilities;

Malcolm W. Klein, Solomon Kobrin, James F. Short, Jr., and Orion M. Barber for their critical and helpful reviews of the manuscript;

and, finally, to Elaine Corry—secretary, research assistant, proof-reader and extraordinary "do-it-all."

**Part I
Theory and Methods**

1 Narrative Statement of Theory

There is a theory of delinquency that has captured the attention of the lay public as well as the scientific community, a theory that appeals to common sense and egalitarian as well as academic traditions. It builds upon the premise that delinquency has its roots in lower-class membership.

Born into conditions of poverty and deprived of the kinds of intellectual and interpersonal experiences that are necessary for achievement in a success-oriented society, lower-class children are terribly handicapped, if not doomed to failure. The result is a growing sense of frustration that not only alienates some of them from conventional rules and expectations, but turns a significant number to membership in delinquent groups where the tendency is to repudiate basic values. Deviant norms, alternative sources of satisfaction, and illegal activities are the result. Delinquency has been spawned. It is the result of the way society is organized; those who are disenfranchised by society often respond to that disenfranchisement by engaging in delinquent activities.[a]

This particular theory relies heavily upon evidence from *official* sources that delinquency is primarily a lower-class phenomenon (Shaw and McKay, 1942; Dirksen, 1948; Wattenberg and Ballistrieri, 1950; Burgess, 1952; Cohen, 1955; Eaton and Polk, 1961). Reflecting this point of view, the recent President's Commission on Law Enforcement and Administration of Justice (1967:56-57) stated that "delinquents tend to come from backgrounds of social and economic deprivation. Their families tend to have lower than average incomes and social status. . . . It is inescapable that juvenile delinquency is directly related to conditions bred by poverty."

This assumption draws support from evidence that lower-class children do not possess the requisite cognitive nor social skills for coping with the grade school environment, and the middle-class people who run it (Deutsch, 1967:31; Dennis, 1960; Goldfarb, 1953; and Hunt, 1961). Furthermore, such problems seem to be most acute for those who eventually become delinquent. The incidence of family disorganization is greater among delinquents than nondelinquents (Schulman, 1949; Monahan, 1957; Toby, 1957; Hirschi, 1969); delinquents score lower on intelligence tests when social class is held constant (Reiss and Rhodes, 1961; Short and Strodtbeck, 1965:237); and experiences in school, rather than reversing these disabilities, seem only to enhance them (Elliott 1966). The longer such children stay in school, the more likely they are to become involved with legal authorities.

---

[a]This theoretical statement formed the basis for the conduct of the Silverlake Experiment (Empey and Lubeck, 1971). For those who are interested, reference can be made to that work for an expanded and more detailed statement of the theory.

The most significant thing about this evidence is its emphasis upon the lack of achievement for this group of young people, particularly those in school. If they are handicapped at this level, then it is assumed that they will not only be failures in legitimate pursuits later on, but may be inclined to become delinquent. Rather than suggesting that the lack of achievement, by itself, leads directly to delinquency, however, the sociological literature suggests that other influences and events, occurring in a series of stages, must intervene.

The first of these stages has to do with the strain that is generated from the lack of achievement. On the surface, it would seem logical to assume that failure on the parts of lower-class juveniles to achieve in school and community would be productive of strain—a lowered sense of self-worth, alienation, or a loss of status. But one cannot make that assumption automatically. A lack of achievement is problematic only if lower-class children have internalized a set of values which define the lack of achievement as "bad." If they have not, then the lack of achievement may be irrelevant in terms of the values they hold.

Theorists have not been in total agreement on this issue. Miller (1958), for example, argues that lower- and middle-class values are not the same. For that reason, lower-class children are not made uncomfortable by the failure to achieve according to middle-class standards. Hirschi (1969) also contends that a theoretical orientation which emphasizes the causal importance of strain is inadequate for a variety of other reasons: e.g., a strain theory hypothesizes far too much pressure, since delinquents are "normal" and law-abiding in most of their behavior; strain theory does not account for maturational reform among delinquents; and delinquency is not necessarily confined to the lower classes. Hirschi argues that delinquency is primarily a function of the adolescent's lack of ties to conventional standards of conduct, whether strain is present or not.

By contrast, other theorists—most notably Cohen (1955), and Cloward and Ohlin (1960)—take an opposing point of view. According to them, the democratic and egalitarian character of American culture results in the indoctrination of all social classes with a desire for success and high social status. Thus, argue Cloward and Ohlin (1960:86),

The disparity between what lower-class youth are led to want and what is actually available to them is the source of major problems of adjustment. . . . Faced with limitations on legitimate avenues of access to [conventional] goals, and unable to revise their aspirations downward, they experience intense frustration; the exploration of non-conformist alternatives may be the result.

Some research evidence has tended to support statements of this type. Studies of levels of aspiration suggest that members of the lower-classes may be motivated, even more than those on strata above them, to escape what seems to be an intolerable situation (Gould, 1941; Empey, 1956). Delinquents, no less than nondelinquents, are inclined to legitimate official values (Kobrin, 1951; Gold, 1963; Short and Strodtbeck, 1965). In fact, their research evidence led Short and Strodtbeck (1965:74) to conclude that existing theories had actually understated the meaningfulness of middle-class values to members of delinquent groups.

If this is true, lower-class youth face a paradoxical problem. Having accepted the view that the way to respect, status, and success lies in pursuing the values of middle-class society, yet finding themselves without the necessary abilities and opportunities for achievement, problems of adjustment are generated which are compelling in their need for resolution. What alternatives, then, are available to resolve the strain that is generated?

Cohen (1959) suggests the availability of three general alternatives. The first is a conformist alternative in which the individual joins others in adhering to conventional expectations despite the likelihood that he will have to carry a chronic and life-long load of frustration. Only a few will be upwardly mobile. The second alternative is one in which the individual breaks with conformist reference groups and joins with new ones whose norms favor a deviant solution. The third alternative is for the individual to "resolve" his problems by "going it alone"–wandering, consciously or subconsciously, into solitary forms of deviant behavior or mental illness.

Of these alternatives, the most common would be the conformist; the majority of lower-class adolescents do not become delinquent, at least not officially. The second most common, and the one with which sociologists have been most concerned, is the collective, deviant adjustment. The idea for which it stands is commonplace in everyday, as well as scientific, thinking; namely, that many people who share common problems of adjustment tend to evolve new and collective, rather than private, solutions. That is why new subcultures, cliques, and power groups evolve. They provide the rationalizations, the techniques, and the socio-psychological support for new, often deviant, patterns of adjustment. Therefore, it is this form of adjustment–identification with deviant peers and subculture–to which greatest attention has been paid in seeking to explain delinquency.

There is some indirect evidence in support of this line of thought. Numerous studies, dating back to the 1930's, have suggested that the majority of delinquent acts are group-related; either the delinquent act is committed in concert with others, or the individual associates differentially with other delinquents (Shaw and McKay, 1931; Fenton, 1935; Healy and Bronner, 1936; Kvaraceus, 1945; Hollingshead, 1949; Glueck and Glueck, 1950; Scott, 1956; Lohman, 1957; Eynon and Reckless, 1961; Geis, 1965).

A basic issue raised by this evidence, however, is whether peer associations actually cause delinquency, or whether both are merely symptomatic of some prior, and more important influences. The Gluecks (1950), for example, rejected peer association as an explanatory variable because they felt it occurred after, not before, the "onset" of delinquency. To them, such things as family dynamics, physique, temperature, or psychological set were far more important as precipitating factors. Eynon and Reckless (1961), by contrast, found that three-quarters of the delinquent boys they studied were with companions when they committed their first delinquent acts, no matter what the age. They concluded, therefore, that companions were highly important, and that the Glueck interpretation was incorrect.

Tannenbaum (1938), indeed the whole "Chicago school" (Thrasher, 1927; Shaw, 1940; Shaw and McKay, 1942), suggested a somewhat different interpretation. They postulated a model of causation in which associations with delinquent peers both cause and result from delinquent behavior. The two were seen as interdependent. At the outset, boys who are unintegrated into the institutional paths of society engage in mischievous and annoying behavior. As the community imposes increasing sanctions upon them, they are forced ever further into delinquent group associations as a refuge. Thus, a self-fulfilling prophecy is set up which tends to evoke and make worse the very behavior which was complained about in the first place.

Other important questions relative to this sequence of events have also been raised: whether the "drift" into delinquency is initiated by a collective reaction formation which involves a repudiation of basic values (Cohen, 1955), by situational and random play activities (Tannenbaum, 1938; Matza, 1964), or by alienation (Cloward and Ohlin, 1960); whether delinquent groups are cohesive and internally rewarding or held together by external pressures (Bordua, 1962; Klein and Crawford, 1967); or whether delinquent subculture(s) is unique and *contra*cultural (Cohen, 1955; Cloward and Ohlin, 1960) or diffuse and *infra*cultural (Matza, 1964; Empey, 1967; Kobrin, 1951; Gordon et al., 1963). Yet few of these questions have entirely discredited the importance of peer influence. Rather, they have simply underscored the importance of attempting to indicate more precisely its nature and impact. From a theoretical standpoint, therefore, its role in providing support for the individual against the moral and legal encroachments of the dominant society still occupies a central position in sociological thinking (cf. Gold, 1963; Rivera and Short, 1967; Short and Strodtbeck, 1965; and Reiss and Rhodes, 1963, for additional evidence on some of these issues).

Thus, the general argument presented above might be summarized as follows:

1. Lower-class boys, especially those who become delinquent, are ill-prepared to achieve in the context of middle-class institutions.
2. The lack of achievement in a success-oriented society produces strain, a serious problem of adjustment.
3. For a significant number of those who have this problem, association with similarly circumstanced peers becomes highly important.
4. This differential association with peers results in the emergence of delinquent groups, possibly delinquent subcultures, through which boys achieve the status, recognition, and sense of belonging which they have not achieved in a conventional way.

In the next chapter, this narrative statement will be presented in formal, axiomatic terms and the steps taken to operationalize it in research terms will be discussed.

2 Formal Theory and Operationalization

Rationale for Formal Statement

The rigors of formalization were imposed upon the narrative statement of the theory for two primary reasons. First, as Gibbs (1967:74) has pointed out, there are compelling reasons in favor of paying greater attention to form. "True," he says,

significant sociological theories have been stated informally, but this mode of construction hardly improves a theory. Even if one grants that formal theory construction does not ensure empirical validity, it may play a crucial role in attempts to *test* the theory. Equally important, it is difficult to assess the logical consistency of a theory without reducing it to formal statements. Moreover, the use of formal statements does not make it impossible for a theoretician to "make a case" for plausibility. The theory can be (and should be) presented in a narrative form, followed by a formal restatement. Finally, a better way than formal construction to reveal the pretentiousness of a theory scarcely can be imagined. When a theory is presented in narrative form, its ostensible significance may evaporate when restated formally. . . . Theories must be testable, which is to say that they must be stated in such a way that they are falsifiable.

Thus, although one must always guard against the problem of substituting form for content in the construction of any theory, that did not seem to be an overriding problem in this case.

Any body of theory such as this often becomes overburdened with a heavy load of rhetorical content that is designed more to persuade the reader of its accuracy by the weight of its elaborations and subtleties than by the strength of its inherent logic. Therefore, given the rich tradition out of which this theory has grown, and the wealth of content from which it springs, it seemed wise to add greater form to it in the interest of enhancing its testability.

The second reason for formalizing the theory had to do with the fact that it implies a sequential series of events leading from membership in the lower class to lack of achievement, to strain, to identification with delinquent peers, to delinquency. Consequently, an adequate test of the theory would require two things: (1) an explicit statement of that sequence in unambiguous and propositional form; and (2) an assessment, not just of adjacent segments of that sequence, but of the sequence in its entirety. It is highly possible that although some of the relationships implied by the theory are valid—e.g., that membership in the lower class results in lack of achievement, or that lack of achievement

7

produces strain—the entire sequence would not be valid. By formalizing the theory, the possibilities of an adequate test might be enhanced.

Formal Statement

Given the rationale just stated, an axiomatic format seemed well-suited to the development of a formal statement (cf. Zetterberg, 1954, 1963, 1965; Gould and Schrag, 1962; Catton, 1961; Gibbs and Martin, 1962).[a] While it is impossible in the formal statement to capture all of the theoretical subtleties implied in the narrative statement, it will be of use in testing the general theme in a rigorous way.

Axiomatically, the theory might be stated in terms of the following postulates:

Postulate I. *The lower the social class, the lower the subsequent achievement.*
Postulate II. *Decreased achievement results in increased strain.*
Postulate III. *Increased strain results in identification with delinquent peers.*
Postulate IV. *Identification with delinquent peers results in delinquency.*

Using the postulates as basic premises, the following first-order theorems can be deduced:

Theorem I. *The lower the social class, the greater the subsequent strain* (deduced from Postulate I and II).
Theorem II. *Decreased achievement results in identification with delinquent peers* (Postulates II and III).
Theorem III. *Increased strain results in delinquency* (Postulate III and IV).

These three theorems exhaust the implications of the four postulates. Using one postulate and one theorem, however, three second-order theorems may also be deduced:

Theorem IV. *The lower the social class, the greater the subsequent identification with delinquent peers* (Postulate I and Theorem II).
Theorem V. *Decreased achievement results in delinquency* (Postulate II and Theorem III).
Theorem VI. *The lower the social class, the greater the subsequent delinquency* (Postulate I and Theorem V).

---

[a]Our earlier work (Empey and Lubeck, 1971) raised a number of questions about the utility of axiomatization, but we wanted to assess its general applicability in this case, especially since we will be testing the theory on samples from both metropolitan (Los Angeles) and non-metropolitan (Utah) environments. The samples will be discussed in chapter 3.

The Price of Abstraction

Whenever one states a theory in propositional form, one pays a price. The various propositions obviously cannot reflect all of the substantive content and specificity that lie in back of them. For example, Postulate III states that "increased strain results in identification with delinquent peers." Put in this form, the proposition may appear to overlook many of the ideas that are included in the narrative statement of the theory regarding the processes by which peer identification occurs.

Actually, the narrative statement suggests that an individual's identification, at least initially, is with peers who, like himself, have tenuous ties to conventional institutions and activities. The strains and alienative effects that can be produced by these tenuous ties may establish the preconditions for the emergence of delinquent activities and deviant norms, but delinquency, as such, need not be the immediate consequence. When, and if, it does occur, it will be the result of complex processes, both within the group and with outsiders as well. The narrative statement suggests a whole sequence of interactional events, not just a single and immediate jump into deviant group activities.[b] Thus, the purpose of the narrative statement is to convey some of these subtleties, while the purpose of the formal statement is to summarize them and to move them to a higher level of abstraction. Postulate III, as a consequence, is not intended to convey all the details that might contribute to peer identification, but merely to indicate their result. The same can be said of all the theoretical propositions.

Nature of Relationships Between Variables

Following the derivation of the postulates and theorems, it is necessary to specify the *nature of the relationships* assumed to exist between variables in the theory and to specify the *rules for deduction* that were used.

Since statements of relationships dealing with absolute certainty are rare or non-existent in the social sciences, the postulates in this theory are meant to be probablistic in nature, even though actual probabilities are not explicitly stated. Furthermore, because of the sequential character of the theory, all of the relationships are assumed to be asymmetric, meaning that the occurrence of a causal factor is followed in time by its effect, rather than occurring simultaneously with it; the observed causal sequence is not reversible.

The utility of stating postulates in asymmetric form lies in the fact that they lead to more powerful deductions in the context of an axiomatic model than statements that are made in symmetric or covariance form, without regard to temporal order (Costner and Leik, 1964:823—825). At the same time, the statement of postulates in this form overlooks the possibility that relationships are interdependent and thus symmetric. Consequently, the choice is obviously a

[b]See Empey and Lubeck (1971: chapter 2) for a greatly expanded narrative statement.

10

debatable one. As suggested above, however, the narrative statement of the theory, indeed, much of the literature on delinquency, implies that relationships within the theory are asymmetric. A diagram of the postulates of the theory, appears in Figure 2-1. They suggest that each causal factor is followed in time by its effect rather than occurring simultaneously with it. But since the issue is such an important one, it will receive careful attention throughout the work. Its resolution will reflect not only upon the choice of a theoretical format made here, but upon the meaning and substance of the theory itself.

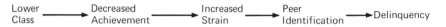

Figure 2-1. The Relationships Between the Postulates of the Theory.

Rules for Deduction

Two rules that have been employed recently were used in performing logical deductions in the statement of this theory. These rules, the sign and transitivity rules, seemed uniquely suited to our purposes.

Costner and Leik (1964) define the *sign rule* very simply: "The sign of the deduced relationship is the algebraic product of the signs of the postulated relationships." In using measures of association, this rule requires that the sign of the relationship expressed in the conclusion or explanandum of an argument must be the algebraic product of the signs of the relationships expressed in the two postulates or explanans of the same argument. This means that if both postulates of an argument express positive correlations, or if both express negative correlations, then the conclusion must be positive. If, on the other hand, the sign of one of the postulates is negative while the other is positive, the conclusion must necessarily be negative. In purely logical terms, this is a simple rule to use. On an empirical level, however, validation of the sign rule can become very complex. Actual correlations among sets of variables do not always conform to the rule. Nevertheless, there are specific, empirical conditions under which the rule must hold true, and these will be observed in testing the theory.

The second rule, the *transitivity* rule, is pertinent to the deduction of the asymmetric relation implied by the theory. It may be stated as follows: "If A implies B, and B implies C, then A implies C" (Schrag, 1967:223; Gould and Schrag, 1962:69). When postulates are presented in asymmetric form, as they are in this theory, the "middle term" of the explanans must occupy a specific position if the transitivity rule is to hold true. It must be the final term of the first postulate and the initial term of the second. For example, in one segment of the theory we have the following set of statements:

Postulate II: *Decreased achievement results in increased strain.*
Postulate III: *Increased strain results in identification with delinquent peers;*
   therefore,
Theorem II: *Decreased achievement results in identification with delinquent peers.*

The conditions of the transitivity rule are satisfied in this case, since the middle term of the argument, *strain*, appeared at the end of the first premise and at the beginning of the second. By giving *strain* this position in the argument, we made it an intervening variable in the causal sequence. We were assuming that *achievement* is related to *delinquent peer identification* only through the intervening variable of *strain*. This is an important assumption and brings us to the conditions necessary to test its validity.

Costner and Leik (1964:819-835) have proposed that if the postulates of an axiomatic theory are stated in asymmetric form, and if the transitivity rule is satisfied, then one additional requirement must be met before valid deductions about the sign rule can be made. One must assume that the theory constitutes a "closed system." There should be no relationships between the variables in the postulates except those stated or implied in them.

Translated into methodological terms, this means that if the closed-system assumption is true, the association between the non-adjacent variables of *achievement* and *peer identification* in the example cited above should be roughly equal to the product of the association between *achievement* and *strain* times the association between *strain* and *peer identification*. By implication, then, the associations between adjacent variables (e.g., *achievement* and *strain*) should be higher than the associations between non-adjacent variables (e.g., *achievement* and *peer identification*). In fact, if the closed system assumption were met completely, we would expect the relationship between *achievement* and *peer identification*, controlling for the effects of *strain*, to disappear. The same would also be true of all the nonadjacent relationships expressed in the theory. Thus, a careful test of the closed system assumption for the entire theoretical sequence should help to indicate whether relations in it are symmetric or asymmetric and how much confidence can be placed in the empirical validity of the sequence as a whole.

Definition and Operationalization of Basic Concepts

It will be recalled that five major concepts were used to construct the theory: social class, achievement, strain, identification with delinquent peers, and delinquency.

Social class was defined as an ordinal concept, used to denote groups of individuals who share similar attributes along a socio-economic continuum. In operational terms, our measure of social class consisted of a scale with ten categories on which the prestige of each subject's father's occupation was ranked (cf. Empey, 1956). However, the original ten categories were collapsed to eight and the ascribed status of each boy was measured in terms of his father's position in one of them.

Achievement was defined as the attainment of goals, through legitimate means, which are endorsed and defined as important by society. For adolescents in the United States, achievement is defined primarily in terms of (1) formal recognition of academic skills, (2) informal recognition associated with the winning of school awards and extracurricular activities, and (3) perhaps some ability to obtain and hold a job. For these reasons, achievement was operationalized as follows:

A. Did subject ever win an award at school?
   1. No
   2. Yes
B. Grade Point Average
   1. F
   2. D
   3. C
   4. B
   5. A
C. Number of jobs held during lifetime.
   1. None   5. 7-8
   2. 1-2   6. 9-10
   3. 3-4   7. 11 or more
   4. 5-6
D. In addition, we measured each subject's "achievement orientation" by coding his occupational aspiration in terms of the occupational prestige scale mentioned above. While this latter measure is not a direct indicator of "achievement," we felt it had special applicability to this theory and might shed light upon the importance of achievement to delinquents.

Strain was the third major concept. It was defined as having two major components: (1) a detachment or disaffection from societal institutions, and (2) a dynamic state of tension which involves a need for resolution. Yet, despite the extended use of this concept in the sociological literature, it remains ambiguous and highly difficult to operationalize. Consequently, two steps were taken. First, two behavioral indicators were used from which strain might be inferred:

A. Did subject ever drop out of school?
   1. No
   2. Yes

Since school and work are two of the most important institutional channels open to the adolescent, it was assumed that failure in either or both of them would be productive of strain—tension and disaffection.

Second, four subjective indicators were used that were designed to have the individual evaluate himself in relation to others and to evaluate his occupational chances:

A. How "smart" did subject feel in comparison to others his own age?
   1. Less smart than average
   2. Average
   3. Smarter than average
B. Did subject consider himself a leader?
   1. No
   2. Not sure
   3. Yes
C. How grown-up did subject feel in comparison to others his own age?
   1. Less grown-up
   2. About the same
   3. More grown-up
D. What were the subject's perceived chances of attaining his vocational aspirations?
   1. Certainly won't
   2. Probably won't
   3. About 50-50
   4. Probably will
   5. Certainly will

The rationale for including this set of items was theoretically based. It springs from two assumptions: (1) that the democratic and success-oriented character of American culture results in the indoctrination of all social classes with a desire for high social status and success despite the fact that the means for reaching these goals are differentially distributed (Merton, 1957:Chaps. 4-5); and (2) that these aspirations constitute the measuring rod for evaluating oneself in comparison with others (Cohen, 1955:121-137). Thus, to devaluations of the non-achieving child by middle-class functionaries is added the likelihood that he will devalue himself. Consequently, it was assumed further that a personal sense of strain would be the product of this devaluation. Whether or not this is true remains a matter of conjecture. Nevertheless, it constitutes one of the basis upon which strain in this study was measured.

In addition, a serendipitous finding occurred in a previous study which indicated that intrafamily difficulties might be strongly related to other variables in the theoretical chain (cf. Empey and Lubeck, 1971). However, since many sociologists have attached only secondary importance to such difficulties, theorizing instead that it is the place of the delinquent's family in the social structure that is at the root of his problems, intrafamily strain was not incorporated into the original theoretical statement. But when indications that it was important continued to appear in the earlier study, the decision was made to relate a study of family problems to the test of the theory. This was done by deriving indicators of family strain and relating them, along with other strain indicators, to other variables in the theory. Therefore, along with, but not necessarily a part of, a test of the theory, the effects of family strain were examined.

The indicators of intrafamily strain that were included in this part of the analysis were:

A. Did subject come from a broken home?
   1. No
   2. Yes (parents divorced, separated, or widowed)
B. How well did subject's parents get along together?
   1. Not at all well
   2. Not so well
   3. About average
   4. Quite well
   5. Very well
C. How well did subject get along with his parents?
   1. Not at all well
   2. Not so well
   3. About average
   4. Quite well
   5. Very well

Identification with delinquent peers was the fourth concept. In definitional terms, it referred to the process of internalizing the norms and beliefs, the subcultural standards, of specific delinquent groups. Identification occurs when the individual makes the delinquent aggregate a primary reference group.

Using a complex, two-stage process—first, factor analysis and then Guttman scaling—scales were developed to measure peer group identification along four dimensions (cf. Empey and Lubeck, 1968 for details):

A. A *Ratfink* Scale which measured whether or not boys would inform on their friends to teachers, parents, or the police;
B. An *Ace-in-the-Hole* Scale which measured whether or not boys would hide their friends in time of trouble;
C. A *Deviance* Scale which measured whether boys would go with their friends to participate in activities of a delinquent nature; and
D. A *Sociability Scale* which measured whether boys would go with friends to participate in activities that were of a social, but non-delinquent nature.

All of the items of which these scales were comprised asked boys to state the extent to which they would engage with others in the activities described. An earlier study indicated that delinquents were more inclined to respond positively to peer expectations than nondelinquents (Empey and Lubeck, 1968). Nevertheless, the scales must be interpreted as attitudinal rather than behavioral measures.

Delinquency was the final concept in the chain. All measurement of it was based upon official data. First, a simple dichotomy was drawn between those who had been officially defined as delinquent and those who had not. This dichotomy was then related to other variables in the theory.

Second, delinquency was also measured in multi-dimensional terms. The official offense patterns of all respondents were organized into a variety of different indicators. The rationale for this kind of measurement, the literature which gave rise to it, and the methods involved are all described in Appendix 1. For the person interested in these matters, attention is invited to the Appendix. Only the indicators themselves are listed below.

The several indicators can be divided into two general categories. Category 1 indexes include those that measure degrees of delinquency, either in terms of frequency or seriousness. A high score on any of them indicates a high degree of delinquency. These indexes include the following:

1. *Number of Offenses*—An enumeration of all offenses appearing on each subject's record was used as an indicator of offense frequency.
2. *Average Seriousness of Offenses*—After constructing an index of offense seriousness, all offenses of each individual were rated and an average score for all the ratings was calculated. This became an index of average seriousness.
3. *Most Serious Offense*—In addition to a measure of average seriousness, we also rated each individual's most serious offense and used it as a second index of seriousness.
4. *Theft Factor*—Using factor-analysis techniques, three indexes were derived. One was a theft factor including such acts as burglary, petty theft, auto theft, and grand theft.
5. *Hell-Raising Factor*—A hell-raising factor was the second of the factor indexes. It included disturbing the peace, use of alcohol, assault, gambling, and curfew violations.
6. *Incorrigibility Factor*—The third factor index was an incorrigibility factor including truancy and malicious mischief.

The delinquency indicators in Category 2 measure offense patterns. These indicators represent the *ratios* of certain types of acts to the total number committed by an individual. Thus, while they do not measure degrees of delinquency in the traditional sense, they do provide some indication of the types of delinquent acts in which different individuals most commonly engaged.

1. *Status Offenses (Adult/Juvenile) Index*—This index indicates the proportion of an individual's offenses that are universally proscribed for everyone, adult as well as juvenile. A high score is indicative of a high proportion of universalistic or adult-type offenses, while a low score suggests that an individual's offenses are primarily juvenile in character; i.e., they are made up largely of such acts as truancy, incorrigibility, or drinking alcohol which are not proscribed for adults.

2. *Felony/Misdemeanor Index*—This index is concerned only with those offenses that are "adult" in character and further subdivides them into felonies and misdemeanors. A high score on the index is indicative of a high proportion of felonious offenses while a low score suggests a pattern of misdemeanors.
3. *Instrumental/Expressive Index*—This index is scored in the same way and indicates whether an individual's offenses can be considered predominantly instrumental (e.g. "utilitarian" acts involving various types of theft, forgery and burglary), or predominantly expressive (e.g., "nonutilitarian" acts, such as fighting, smoking, taking drugs, etc.).
4. *Retreatism Index*—Three theoretically-based indexes were created, the first of which is a measure of retreatism. Besides all drug-related offenses, it includes such things as running away and truancy, and indicates whether an individual's offenses are predominantly retreatist in character, in contrast to being conflict- or criminally oriented.
5. *Conflict Index*—The conflict index indicates the extent to which a person's offenses are hostile and often violent in character. It includes such offenses as defiance of authority, disturbing the peace, and simple and serious assault.
6. *Criminalism Index*—As the last of the three subcultural indexes, the criminalism index indicates the extent to which offenses are predominantly criminal as contrasted to retreatist or conflictive, including such things as burglary, all kinds of theft, robbery, and forgery.

Some of these indicators obviously overlap and it is likely that when their relationships to other variables are assessed they will reflect that overlap. Nevertheless, there seemed to be considerable utility at this stage, first, in distinguishing between amounts and patterns of delinquency in the measures that were used and, second, in determining whether some indicators are differentially associated with other variables while some are not. The task of determining whether or not only a few offenses are actually responsible for observed relationships might be better reserved for future inquiry.

Study Limitations

A closing comment is in order on some of the limitations of this investigation. The data on which it is based were derived from the Provo (Empey and Rabow, 1961) and Silverlake (Empey and Lubeck, 1971) experiments. Since these experiments, one in Utah and one in Los Angeles, were designed primarily for the purposes of intervention rather than as a test of causation theory, limitations on the causation test were imposed.

On the one hand, although the theory described above was an integral component of both studies, they were not designed with the explicit objective of providing the most effective test of it. Had that been done, some of the operational indicators might have been improved. On the other hand, the nature of both of these studies lent some strengths. Not only did they provide the opportunity to obtain considerable data from samples of serious delinquents and comparison samples of nondelinquents, but the data were collected in both metropolitan Los Angeles and nonmetropolitan Utah. Thus, by conducting a test of the theory, it was possible to compare findings from two, strikingly different locations and subcultures.

Speaking specifically of the various indicators, it is our opinion that those which represent social class and delinquency are the most valid. Of all single indicators of the complex class concept, occupation has probably been the most useful. With respect to delinquency, the twelve separate indicators seem to provide a rather broad sampling of the various dimensions of that concept, at least in official terms. One can gain some notion, not only of the frequency and seriousness of the official offenses committed by these samples, but of the various offense patterns that are involved as well. The chief limitation of the indicators, however, is that one does not know how well they represent the total iceberg of which unofficial, as well as official, delinquency is composed. But rather than discussing the matter further here, it will be treated throughout the manuscript, especially in chapter 10 where its implications for further research are treated at length.

The four peer scales probably rank next in their capacity to represent the concept of peer identification. This is a most difficult area to conceptualize as well as to measure (cf. Empey and Lubeck, 1968) and not many available indicators have received greater attention in their construction than these.

The two weakest sets of indicators may be those that represent achievement and strain. It is difficult to know how achievement, for example, should be measured, especially in terms that are meaningful to young people themselves. Nevertheless, one reason we limited our indicators to those that measure school performance, aspirations for the future, and youthful employment is because they are institutionally related. They represent probably the most universal criteria that are used. A second reason is that we had to use data that were accessible and could be matched in two very different places—Los Angeles and Utah—and which could be collected under the usual budgetary and time constraints. Given other circumstances, better measures might have been used.

An even more difficult problem had to do with the concept of strain. Because it was conceptually ambiguous, as are such related concepts as status frustration and alienation, it was the most difficult of all to operationalize. Thus, with such indicators as dropping out of school or being fired from a job, its existence, in terms of some psychological state, can only be inferred. About the only measurements of an internal, psychological state are the self-evaluation measures, but again one can only assume that a low self-evaluation implies strain; it is not really a documentation of strain. Much more could be said on these matters, but the point is clear that some indicators might have been improved, and that the following test of the theory will be valid only insofar as the indicators are valid.

Implications and Conclusions

One other comment is in order regarding the approach that is taken in the test of any theory. It is not uncommon in scientific research to test only one, or an incomplete number, of all the possible relationships implicit in a theory. In the theory to be tested here, for example, it is easily possible that one might want to make a single, bivariate test of the relationship of social class to delinquency or poor achievement to peer identification without taking other variables into account. In addition to the possible benefits from such a test, there are also some liabilities. If it turned out that class was only weakly related to delinquency, one might be inclined to conclude that class is not of causal importance. This may, or may not, be true. It is also possible that, although class does not have a strong direct relationship to delinquency, it does have an important indirect effect through the intervening variables of achievement, strain, and peer identification. In order to make an exhaustive test of the relationship, therefore, one may have to design research that takes all these variables, and their indirect effects, into account.

There are two ways in which the formal construction of the theory described in this chapter may be helpful in taking that step. First, by placing the entire theory in propositional form, it is possible to exhaust its major implications. All of the possible relationships among key concepts are indicated. Thus, in the analysis that follows, it will be possible to make a bivariate test of all the two-variable relationships implicit in the theory. It will be possible to indicate which relationships are strong, and which are weak, which postulates and theorems receive support, and which do not. This kind of analysis will be analogous to that described above, except that all, rather than a few, of the relationships will be examined. Hopefully, new insights will be gained, some anticipated, some unanticipated.

Following that, the closed system assumption will be examined. This part of the analysis will be an important supplement to the first because it will provide some indication of the extent to which confidence can be placed in the entire causal sequence, whether the assumption is valid that relationships among variables are asymmetric, and whether the indirect effects of some variables on others are important even though their direct effects are weak. By taking both steps in the analysis, it should be possible not only to give some general indication of the extent to which strong or weak bivariate relationships exist, but whether these relationships occur in the sequence suggested by the theory. The entire theory, with all its implications, may then be submitted to test.

It should be noted as well that the concern of this analysis is with the explanation of individual behavior. It is important that this point be made because, if the different faces of delinquency are to be understood, one must be clear as to whether he is concerned with delinquent norms, acts, persons, or some other dependent variable. For example, many of the earlier studies upon which conclusions were reached regarding the relation between individual delinquency and such variables as class or achievement were ecological studies.

Yet, as will be documented later, there is serious doubt that extrapolations can be made from ecological units of analysis to individual behavior. Serious distortions are probably introduced when this is done.

In addition, many of the theories which contribute to the theoretical framework under study in this analysis are concerned with delinquent groups or subcultures. They are focused upon what it is about cultural and social structures that lead to the emergence of delinquent collectivities. Therefore, it is important that the reader understand that, while this study uses some of the same theoretical variables—class membership, achievement level, strain, and peer relations—the analysis attempts to determine how they are related to individual, not group, conduct. This analysis examines the individual's behavior as it relates to the institutional context of home, school, and work, on the one hand, and to the context of peer groupings on the other.

3 Sampling and Methods

The Samples

The theory was tested on a purposive sample of 482 serious delinquents, 249 in Utah and 233 in Los Angeles, and 185 nondelinquents, 100 in Utah and 85 in Los Angeles. To qualify for inclusion in the study, delinquents had to meet the following criteria:

1. They had to be persistent offenders. This criterion was met by the fact that the average number of recorded offenses for the Los Angeles delinquents was 4.5 and for the Utah delinquents, 6.2.
2. They had to range in age from 15 to 18. As it turned out, the modal age for both samples was 16, with only 1 per cent in Los Angeles and 12 per cent in Utah being over 17 years.
3. They could not be psychotic, mentally retarded with a measured I.Q. below 80, heroin addicts, or assaultive sex offenders.

Data were gathered in Los Angeles from all delinquents from Los Angeles County who met the above criteria and who were assigned to Boys Republic, a private correctional institution, for the period 1964 through 1967. Since Boys Republic maintains an ethnic balance which approximates that of the county, this delinquent sample is slightly over three-quarters Caucasian, one-tenth Negro, and one-tenth Mexican American.

Data were gathered in Utah from two major sources: (1) an enumeration of all delinquents who met the above criteria, and who were incarcerated in the Utah State Industrial School during the years 1962-64; and (2) a total enumeration of all offenders who met the above criteria and who were processed by the juvenile court in Utah County, Utah, during the years 1959-1964. In Utah, however, no minority subjects were included, since their respective populations in that state are extremely small.

Nondelinquents, by contrast, were randomly selected from a local high school in Utah County and purposively selected from one in Los Angeles. To qualify for inclusion, they also had to meet relevant criteria:

1. They had to be without delinquent histories, with the exception of minor traffic offenses.
2. They had to be of the same age range as the delinquents. As it turned out, they were slightly older in Utah.
3. They could not be psychotic or mentally retarded.

In terms of sample generalizability the following things should be noted. Since neither delinquent nor nondelinquent subjects were chosen randomly from totally representative populations in either Utah or Los Angeles, one cannot generalize from the subjects to delinquents in general with complete confidence. The Utah sample of delinquents is probably more representative of officially persistent offenders in that state than the Los Angeles sample, however, since it is a virtual enumeration of the most serious offenders in a three-year time period. The Los Angeles sample of delinquents clearly includes only the more serious offender group, since all subjects had been assigned to a correctional institution, and most had already failed on probation. However, this sample probably suffers from an underrepresentation of ethnic minorities. What the effects of this and other possible biases may be, we cannot say, since we have no way of documenting why judicial and court personnel assigned offenders to this institution rather than some other. A singular benefit of the samples lies in the fact that, in providing a test of the theory, they permit a comparison of serious delinquents and nondelinquents from such disparate places as sparsely populated, non-metropolitan Utah and densely populated, metropolitan Los Angeles.

Methods for Testing the Theory

The causation theory will be assessed through the use of two statistical techniques. First, the postulates and theorems will be examined with the use of gamma coefficients. Second, the causal sequences implied by the postulates will be assessed by the use of path analysis. Although these two approaches are essentially different, each possesses a distinct set of advantages and disadvantages when compared to the other. By using them both, we hope to capitalize on their relative strengths and to provide as sensitive and complete test of the theory as possible.

The Use of Gamma Coefficients

Goodman and Kruskal's gamma (1954; Costner, 1965:347) will be used to measure the bivariate relationships among the operational measures of the theory. The absolute value of gamma has a "proportional reduction in error" interpretation which enables the researcher to determine how much error is eliminated in predicting the rankings of a given variable through knowledge of the rankings of a second variable. For example, social class was postulated as an important determinant of adolescent achievement. How accurate is that postulate? Gamma helps to answer that question by indicating how much error is eliminated in predicting rankings of achievement for a group if their class levels are known. Thus, it is highly useful in helping us to realize the first of our major objectives; namely, to examine exhaustively all of the bivariate relationships specified in the postulates and theorems of the formal theory.

Gamma was also chosen (1) because all of our operational measures were dichotomous or in at least rank-order form, and (2) because the gamma coefficient yields a relatively clear and unambiguous operational meaning when compared to other ordinal-based measures of association. Moreover, gamma analysis was chosen to complement path analysis because of a difference of opinion in the literature regarding the assumptions to be made if path analysis is used. Since path analysis is an adaption of regression analysis, it implies that the assumptions of interval level measurement and linear and additive relations among variables must be met (Land, 1969:32-33). Additionally, the proper interpretation of path analysis requires a recursive system with established causal priorities among the variables (Heise, 1969:44, 50).

Strictly speaking, it cannot be maintained that our data meet all these assumptions, since our measures are largely ordinal. Thus, although Boyle (1970) maintains that the use of path analysis with ordinal data is acceptable, we chose to complement our use of path analysis with the gamma analysis.

The following are the criteria that were used in determining whether any particular theoretical statement was supported, or not supported, by the gamma coefficients:

1. The sign of each coefficient was examined to see whether it was commensurate with, or contrary to, theoretical expectations. If, for example, the theory specified that a given relationship would be inverse and its respective coefficient was direct or positive, then the coefficient would not be supportive of the theory.
2. A cutting point of .20 was used in deciding whether any *particular* gamma coefficient was acceptable, by itself, as supporting a particular postulate or theorem. There is nothing sacred about the .20 cutting point, but, as will be seen, it proved to be of heuristic value in organizing our findings.
3. The total context of the findings, however, was also considered. That is, both the signs and magnitudes of all coefficients used to test a particular statement were taken into account. For example, in some cases the magnitudes of the various gammas, taken singly, did not exceed the acceptable cutting point of .20. However, when they were considered in total, it was sometimes found that all, or most, of their signs conformed to theoretical expectations. When this occurs, it should not be ignored.

Path Analysis

Path analysis is the second of the two major techniques used. It is a measurement device that has enjoyed recent popularity in the social sciences because it is particularly well suited to the analysis of recursive causal models such as the one developed in this work (cf. Boyle, 1968 and 1970; Duncan, 1966; Heise, 1969; and Land, 1969). Through the use of standardized partial regression (or path) coefficients, one is in a better position to assess the complexities involved in the postulated causal sequences than one would be with the bivariate gamma coefficients. Not only can one examine the direct causal effects among indicators, but their indirect and combined effects as well. One should be able to tell, for example, whether the assumption is valid that relationships are asymmetric, and whether the indirect effects of some variables on others are important even though their bivariate relationships may be relatively weak. Before dealing with path analysis in detail, however, some problems relative to its use in this study must be presented.

In this study, as in virtually all studies, we were faced with a missing data problem. For the usual host of reasons, complete information for all individuals on all variables was not always available. This did not seem to be too serious a problem in the gamma analysis, since we were concerned with the bivariate, zero-order gamma coefficients between different combinations of variables; the problem would affect each coefficient differently, depending upon the amount of missing information involved.[a]

In the conduct of the path analysis, however, missing data consitutes a more serious problem since the analysis is not always based upon bivariate, zero-order coefficients. Instead, it usually calls for the computation of beta coefficients derived from multiple regression analysis. Ideally, therefore, it requires that complete information be available for all individuals on all variables. Thus, given the fact that some data were missing, we were faced with a difficult choice, either to eliminate all individuals or variables on which there was incomplete information, or to substitute the arithmetic mean on each person or measure where data were missing. We chose a modified form of the first alternative, deciding to eliminate either individuals or measures so that losses would be minimized. This was a debatable choice, but it was the one we followed.[b]

With regard to the loss of individuals, we found it necessary in Los Angeles to drop 99 delinquents from our sample of 233 and 7 nondelinquents from our sample of 85. Thus, in the path analysis, these two groups number 134 and 78 subjects, respectively. In Utah, we dropped 110 delinquents, leaving an N of 139, and 22 nondelinquents, leaving an N of 78.

With regard to variables, the loss was less serious. The measure of *social class*, of course, was retained and it was necessary to alter the measures of *achievement* only slightly. The two major achievement indicators of "grades in school" and "awards in school" were retained with only the measure of occupational aspiration being eliminated. Indicators of *strain* were the hardest hit. While the major indicators of "dropping from school" and "being fired from a job" were

---

[a]In Appendix 2, the frequency distribution of each of the operational measures is listed. From these distributions, the reader can assess where, and the extent to which, data were missing.

[b]The alternative of substituting an arithmetic mean was an attractive one because we would have suffered no data losses. However, we followed the conservative course because our use of ordinal data already tended to violate the assumptions of path analysis. Thus, had we substituted means calculated on ordinal scales, and substituted them for missing data, we would have violated basic assumptions even further with the result that some findings might have been severely distorted.

kept, the three self-concept indicators—personal estimates of leadership, smart-ness, and maturity—were dropped. (In our parallel analysis of family strain, we retained the measure of boy-parent harmony but eliminated the measures of family separation and parental harmony.) Finally, we retained all of our indicators of *peer identification* so there was no loss of measurement on that concept.

A key issue in eliminating some subjects from the path analysis was whether it would seriously bias the results. As may be seen in Table 3-1, that did not seem to be the case. Shown in the table are the effects of sample loss on such key variables as number of delinquent offenses, social class, school grades, number of school awards, school dropout, and being fired from a job.

Table 3-1

Comparison of Total Sample with Sub-Sample Used in Path Analysis

Variable	Los Angeles		Utah	
	Total Sample N=332	Path Analysis Sample N=212	Total Sample N=339	Path Analysis Sample N=217
Number of Offenses[a]	$\bar{x}$=4.2	$\bar{x}$=4.4	$\bar{x}$=6.2	$\bar{x}$=6.4
Social Class	$\bar{x}$=5.2	$\bar{x}$=5.1	$\bar{x}$=4.3	$\bar{x}$=3.9
Grades	$\bar{x}$=3.1	$\bar{x}$=3.0	$\bar{x}$=3.0	$\bar{x}$=3.0
Awards	48%	47%	29%	30%
Left School	58%	56%	45%	44%
Fired from Job	20%	19%	21%	18%

[a]Number of offenses were compared on delinquents only. All other comparisons included delinquents as well as nondelinquents.

The means or percentages of these variables for the total sample are compared with those of the sub-sample upon which the path analysis was based. The overall figures in these comparisons are remarkably similar and suggest that subject loss did not greatly affect the validity of the analysis. Apparently, the reasons for data loss were randomly distributed. Further, when comparisons of the gamma and path analyses are made in the chapters that follow, it will be seen that the findings resulting from these two techniques are highly similar. The loss of subjects, although high, did not seem to distort comparable findings to any serious degree.

Steps in Path Analysis. When dealing with complex, multi-stage models, Land (1969:28) has suggested at least four steps in conducting a path analysis. The first step involves the construction of a path diagram. In the diagram, all of the variables used to test a given theory should be specified and unidirectional arrows drawn to indicate causal relationships. Figure 3-1 depicts the path diagram to be used in the present analysis.

Notice that causal arrows are provided to indicate the appropriate relationships specified in the theoretical statement. Social class is causally connected to two indicators of achievement which, in turn, are connected to two indicators of strain. These, in turn, are connected to the four indicators of peer identification. And, although each peer identification scale is intended to be causally connected to each of the twelve delinquency measures, all of the relevant arrows were not drawn into the diagram in the interest of keeping it as intelligible as possible.

It will also be noted that family relationships, as measured by boy-parent harmony, have also been included in the diagram. However, arrows were not drawn between the achievement measures and the measures of boy-parent harmony for two reasons. First, boy-parent harmony was not originally conceptualized as a part of the theory but was included here because, as indicated in chapter 2, previous research suggested it could be important. Second, it does not make theoretical sense to posit a direct, asymmetric relationship from a boy's achievement to his relationship with his parents. It is sensible, however, to expect boy-parent harmony to be one of the causal antecedents to delinquent peer identification. Therefore, arrows were included to indicate this relationship.

Arrows have not been drawn among multiple indicators of the same concept. This is because the theory did not specify any causal relationships within sets of measures, even though such assertions of causality might be plausible in certain instances.

Finally, causal paths can be seen leading from sources indicated by the letter Z. These paths represent "residual paths," and are included to represent the variance in a given variable that is *not* explained by the theory. As will be seen in the following chapters, these residuals have the advantage of making the researcher aware (painfully, at times) of what he is *not* explaining in the context of his analysis.

The second step suggested by Land involves a delineation of the "path model" or set of recursive equations implied by the path diagram. Our path model may be found in Figure 3-2. The path model is comprised of a set of regression equations and a set of path coefficients that are nothing more than a combined group of standardized partial regression coefficients, or beta weights. The number of independent, or predictor, variables included in a given regression model is equal to the number of causal paths (indicated by arrows in Figure 3-1) that lead into a given dependent variable. For example, the Ratfink Scale is the recipient of four causal paths leading from boy-parent harmony, school dropout, fired from a job, and a residual path. Therefore, in constructing a regression model to predict the Ratfink Scale, four separate coefficients would be

27

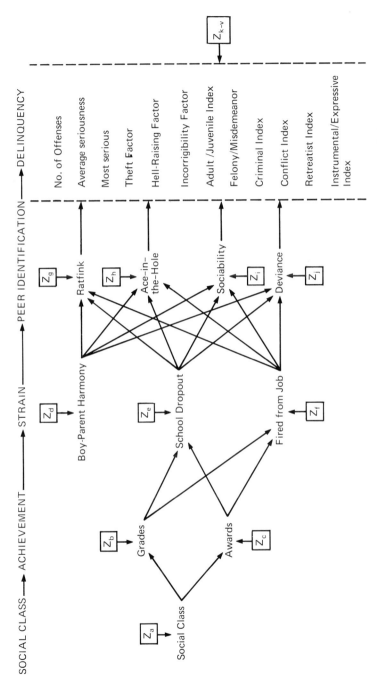

Note: Each peer identification scale is conceived to be causally connected to each delinquency measure. Only one arrow was drawn from each scale, however, in the interest of intelligibility.

*Residuals k through v respectively account for the unexplained variation of each delinquency indicator.

Figure 3-1. The General Path Diagram.

computed for each of the independent variables involved in the causal relationship. In the case where only one causal arrow leads into a variable, the path coefficient would be comparable to the zero-order correlation between a dependent variable and its causal antecedent. (In standard score form, the beta weight of a zero-order correlation is equal to its correlation coefficient.)

$$X_1 = P_{1a}Z_a = \text{variation in class}$$
$$X_2 = P_{2b}Z_b + P_{2.1}X_1 = \text{variation in school grades}$$
$$X_3 = P_{3c}Z_c + P_{3.1}X_1 = \text{variation in awards won}$$
$$X_4 = P_{4d}Z_d = \text{variation in boy-parent harmony}$$
$$X_5 = P_{5e}Z_e + P_{5.2}X_2 + P_{5.3}X_3 = \text{variation in school dropout}$$
$$X_6 = P_{6f}Z_f + P_{6.2}X_2 + P_{6.3}X_3 = \text{variation in fired from job}$$
$$X_7 = P_{7g}Z_g + P_{7.4}X_4 + P_{7.5}X_5 + P_{7.6}X_6 = \text{variation in Ratfink}$$
$$X_8 = P_{8h}Z_h + P_{8.4}X_4 + P_{8.5}X_5 + P_{8.6}X_6 = \text{variation in Ace-in-the-Hole}$$
$$X_9 = P_{9i}Z_i + P_{9.4}X_4 + P_{9.5}X_5 + P_{9.6}X_6 = \text{variation in Sociability}$$
$$X_{10} = P_{10j}Z_j + P_{10.4}X_4 + P_{10.5}X_5 + P_{10.6}X_6 = \text{variation in Deviance}$$
$$X_w = P_{wk}Z_k + P_{w.7}X_7 + P_{w.8}X_8 + P_{w.9}X_9 + P_{w.10}X_{10} = \text{variation in Delinquency}$$

Where X_1 = social class; X_2 = school grades; X_3 = awards;
X_4 = boy-parent harmony; Z_5 = school dropout;
X_6 = fired from job; X_7 = Ratfink; X_8 = Ace-in-the-Hole;
X_9 = Sociability; X_{10} = Deviance;
X_w = each of 12 measures of delinquency; and
Z_k = each of 12 residuals of delinquency.

Figure 3-2. The Path Model.

The third step in the path analysis involves the computation of the residual path coefficients. In each of the models (see Figure 3-2), the residual coefficients are included as the first term to the right of the first equal sign. They are computed simply by subtracting the squared multiple correlation coefficient (R^2) involved in a given causal relationship from unity and taking the square root of the difference. A squared residual path coefficient indicates what proportion of variance in a given dependent variable is explained by factors not measured by the causal model.

The fourth step involves the estimation of the *indirect* and *shared* effects of prior variables in the causal sequence on subsequent variables (see Duncan, 1970, for an extension of Land's treatment of this step). In order to describe what these effects are, let us refer to Figure 3-3, below, which focuses on a specific aspect of the causal chain presented in Figure 3-1. The path coefficients for this example would be estimated according to the procedures described in steps two and three. This would involve an assessment of the direct effects of school dropout (P_{13}) and fired from a job (P_{23}) on deviance (P_{13} and P_{23}), of deviance on number of offenses (P_{34}) and of the residuals Z_e, Z_f, Z_j and Z_k.

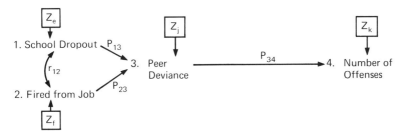

*The curved arrow indicates a "correlation effect" of a non-causal nature.

Figure 3–3. Indirect and Shared Effects.

There are (discounting residuals) two types of *indirect* effects possible within the diagram. First, it is possible that school dropout might affect number of offenses through the intervening variable of the deviance scale. This indirect effect could be computed by multiplying P_{13} by P_{34}. Similarly, the indirect effect of fired from job on number of offenses (through deviance) could be computed by multiplying P_{23} by P_{34}.

Several *shared* effects are also possible. A shared effect is present when two or more variables, because of their non-causal intercorrelatedness, join together in order to affect a causal sequence. For example, it is possible that school dropout and fired from job might have a shared affect on deviance through either path 13 or path 23. The former shared effect could be estimated by multiplying r_{12} by P_{13}, while the latter could be estimated by multiplying r_{12} by P_{23}. Furthermore, it is possible that the two strain measures might have shared effects on number of offenses through the intervening influence of deviance. Shared effects in this area could be estimated by the following multiplications: $(r_{12})(P_{13})(P_{34})$ and $(r_{12})(P_{23})(P_{34})$.

As a final point, it should be mentioned that the criteria used to assess the gammas—those of sign and magnitude—were also used in assessing the paths. However, because path coefficients, as a rule, are lower than gammas, a lower cutting point of .10 was adopted in deciding which to accept.

Summary

In summary, two statistical techniques will be used to test the theory. First, using gamma analysis, all of the bivariate relationships specified in the postulates and theorems will be examined. This analysis will involve all 482 serious delinquents and 185 nondelinquents included in the study. Second, path analysis will be used to complement the gamma analysis. This technique will permit us to examine not only the direct causal effects among our indicators, and thus provide a check on the gamma analysis, but to test the closed system assumption as well by assessing the indirect and combined effects of the various measures. The path analysis may be limited in some way due to non-response, but the fact that it is combined with the gamma analysis should help to isolate any glaring inconsistencies.

Part II
Test of Theory

4 Social Class as a Causal Antecedent

This is the first of three chapters devoted to an examination of all the bivariate relationships expressed in the propositions of the theory. This chapter will examine the relationship of *social class* to all other concepts; chapter 5 will examine all of the relationships among the concepts of *achievement, strain,* and *peer identification*; and chapter 6 will be concerned with the single relationships of all three variables to *delinquency*.

The propositions to be treated in this chapter in which social class is involved are as follows:

Postulate I. *The lower the social class, the lower the subsequent achievement.*
Theorem I. *The lower the social class, the greater the subsequent strain.*
Theorem IV. *The lower the social class, the greater the subsequent identification with delinquent peers.*
Theorem VI. *The lower the social class, the higher the subsequent delinquency.*

It is difficult to overstate the importance of these propositions to contemporary delinquency theory. They form the basis not only for arguments favoring the idea that delinquency is primarily a lower-class phenomenon, but for arguments that class membership is also a primary determinant of childhood and adolescent achievement, strain, and peer identification. For these reasons, extended tests of them are of significance.

As promised earlier, the findings for this and subsequent chapters are presented, first, in summary and, then, in detailed form. The summary provides a general statement of findings and implications while the detailed statement provides a much greater explication of both method and content.

Summarized Findings

The findings failed to support any of the four propositions stated above. In neither Los Angeles nor Utah was membership in the lower-class related significantly to poorer levels of achievement, nor to higher levels of strain, peer identification, and delinquency. In fact, there were some hints of a possible tendency for the reverse to be true in Utah, but the most likely interpretation would be that class membership per se, either high or low, is a poor predictor of a variety of different and specific kinds of adolescent behavior.

An evaluation of this conclusion in light of other recent studies provided some confirmation for it. Few investigators would argue that factors related to class are unimportant. However, when class is treated as an all-inclusive and global concept, without regard to familial, ethnic, sub-cultural, and other differences within it, one should not expect it to have much predictive efficiency. While some theorists have attempted to incorporate this idea in their theories, the prevailing interpretations that are placed upon them tend to ignore it.

In light of this and other findings, this seems to be a serious mistake. If our understanding of delinquency and other childhood difficulties is to be improved, a concentration upon other determinants, for which social class by itself may be a poor clue, would seem to be warranted. The issue is such an important one that a review of the interpretations beginning on page 43 is recommended.

Detailed Findings

In reviewing the detailed test of the four postulates listed above, recall the criteria that were set up by which the relationships between the various operational indicators of class and the other concepts are to be evaluated.

1. The sign of each gamma and path coefficient will be examined to see if it is commensurate with theoretical expectation. If it is not, an asterisk will be used to so indicate. A negative sign in front of a coefficient simply indicates that an inverse relation between variables was observed.
2. Cutting points of .20 for gamma coefficients and .10 for path coefficients were used in deciding whether any particular coefficient, by itself, could be accepted as supporting a proposition.
3. The combined criteria of both sign and magnitude for all coefficients in total will also be used in assessing a proposition; that is, the overall context of the findings as well as the values of single coefficients are important.
4. The findings using the gamma coefficients will be discussed first, followed by a presentation of path findings. With these criteria in mind, let us turn to an examination of the propositions.

Postulate I. *The lower the social class, the lower the subsequent achievement.*
In testing this postulate, it will be recalled that the following operational indicators were used: the occupational status of the father as an indicator of social class, and several indicators as measures of achievement: school grades, awards in school, and occupational aspirations.

Gamma Analysis

According to the criteria listed above for gamma coefficients, this postulate received virtually no support (Table 4-1). In neither Los Angeles nor Utah did

Table 4-1

Support for Postulate I (Class Determines Achievement)

Sign Commensurate with Theory	Los Angeles		Utah	
	Gamma ≥ .20	Gamma < .20	Gamma ≥ .20	Gamma < .20
Yes	0	2 (67%)	0	0
No	0	1 (33%)	1 (33%)	2 (67%)

any of the relationships between social class and the indicators of achievement exceed the .20 cutting point *and* possess signs commensurate with the postulate.

As may be seen in Table 4-2, the gamma coefficients were either so low that their signs, positive or negative, either suggested the lack of a significant relationship or, in the case of Utah, were contrary to expectation.

Table 4-2

Gamma Coefficients from Class to Achievement

Achievement Measure	Los Angeles	Utah
School grades	−.01*	−.24*
School awards	.01	−.03*
Occupational aspiration	.15	−.17*

*Contrary to expectation.

In Utah, the contrary findings, although fairly weak, implied that the higher the class, the lower the achievement. However, the findings may be questionable because of the way the *nondelinquents* in Utah were distributed on the class ladder. It will be recalled that social class was measured in terms of father's occupational prestige, which was ranked initially on a ten point scale. This scale was then collapsed into eight categories for convenience in analysis. The lower three categories include unskilled or semi-skilled occupations; the middle three include skilled occupations, owners of small businesses and a variety of white collar jobs; and the latter two include most of the professions, corporate positions, scientists, and artists. As will be noted in Table 4-3, a possible problem may be inherent in the distribution of the Utah *non*delinquents on the prestige scale. While the other samples seem reasonably well distributed over the various

36

Table 4-3

Distribution of Samples on Occupational Prestige Scale

Prestige Ranking	Los Angeles		Utah	
	Delinquents	Non Delinquents	Delinquents	Non Delinquents
1	3%	1%	4%	12%
2	4	9	13	20
3	21	15	12	14
4	17	13	26	36
5	15	21	32	16
6	15	23	10	2
7	6	4	3	0
8 (8-9-10)	17	15	1	0
Totals	98	101	101	100

Note: The lower the ranking, the lower the prestige.

categories of the scale, the distribution for the Utah nondelinquents is attenuated at the upper end. Despite the fact that this sample was randomly selected, it may be biased in the sense that nondelinquent subjects whose fathers are the most prestigious are underrepresented. Thus, in relating class to achievement in Utah, an association may have been suggested that is spurious. Had the *nondelinquent* sample been better distributed over the class ladder, as were the other three samples, it is highly possible that the findings for Utah would have been much like those for Los Angeles. In any event, whether the observed relationship is spurious or not, it does not support the postulate.

Path Analysis

Path coefficients for the relation between class and the two school indicators—grades and awards—are listed in Table 4-4. The findings were highly similar to those in which the gamma analysis was used. The path coefficients (P) were low in Los Angeles and the residuals (Z), which indicate the amount of variance in achievement that is *unexplained* by class membership, were high, suggesting that little variance was being explained. In Utah, the relation between class and school grades was again contrary to expectation, although there was little relationship between class and school awards. Thus, the data simply did not support the theoretical premise that membership in the lower class predisposes

Table 4-4

Path Coefficients from Class to Achievement

Achievement Measure	Los Angeles		Utah	
	P	Z	P	Z
Grades	.05	1.00	−.26*	0.93
Awards	.08	0.99	−.01*	1.00

*Contrary to expectation.

delinquents to poor levels of school performance. In fact, in Utah a tendency toward the reverse may be true, although, because of the nature of our nondelinquent sample, we would question that conclusion. It is our feeling that an interpretation favoring no strong relationship between the two indicators in either location would be the most accurate.

Theorem I. *The lower the social class, the greater the subsequent strain.*
In testing this theorem, the relationships of several indicators of strain to our measure of social class were examined: dropping out of school, being fired from a job, estimates of future occupational chances, and three evaluations of self (as compared to others)—leadership, smartness, and maturity.

Gamma Analysis

The theorem, as will be observed in Table 4-5, was not supported for either sample. Of the six coefficients used to assess the theorem, in each location, none was supportive when both sign and magnitude were considered.

Table 4-5

Support for Theorem I (Class Determines Strain)

Sign Commensurate with Theory	Los Angeles		Utah	
	Gamma ⩾ .20	Gamma < .20	Gamma ⩾ .20	Gamma < .20
Yes	0	4 (67%)	0	2 (33%)
No	0	2 (33%)	2 (33%)	2 (33%)

As may be seen in Table 4-6, the size of the coefficients in Los Angeles, either in support of or against the theorem, were so small that they implied the lack of a relationship. In Utah, the picture was like that for the relation between class and achievement. Although only two of the gamma coefficients were of sufficient magnitude to exceed the .20 cutting point, the overall set of relationships was contrary to expectation, suggesting that the higher the class the greater the inclination to drop out of school, to be fired from a job, and to have poor evaluations of self.

Table 4-6

Gamma Coefficients from Class to Strain

Strain Measure	Los Angeles	Utah
School dropout	−.07	.15*
Leadership self-concept	−.06*	−.24*
Smartness self-concept	.10	−.27*
Maturity self-concept	−.02*	−.15*
Occupational chances	.13	.00
Fired from job	−.01	.10*

*Contrary to expectation.

We suspect that the Utah findings may again be due to the distributions of the delinquent and nondelinquent samples on the class ladder, and not to any generalizable characteristics. Thus, if upper-class nondelinquents had been better represented, the size of these relatively weak and contrary coefficients might have been lowered and become much like those for Los Angeles. Nevertheless, even if they had, the data would not have supported the theorem. There was little evidence derived from these Los Angeles or Utah samples to support the theorem that being lower-class produces greater strain.

This conclusion was supported as well by family data. The reader will recall that, although sociological theory in recent years has tended to pay greater attention to the place of the family in the social structure, in its relationship to delinquency than to intrafamily strain, we decided to examine this assumption. A parallel analysis of family strain was conducted, therefore, along with our test of the theory. The findings are shown in Table 4-7.

It will be observed that in neither Los Angeles nor Utah was there a clear-cut trend. Being lower class was clearly not predictive of greater family strain, nor was the reverse true. If anything at all is revealed, it is that family separation was

Table 4-7

Gamma Coefficients from Class to Family Strain

Family Strain Measure	Los Angeles	Utah
Family separation	.13*	−.03
Parental harmony	.10	−.14*
Boy-parent harmony	−.01	−.09

*Contrary to expectation.

slightly more likely in Los Angeles to be associated with middle or upper-class membership, rather than lower, or in Utah that parental disharmony was more likely to be a middle than upper-class phenomenon. However, given the small size of the coefficients, the safest interpretation would be that the observed associations are of little importance.

Path Analysis

In the path diagram described in chapter 3 (Figure 3-1), it was indicated that the path analysis could be devoted only to a test of the postulates of the theory. Consequently, path coefficients were not calculated to test this theorem. However, zero-order correlation coefficients (Pearsonian *r*'s) were calculated, but only for those indicators that were retained in the path analysis.[a] They are shown in Table 4-8.

Table 4-8

Zero-Order Correlations Between Class and Strain

Strain Measure	Los Angeles	Utah
Dropout	.05*	.15*
Fired from job	−.01	−.04
Boy-parent harmony	−.08	−.13

*Contrary to expectation.

[a]As indicated in chapter 3, some indicators were dropped because path analysis requires that complete data be available on all respondents for each item. The losses, in this case, included the indicators of self-concept, occupational aspiration, and family separation (cf. chapter 3, pp. 24-25.

Again the findings failed to support the theorem that the lower the class the greater the strain. The small size of the zero-order coefficients, like the gamma coefficients, implies that no class pattern exists for these groups.

Theorem IV. *The lower the social class, the greater the subsequent identification with delinquent peers.*

In testing this theorem, four indicators of peer identification were used, all derived from factor analysis and Guttman scaling: *Ratfink* (willingness to tell on others), *Ace-in-the-Hole* (willingness to hide another being sought by police or parents), *Deviance* (willingness to engage with others in clearly delinquent acts), *and Sociability* (willingness to participate in group but non-delinquent activities).

Gamma and Zero-Order Analysis

As was the case with the other propositions involving social class, this theorem was not supported by empirical evidence (Table 4-9). None of the gamma coefficients exceeded the cutting point and in Utah three-quarters of them, although small in magnitude, were contrary.

Table 4-9

Support for Theorem IV (Class Determines Peer Identification)

Sign Commensu-rate with Theory	Los Angeles		Utah	
	Gamma ⩾ .20	Gamma < .20	Gamma ⩾ .20	Gamma < .20
Yes	0	3 (75%)	0	1 (25%)
No	0	1 (25%)	0	3 (75%)

As may be seen in Table 4-10, which includes zero-order as well as gamma coefficients, the lack of a definitive relationship between class and peer identification is so pronounced that whether the signs of the coefficients are supportive or contrary, their magnitudes are so low that one could have little confidence in the empirical validity of this theorem. If there is any trend whatsoever, it is one favoring a slight relationship between higher class membership and peer identification. However, the coefficients favoring this relationship for the Utah sample would have been more like those for Los Angeles had the nondelinquent group in Utah not been skewed toward the middle and lower end of the class ladder. The soundest interpretation, therefore,

Table 4-10

Associations Between Class and Peer Identification

Peer Identification Measure	Los Angeles		Utah	
	Gamma	Zero Order r	Gamma	Zero Order r
Ratfink	.07	.03	.09	.14
Ace-in-Hole	.00	.01*	.12*	.11*
Sociability	.01*	.05*	.09*	.12*
Deviance	−.01	−.02	.12*	.17*

*Contrary to expectation.

would probably be that delinquent peer identification is spread across class levels and is not uniquely characteristic of lower-class juveniles, at least in these samples. The findings simply do not conform to the rather common assumption that it is lower-class boys who are most inclined to peer influence. If the peer scales are at all reflective of those social and psychological forces that encourage group identification, then one might be as likely to find them among middle- and upper-, as among lower-class boys.

Theorem VI. *The lower the social class, the higher the subsequent delinquency.* Given the emphasis which this and other theories have placed upon the relation of class to delinquency, this may be the last of the theoretical statements, but it certainly is not the least important. A test of it involved the computation of one gamma coefficient relating class to delinquency via a single dichotomous indicator (delinquent or not delinquent), and several zero-order coefficients between class and the twelve multiple indicators of delinquency.[b]

For neither sample were the findings supportive. In Los Angeles, the sign of the gamma coefficient for the dichotomous indicator was in the expected direction, but its magnitude (−.02) was far below an acceptable level. For the Utah sample, the magnitude was acceptable (.39), but its sign was contrary. It suggested a direct rather than an inverse relation: the higher the class, the higher the delinquency.

The twelve multiple indicators conveyed the same general message. However, before turning to them it must be noted that not all of them can be used as a direct test of the theorem. Six of the twelve can be used because a low score on them is indicative of a low degree of delinquency, either in terms of frequency or seriousness. These are the Category 1 indicators described in chapter 3. The

[b]For a detailed description of these indicators, refer to chapter 2, pp. 15-16, or Appendix 1.

remaining six (Category 2) indicators cannot be interpreted as a direct test because they represent the ratio of certain types of acts to the total number committed by a given individual. For example, a high score on the Felony/ Misdemeanor index indicates that an individual's offenses are mainly felonies, while a low score indicates that they are mainly misdemeanors. The same is also true for such other indexes as Status Offenses (i.e., adult vs. juvenile), Instrumental/Expressive, Retreatism, Conflict, and Criminalism. Therefore, while these indexes will provide some information regarding the relation of social class to certain kinds or patterns of offense, they will not provide a relative measure of the extent of delinquent behavior per se.

With these qualifications in mind, consider the zero-order coefficients shown in Table 4-11.

Table 4-11

Zero-Order Correlation Between Class and Delinquency

	Delinquency Indicator	Los Angeles	Utah
	Number of offenses	−.04	.27*
	Average seriousness	.01*	.31*
	Most serious offense	.01*	.32*
Category 1	Theft factor	−.04	.26*
	Hell-raising factor	−.07	.10*
	Incorrigibility factor	−.01	.06*
	Adult/juvenile	−.01	.13
	Felony/misdemeanor	.03	.22
Category 2	Instrumental/expressive	−.04	.16
	Retreatism	.03	.06
	Conflict	−.02	.13
	Criminalism	−.04	.21

*Contrary to expectation.

For the Los Angeles sample, no relationships of any magnitude were observed, either contrary to or in support of the theorem. But for Utah most of the Category 1 coefficients were relatively high and contrary to the theorem. They suggested that the higher the class, the higher the delinquency. However, given the problems described for the distribution of the Utah nondelinquent sample, we would guess that the sizes of the contrary relationships are spuriously high, that if the distribution had been normal, the coefficients would have declined. Nevertheless, it is possible that a relationship does exist in Utah which indicates that the higher the class, the higher the delinquency. Both the gamma and zero-order coefficients, if accepted at face value, would suggest that this is the case. But whichever interpretation is preferred, the data clearly do not support the theorem that the lower the class, the higher the delinquency.

Interpreting the Findings

Given the dominant emphasis of delinquency theory, indeed, the almost universal assumption that membership in the lower class is a precursor of poor adolescent achievement, of delinquency, and of many other social problems, how can findings such as these be reconciled? They seem to be at odds with virtually all thinking on the matter, lay as well as scientific.

Two possible explanations are in order. First, the findings could be due to the nature of the samples involved. Since they were not randomly selected from a general population of all known delinquents, or of all law violators, they may not be representative. If new samples were to paint a different picture, however, they would have to change markedly. In Utah, for example, the sample represented (1) an enumeration of all of the most serious offenders incarcerated in the Utah State Industrial School over a period of three years, and (2) a total enumeration of all of the most serious offenders to come before the juvenile court in Utah County during the years 1959-64. Yet these two groups of delinquents were quite well-distributed over the class ladder, coming from families of moderate and high as well as low prestige. Thus, if some more representative sample of serious offenders exists, its distribution over the class structure would have to change drastically before much of an inverse relation between class and delinquency could be documented. The change that would be required would not be merely a moderate one, but a significant one.

Perhaps if ethnic minorities had been more highly represented, the findings would have been different. Again, however, one must exercise caution. The concepts of race and class are not equatable; they are conceptually distinct. Thus, although a greater representation of black and other minorities might have changed the findings, it cannot be assumed automatically that they would have been totally reversed. Thus, even though the issue of sampling remains a major one, there are other issues to be considered.

A more plausible interpretation, it seems to us, is that class membership, by itself, may simply be too global a concept to be of much utility in predicting a long list of specific behaviors such as delinquency. There are some compelling reasons for this conclusion.

The first is related to the use of ecological vs. individual correlation in the study of class and delinquency. As Robinson (1950:351) points out, when an ecological correlation is used, the object of study is a group of persons often delimited by residence in a social area such as a census tract or some larger entity. By contrast, an individual correlation is one in which the object of study is a person or thing. In this case, any variables are descriptive properties of that individual and not of group rates or means, as in the case of the ecological correlation.

The reasons the measurement issue is an important one are that some of the major studies upon which conclusions have been reached regarding the relation between class and delinquency have been ecological studies (Shaw, 1929; Shaw and McKay, 1942), and that vastly different conclusions can be reached depending upon the nature of the correlation used. Robinson (1950:352-3) cites an example in which, when an ecological correlation was calculated between membership in the Negro race and illiteracy, using nine geographic divisions in the United States, a coefficient of .946 was obtained. The finding would suggest that illiteracy was primarily a black phenomenon. Yet when the same variables were correlated on the same population, using the properties of individuals rather than areas, the value of the correlation declined to .203, slightly more than one-fifth of the original, ecological correlation. Robinson (1950:357) concluded, therefore, that an ecological correlation cannot be used as a valid substitute for an individual correlation; it is almost certain that the two will not be equal. He also pointed out, however, that most ecological studies have been used to make conclusions about individuals. It is highly possible, therefore, that the role of social class has been misinterpreted, perhaps overstated. That may be one reason that the results of earlier ecological studies differed so much from a study such as this one where the properties of individuals, not areas, were the object of analysis.

What is also significant is the fact that several recent ecological studies have failed to support the findings of earlier ones. As Polk (1967) points out in a summary article, newer studies have failed to document a consistent relationship between a number of different economic-status variables and delinquency. This failure, he says, presents a major disjunction between current fact and delinquency theory. It is possible, of course, that differences between older and newer ecological studies are due to the changing character of American cities and the class structures within them. Polk feels, however, that a more likely interpretation is that they are due to methodological and theoretical inadequacies.

With reference to methodology, he argues that any method which does not permit the examination of characteristics *within*, as well as between, urban social areas is hopelessly inadequate. "It is only when we examine specific types of areas that differential rates of delinquency between neighborhood status levels, or even differentials *at the same economic level*, can be understood and interpreted" (1967:305). What is needed are techniques that are sensitive to familial and ethnic as well as economic status.

Polk (1967:305-6) also feels that the ecology of the modern city is more complex than contemporary theory indicates:

It is not sufficient to say that delinquency is higher in 'lower-class areas,' because low economic status areas will differ considerably when family status and ethnic status vary. . . . If class-linked theories are to be expressed in such a way that their implications are to be seen in the ecological structure of the city, more than simple economic characteristics will have to be specified. There is no such thing as *a* lower class area, or *a* lower class culture. There are a number of such cultures, and it is the task of the theorist to specify which is being discussed.

The relevance of Polk's remarks would seem to be without question. A number of studies have suggested why there is merit in his conclusions.

Based upon their findings, Reiss and Rhodes (1961) suggest that there are community aggregates and social milieus whose influences cut across class lines and thus transcend the influences of class differences within them.

While the life-chances of low ascribed status boys becoming delinquent are greater than those of high status ones, a low status boy in a predominantly high status area with a low rate of delinquency has almost no chance of being classified a juvenile court delinquent. . . . The more the lower class boy is in a minority in the school and residential community, the less likely is he to become delinquent [p. 729].

They also suggest that

the factors related to where a family of a given ascribed status will live are important in predicting the delinquency life-chances of a boy of any ascribed status. . . . Lower class status is not a necessary and sufficient set of conditions in the etiology of any type of delinquency [p. 730].

Similarly, Clark and Wenninger (1962:833) conclude that although delinquent behavior is affected by the predominant class of the area in which a juvenile lives, *his* particular class level may not be the deciding factor. If he is a lower-class person, living in a middle-class area, his behavior will reflect that of the prevailing class, not his own, and vice versa. "Social class differentiation with these areas," they observe, "is apparently not related to the incidence of illegal behavior."

While these studies provide obvious and important support for Polk's position, one would be remiss in suggesting that current theory has failed entirely to take subcultural and other community factors into account. There is a difference between the interpretations of prevailing theories and what theorists have actually said. For example, if one theme can be said to characterize current interpretations of class-based theories, it is that poverty is the primary cause of delinquency. Witness the statement of the President's Commission on Law Enforcement and Administration of Justice (1967:56-57):

Delinquents tend to come from backgrounds of social and economic deprivation. Their families tend to have lower than average incomes and social status. . . . It is inescapable that juvenile delinquency is directly related to conditions bred by poverty.

Taken at face value, such statements would suggest that economic factors are the deciding influence. Yet Cohen (1955) or Cloward and Ohlin (1960) go to great length to point out, first, that all lower-class youth do not become delinquent, and, second, that for those who do, it is their contact with, and involvement in, delinquent subculture(s), not class alone, that will be the deciding factor. Failures and frustrations resulting from membership in the lower class may make the lower-class youth a likely candidate for a delinquent solution, but unless delinquent structures and associations are available into which he can be inducted, delinquency on his part will be less likely to occur.

While Miller (1958) disagrees with many of these ideas, he does posit varieties of lower-class culture which, he says, account for variations in behavior and values. Lower-status groups, he believes, vary in the degree to which they display the core features of lower-class culture. Thus, one might anticipate variations in the degree to which delinquent as well as other kinds of behavior might be expected and reinforced.

The formal theoretical statement tested in this work, which was designed to capture some of the major themes of these theorists, also incorporates the ideas just suggested. It postulates that it is not mere class membership alone that will determine whether the individual will become delinquent or not, but a host of other experiences as well, in the school and community, and with his peers. Thus, according to the logic of the theory, one would not expect to find strong, direct relationships between class membership on one end of a long chain of events and delinquency on the other.

Interestingly, causal inference based upon correlational analysis might suggest the same conclusion. Refer again to Figure 2-1. According to the causal sequence outlined there, social class was the first in a long series of factors said to produce delinquency. By way of illustrating why it might be expected to have a low relationship to delinquency, let us assume that the absolute value of the correlation between each of the adjacent variables in the chain is .70. What, then, would be the separate relationships of each of the causal variables to delinquency? Even though a correlation of .70 is relatively high, and appeared in few cases in this test of theory, the principle that it illustrates is useful.

Assuming that the causal model is valid, and by using the analytical techniques suggested by path analysis, we could expect the following effects between each variable and delinquency:

$r_{1,5}$ (lower-class and delinquency) = $(r_{1,2}) \times (r_{2,3}) \times (r_{3,4}) \times (r_{4,5}) = (.70)^4 =$ .24.

$r_{2,5}$ (achievement and delinquency) = $(r_{2,3}) \times (r_{3,4}) \times (r_{4,5}) = (.70)^3 = .34$.

$r_{3,5}$ (strain and delinquency) = $(r_{3,4}) \times (r_{4,5}) = (.70)^2 = .49$.

$r_{4,5}$ (peer identification and delinquency) = $(r_{4,5}) = (.70)^1 = .70$.

In other words, the model indicates rather clearly that the closer any theoretical antecedent is to delinquency, the greater will be its association with delinquency, and, conversely, that the further that antecedent is in the developmental sequence from delinquency itself, the lesser will be its direct association. Thus, there are a number of reasons, aside from sampling, why social class might not be expected to have a very strong, direct relationship to delinquency. If any relationship exists at all, it may be an indirect one that is mediated by several intervening influences: family and ethnic status, the prevailing ethos of a community, and the existence of particular kinds of peer subcultures.

What is more, one can ill afford to forget two other bodies of information that have not yet been presented. The first is derived from a growing number of studies which, on the level of self-reported, if not official, lawbreaking, question the existence of a universal and unqualified relationship between social class and delinquency (Porterfield, 1946; Nye, Short, et al., 1958; Dentler and Monroe, 1961; Reiss and Rhodes, 1961; Empey and Erickson, 1966; Gold, 1966; and Empey, 1967). These self-report studies have yielded very low correlations between class and delinquency such that the degree of variance that could be explained by them is small indeed. The chief limitation in comparing these studies with the present findings, however, is the fact that different criteria for delinquency were used, official delinquency in this case, and self-reported lawbreaking in the others. Nevertheless, the striking similarities cannot be ignored.

The second body of information relates to the school. Call (1965) and Polk and Halferty (1966) both found that delinquency was more highly related to poor adjustment in the school than to social class. While delinquency was uniformly low among boys from all class levels who were doing well in school, it was uniformly high among those who were doing poorly.

A later analysis helps to explain why this may be so. Schafer, Olexa, and Polk (1970), in their study of two midwestern high schools, found that students could be classified by their placement in two general "track positions" in the school. The first track was college preparatory and stressed the acquisition of skills in such areas as mathematics, foreign language, and English. The second track was more general in nature and emphasized business and vocational training. It was found that these track positions were virtually irreversible once they were started, and that there was very little mobility between them.

Several important differences were found to exist between students in the two tracks. The academic performances of college prep students far exceeded those of lower track students and the latter group were much more likely to drop out of school prior to graduation. High track students were also more likely to participate in extracurricular activities.

Finally, track position was found to have a high relationship to delinquency, both in and out of school. Only 19 per cent of the high track students committed three or more violations of school rules, while the figure for low track students was a striking 70 per cent. Further, only 6 per cent of the high track students were official delinquents, while the figure for low track students was almost three times as high at 16 per cent.

Although the investigators found that upper- and middle-class whites were more likely to be found in the college-prep track than lower-class and black students, they also found that the effects of track position on the performance criteria of grade point average and dropping out were largely independent of, and considerably higher than, the effects of IQ, past performance, and social class. Thus, within the high school setting, a very rigid—indeed, almost caste-like—stratification system was present. The effects of this system on the performances of students were significant and independent of such factors as social class and intellectual ability.

This led the authors of the study to conclude that

delinquency may well be largely a rebellion against the school and its standards by teenagers who feel they cannot get anywhere by attempting to adhere to such standards. Our analysis suggests that a key factor in such rebellion is non-college prep status in the school's tracking system, with the vicious cycle of low achievement and inferior self image that go along with it [Schafer, Olexa, and Polk, 1970:45].

What is significant about these findings is their similarity to later chapters of this book where it will be shown that it is performance in, and dropping out of, school, not social class, that are related most strongly to official delinquency.

In conclusion, this review has seemed to suggest a number of reasons why, when the global concept of social class was correlated on an individual basis with a number of indices of adolescent difficulty, relationships were small or nonexistent. By itself, the concept could not possibly reflect all of the factors that might have affected the relationship: familial and ethnic status, community milieus that cut across class lines, school influences, peer subcultures, or the discretionary acts of police, courts, and correctional agencies. By the time the effects of class membership had been mediated by all these influences, they might have been so diluted that their impact could not be discerned with any precision.

This conclusion is not meant to suggest that class differences do not exist, especially when ecological rather than individual measurement is used. But what it does imply—reinforced by the findings of other recent studies—is that our understanding of delinquency and other adolescent difficulties might be enhanced if we concentrate our search upon other determinants for which social class, by itself, may be a poor clue. The fact that delinquency is not limited to the lower class suggests that we might discover as many differences *within* classes as we discover between them. Instead of comparing lower-, middle-, and upper-class groups across class lines, we might be well-advised to study the behaviors of subgroups within classes. Precise distinctions of this type might provide better clues to the nature of delinquent behavior than do gross comparisons between classes.

5 Examination of Causal Sequence Involving Achievement, Strain and Peer Identification

The relationships among *achievement, strain,* and *peer identification* are expressed in the following theoretical propositions:

Postulate II. *Decreased achievement results in increased strain.*
Postulate III. *Increased strain results in identification with delinquent peers.*
Theorem II. *Decreased achievement results in identification with delinquent peers.*

The sequence embodying these propositions is shown in Figure 5-1.

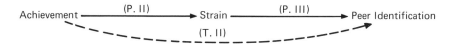

Figure 5-1. The Relationships Among Achievement, Strain, and Peer Identification.

The significance of this sequence in the original theoretical statement was great. First, it was used to represent an intervening set of forces thought to be present between social class and delinquency. According to much of sociological theory, the forces set in motion by membership in the lower class are mediated through the variables of achievement, strain, and peer identification prior to any onset of delinquency. Second, it is this aspect of the theory which makes it a dynamic rather than static formulation. Hypothetically, the strain generated by the lack of achievement, in an achievement-oriented society, creates a psychological dissonance in the individual demanding resolution. Although it is not the only way he has of resolving strain, a common means involves a collective (and often deviant) adjustment among like-minded peers. By identifying with others, and by seeking alternative sources of satisfaction to legitimate ones, the individual is able to reduce some of the strain he feels. Basic to this whole section of the theory, however, is the assumption that the series of events leading to delinquency must occur in sequence. If they do not, then delinquent behavior will probably not occur. Consequently, an examination of the sequence is vital to a test of the theory.

Summarized Findings

Consistent support appeared in both Los Angeles and Utah for the postulate that decreased achievement results in increased strain. Poor school performance in both locations was associated with such strain measures as school dropout, lowered self-estimates of maturity, smartness, and leadership, and lowered estimates of future occupational chances.

There was also some support for the postulate that increased strain results in identification with delinquent peers, but this support was of a limited nature. While dropping out of school, as a measure of strain, was related consistently to peer identification, the relations of all the self-concept indicators to peer identification were extremely weak. Thus, although the data supported the theoretical notion that poor achievement in school results in a loss of self-esteem and the belief that one's future is limited, they did not support the notion that these same indicators enhance peer identification. The two non-adjacent concepts—achievement and peer identification—were linked only through dropping out of school, not through a lowered sense of self-worth.

Finally, the data tended to support the theorem that the lack of achievement—most notably, poor school grades—results in identification with delinquent peers. Thus, this finding tended to reinforce the idea that strain, as an intervening variable between achievement and peer identification, may not be a necessary one. However, a definitive test of that issue will be made when the closed system assumption is tested in chapters 7 and 8.

The most significant thing about these findings is the implication that it is the lack of institutional ties to the school (as measured by poor grades and dropping out), and *not* a lowered sense of self-esteem, that is of greatest importance in leading to identification with delinquent peers. The findings are such as to suggest that "strain," at least as measured by self-concept, may not be a crucial concept in the theoretical sequence being considered.

The possible importance of an individual's institutional ties is underscored by another finding presented in this chapter. It is that intrafamily difficulties—physical separation and interpersonal disharmony—may be associated with peer identification as strongly as, if not more strongly than, the school measures. Consequently, the omission of family variables from the theoretical statement seems to have been a significant one.

It is significant because a generation of sociologists seem to have decided that if delinquency is to be seen as a response to institutional or personal stress, that stress cannot have come from the family. Family variables have largely been omitted from current sociological theory on delinquency. Yet these findings imply that the lack of institutional ties to home, as well as to school, perhaps more than measures of self-concept, are important in leading to peer identification.

In carrying the analysis further into subsequent chapters, the first step will be to examine the relationships of achievement, strain, and peer identification, along with family variables, to delinquency. This step should help to clarify some of the issues raised in this chapter. Then, in subsequent chapters, the entire causal sequence will be examined, paying special attention to the closed system assumption, to whether much confidence can be placed in the idea that the series of events thought to lead to delinquency actually follow a sequential pattern.

Detailed Findings

The data are presented in two ways. First, they are summarized in Tables 5-1, 5-2, and 5-3. Tables 5-1 and 5-2 are correlation matrices for the Los Angeles and Utah samples presenting the gamma coefficients for all of the bivariate relationships specified in the propositions being tested. They also indicate the relationships of family variables to other variables in the chain. All coefficients exceeding the .20 cutting point are enclosed in brackets. Since correlations involving family variables are not crucial to a test of the theory, they are enclosed in double lines so that the reader will recognize them easily.

Table 5-3 presents the path coefficients for all the relationships being examined. Again, all path coefficients exceeding the .10 cutting point are enclosed in brackets, and the family variables are enclosed in double lines. These three tables are presented so that the reader may have all of the data easily accessible to him.

As a second way of presenting the data, each of the three propositions will be examined singly and in detail.

Examination of Individual Propositions

Postulate II. *Decreased achievement results in increased strain.*
The bivariate test of this postulate involves the following sets of indicators. For achievement, they include the measures described earlier: school grades, school awards, and occupational aspirations. For strain, they include school dropout, the three self-concept indicators, estimates of future occupational chances, and being fired from a job.

Gamma Analysis

As may be seen in Table 5-4, the gamma findings for this postulate are generally supportive. Thirty-nine per cent of the Los Angeles coefficients and 50 per cent of the Utah coefficients provided optimum support in the sense that both their signs and magnitudes were in accord with theoretical expectation. When sign alone was considered, the figures in support of the postulate rose drastically to 83 and 100 per cent, respectively. Only a very small percentage of the gammas were contrary to expectation in terms of both sign and magnitude.

52

Table 5-1

Gamma Coefficients for Los Angeles Sample

	4	5	6	7	8	9	10	11	12	13	14	15	16
Achievement													
1. Grades	[-.65]	[.33]	[.57]	.15	.19	[-.20]	[-.27]	[.25]	.16	[-.21*]	[-.28]	[-.21]	[-.26]
2. Awards	-.15	[.44]	[.41]	.13	[.21]	.10*	-.04	-.02	-.04	-.03*	-.13	.00	.00
3. Occupational Aspirations	-.19	.11	[.26]	-.16*	.11	.17*	-.02	-.02	.02	[-.20*]	.04*	.04*	-.07
			Postulate II									Theorem II	
Strain													
4. School Drop-out										-.12	[.31]	[.23]	[.22]
5. Leadership Self-Concept										.02	-.17	-.10	-.03
6. Smartness Self-Concept										-.07*	-.16	-.19	-.06
7. Maturity Self-Concept										-.16*	-.10	-.13	-.13
8. Chances of Getting Occupational Aspiration										-.13*	.00	-.05	-.14
9. Fired from Job										[-.21*]	-.03	-.08	-.12
												Postulate III	

Family
Strain

10. Family Separation	.06	[.24]	.10	.16
11. Parental Harmony	-.06*	[-.32]	[-.27]	[-.24]
12. Relations with Parents	[-.39]	[-.35]	[-.32]	[-.31]

Peer
Identifica-
tion

13. Ratfink

14. Ace-in-the-Hole

15. Sociability

16. Deviance

Note: In this table and in subsequent tables, coefficients exceeding the cutting point are in brackets, [ ]. Coefficients involving family strain are enclosed in double lines. Coefficients showing the relationship of family to other types of strain are not included, since such relationships were not specified by the theory. Column numbers at the top of the table refer to causal measures shown in left-hand column.

*Contrary to expectation.

Table 5-2

Gamma Coefficients for Utah Sample

	4	5	6	7	8	9	10	11	12	13	14	15	16
Achievement													
1. Grades	[-.44]	[.49]	[.41]	[.23]	[.23]	-.08	-.11	.18	[.27]	[-.27*]	[-.37]	[-.35]	[-.24]
2. Awards	-.12	.14	.14	.19	.14	-.05	.12	.09	.00	-.18*	.02*	-.03	-.03
3. Occupational Aspirations	[-.36]	[.33]	[.32]	[.15]	[.21]	-.19	-.05	.03	.04	-.08*	[-.25]	[-.23]	-.14
			Postulate II									Theorem II	
Strain													
4. School Drop-out										-.14	[.33]	[.25]	[.24]
5. Leadership Self-Concept										-.12*	-.04	.00	-.06
6. Smartness Self-Concept										-.12*	-.01	.07*	.03*
7. Maturity Self-Concept										.04	-.03	.15*	-.04
8. Chances of Getting Occupational Aspiration										-.16*	-.09	-.10	-.14
9. Fired from Job										-.09	.02	-.01*	.14
												Postulate III	

55

Family
Strain
10. Family
    Separation
11. Parental
    Harmony
12. Relations
    with
    Parents

Peer
Identifica-
tion
13. Ratfink
14. Ace-in-the-
    Hole
15. Sociability
16. Deviance

−.03	.04	.02	.04
.03	−.12	−.06	−.05
[−.21]	[−.26]	[−.30]	[−.26]

Note: See note to Table 5-1.
*Contrary to expectation.

Table 5-3

Path Coefficients for Los Angeles and Utah Samples

Los Angeles Sample

	Boy-Parent Harmony	School Dropout	Fired from Job	Ratfink	Ace-in-the-Hole	Sociability	Deviance
Grades	[.21]	[−.50]	[−.16]	[−.13]	[−.22]	[−.22]	[−.30]
Awards	−.08*	.04*	.09*	−.03	−.09	−.05	−.05
Squared Residuals	(.96)	(.76)	(.97)				
Boy-Parent Harmony				[−.32*]	[−.21]	[−.23]	[−.23]
School Dropout				.07*	[.22]	[.15]	[.13]
Fired from Job				−.03	−.04*	−.04*	[.10]
Squared Residuals				(.88)	(.88)	(.91)	(.90)

Utah Sample

	Boy-Parent Harmony	School Dropout	Fired from Job	Ratfink	Ace-in-the-Hole	Sociability	Deviance
Grades	[.26]	[−.26]	−.04	[−.22]	[−.24]	[−.34]	[−.29]
Awards	−.04*	.05*	−.02	[−.11]	−.03	−.08	−.07
Squared Residuals	(.94)	(.93)	(1.0)				
Boy-Parent Harmony				[−.17*]	[−.19]	[−.32]	[−.31]
School Dropout				−.06	[.22]	[.18]	[.18]
Fired from Job				[−.12]	−.03*	−.04*	.02
Squared Residuals				(.95)	(.92)	(.87)	(.86)

Note: The figures enclosed in double lines are not path coefficients, but represent zero-order correlations. The figures in parentheses ( ) are *squared* residual path coefficients.
*Contrary to expectation.

Table 5-4

Support for Postulate II (Achievement Determines Strain)

Sign Commensu-rate with Theory	Los Angeles		Utah	
	Gamma ≥ .20	Gamma < .20	Gamma ≥ .20	Gamma < .20
Yes	7 (39%)	8 (44%)	9 (50%)	9 (50%)
No	0 (0%)	3 (17%)	0 (0%)	0 (0%)

The gammas whose signs and magnitudes were supportive for both samples are listed in Table 5-5. However, since the findings were not always the same for both samples, those coefficients for one sample or the other which did not exceed the .20 cutting point are listed in parentheses. This common listing will facilitate comparison. It will be observed that school grades were highly important in both location, predicting several kinds of strain, especially dropping out of school, lowered estimates of self, and lowered estimates of occupational chances. School awards (or their lack) seemed more predictive of strain in Los Angeles, while in Utah, lowered occupational aspirations (as a measure of achievement orientation) were of greater importance. In fact, this latter trend is worth noting because it shows up later in other sections of the analysis, and because it seems contrary to theoretical expectation. In contrast to the notion that high aspirations are associated with high degrees of strain, these data suggest that in Utah, especially, it is boys with lowered aspirations who are most likely to have dropped out of school and to have experienced lowered estimates of self.

A second matter of importance for both samples had to do with the family data. Although, as mentioned previously, they do not reflect directly on a test of the theory, they did turn out to be of importance in the analysis. In Los Angeles, for example, a negative relationship (-.27) was found between school grades and *family separation*—death or divorce; the greater the separation, the poorer the grades. In Utah, school grades were more strongly associated with the degree of harmony between a boy and his parents (.27) than with physical separation; the better the harmony, the better the grades. Further, this is but the first of a number of examples indicating that although provision was not made for family variables in this theory, their relationship to other variables in the chain may be important in any future revision of the theory.

Path Analysis

The path analysis (Table 5-3) also provided a moderate amount of support for the postulate that lowered achievement and strain are related. In Los Angeles, although none of the coefficients between school awards and the measures of

58

Table 5-5

Supportive Relationships Between Achievement and Strain

Variables	Los Angeles	Utah
School Grades and Dropout	−.65	−.44
School Grades and Estimate of Leadership	.33	.49
School Grades and Estimate of Smartness	.57	.41
School Grades and Estimate of Maturity	(.15)	.23
School Grades and Occupational Chances	(.19)	.23
School Grades and Fired from Job	−.20	(−.08)
School Awards and Estimate of Leadership	.44	(.14)
School Awards and Estimate of Smartness	.41	(.14)
School Awards and Occupational Chances	.21	(.14)
Occupational Aspirations and Dropout	(−.19)	−.36
Occupational Aspirations and Estimate of Leadership	(.11)	.33
Occupational Aspirations and Estimate of Smartness	.26	.32
Occupational Aspirations and Occupational Chances	(.11)	.21

Source: Tables 5-1 and 5-2.
Note: Parentheses indicate coefficients not exceeding the cutting point.

strain exceeded the cutting point of .10 which was adopted for the paths, the coefficients involving grades were highly supportive. The paths between grades and the strain measures of boy-parent harmony, school dropout and fired from a job were .21, -.50 and -.16, respectively, and all signs were in the expected direction. However, the squared residual coefficients for the strain indicators of boy-parent harmony and fired from a job were .96 and .97, indicating that most of their variation for these factors was unexplained by the analysis. On the other hand, the squared residual coefficient for school dropout was .76, indicating that for this measure, at least, 24 per cent of the variance was explained by the direct, indirect, and combined effects of our measures of achievement (grades and awards).

In Utah, the path findings for this postulate were slightly less supportive. Again, none of the paths involving school awards exceeded the cutting point, while two of the three coefficients involving grades did exceed it. Grades appeared to be causally associated with boy-parent harmony (.26) and school dropout (−.26), and the directions of neither of these two paths contradicted theoretical expectations. However, the squared residual paths for the strain measures were high: for boy-parent harmony, .94, for school dropout, .93, and for fired from a job, 1.0. Thus, in testing the postulate that decreased achievement results in increased strain, two things stand out. Both the gamma and path analyses lend support to the notion that the relation is an important one. Yet, the magnitude of the path residuals suggests that much of the variation for the strain indicators is unexplained by the achievement measures which are antecedent to them. The amount of variance being explained is far lower than might have been hoped.

Postulate III: *Increased strain results in identification with delinquent peers.*
The bivariate test of this postulate involved the strain indicators just described, plus the four peer scales—Ratfink, Ace-in-the-hole, Deviance and Sociability—as measures of peer identification.

Gamma Analysis

As shown in Table 5-6, the support this postulate received from the gamma coefficients was less pronounced than that for Postulate II.

In terms of both sign *and* magnitude, only 13 per cent of the twenty-four gammas were supportive of the theory for both groups (Tables 5-1 and 5-2). However, when sign alone was considered, support rose considerably to 84 per cent for the Los Angeles group and 71 per cent for the Utah group. Further, of those gammas which were contrary to sign, only one was of a high magnitude. Thus, it was not so much that the findings were contrary to the postulate, but that the observed relationships were relatively weak in their support.

Table 5-6

Support for Postulate III (Strain Determines Peer Identification)

Sign Commensu-rate with Theory	Los Angeles		Utah	
	Gamma $\geq$ .20	Gamma $<$ .20	Gamma $\geq$ .20	Gamma $<$ .20
Yes	3 (13%)	17 (71%)	3 (13%)	14 (58%)
No	1 (4%)	3 (13%)	0 (0%)	7 (29%)

Those gammas whose signs *and* magnitudes were supportive are listed in Table 5-7.

It is significant that, of the several indicators of strain—dropping out of school, lowered self-evaluations, and being fired from a job—only dropping out of school in both locations was related to indicators of peer identification.

Table 5-7

Supportive Coefficients Between School Dropout and Peer Identification

Peer Identification Measure	Los Angeles	Utah
Ace-in-the-Hole	.31	.33
Sociability	.23	.25
Deviance	.22	.24

Source: Tables 5-1 and 5-2.

According to some theorists, this should not have been the case. Cohen (1955:121-137), for example, and Cloward and Ohlin (1960:86) suggest that when young people suffer a loss of self-esteem, when, according to their own estimates, they compare poorly with others, they experience intense frustration. This frustration, in turn, should encourage identification with like-minded, and often deviant, peers. Yet although poor achievement in school was related to such strain indicators as lowered estimates of personal maturity, smartness, and leadership, these indicators, in turn, were not associated to any degree with peer identification. Instead, of all the strain indicators, it was only the lack of institutional ties to the school that was predictive of peer identification, not the psychological indicators.

Moreover, the importance of institutional ties was underscored by a review of the family data. As may be seen in the coefficients listed in Table 5-8, our parallel study of the relation of intrafamily strain indicated that it may be as good, or even a better predictor of peer identification, than dropping out of school.

What is revealed is the first of a series of findings which support both those of Hirschi (1969) and DeFleur (1969) suggesting that marginal integration in basic institutions is more predictive of deviant associations than other antecedents. In addition, two other findings are worth noting. First, evidence suggests that strained relations within the family—a lack of parental harmony or a boy's poor relations with his parents—were more predictive of peer identification than disruption by death or separation. Second, it will be observed that family strain was more predictive of peer identification in Los Angeles than Utah. Why this was so, we do not know. However, it may reflect the possibility that boys in an impersonal, metropolitan environment are more affected by internal disharmony within the family than in a more integrated, nonmetropolitan environment. If so, the disruption of this important primary group for them may precipitate a more rapid rush to the peer group. In any event, these overall findings indicate that the failure to include intrafamily problems in the theoretical statement may have been a serious omission.

In noting this fact, one is reminded of Bordua's comment (1962:249) that

Table 5-8

Gamma Coefficients from Family Strain to Peer Identification

Variables	Los Angeles	Utah
Relations with Parents and Ace-in-the-Hole	−.35	−.26
Relations with Parents and Sociability	−.32	−.30
Relations with Parents and Deviance	−.31	−.26
Parental Harmony and Ace-in-the-Hole	−.32	(−.12)
Parental Harmony and Sociability	−.27	(−.06)
Parental Harmony and Deviance	−.24	(−.05)
Family Separation and Deviance	(.16)	(.04)

Source: Tables 5-1 and 5-2.
Note: Parentheses indicate coefficients not exceeding the cutting point.

the "discussion of the family in recent sociological theory of group delinquency seems to be distinguished more by a desire to avoid 'psychologizing' than by a desire to understand delinquency." He goes on to suggest (p. 250) that the case of sociological theory against psychology might be caricatured as follows:

1. If a lower-class boy is humiliated by his teacher, then that is social class and admissible. If he is humiliated by his father, that is child psychology and inadmissible.
2. If a boy is hostile because of deprivation of legitimate means to success goals, then it leads to 'alienation' which is sociological and admissible. If a boy is hostile because of deprivation of love and affection in his family, then it leads to 'disturbance' which is psychological and inadmissible.
3. If many families whose heads have similar occupations deprive boys similarly, then that makes the deprivation 'patterned' and part of a 'class culture' and it does not hurt.

In other words, sociologists seem to have decided that if delinquency is a response to stress, it cannot have come from the family. The result has been an inadequate bridging between areas having to do with personal and social systems.

Finally, to return to the analysis, it should be observed that neither in Los Angeles nor Utah did the several indicators of strain correlate significantly with the Ratfink peer scale—the scale that measured whether a boy would inform on his friends. This finding, coupled with later and inconsistent findings, raised serious question whether an unwillingness to inform on friends is a good measure of a norm shared exclusively by delinquents; that is, it may be a norm that is widely shared and thus is not the unique property of delinquent groups.

Path Analysis of Strain and
Peer Identification

The results of the path analysis (Table 5-3) were very similar to the gamma analysis. In both Los Angeles and Utah, the path coefficient between dropping out of school and three peer scales exceeded the .10 cutting point, as shown in Table 5-9. And, just as evidence indicated that the relationship between boy-parent harmony and peer identification was an important one, so the path coefficients shown in Table 5-10 supported that notion. However, the path coefficient involving the Ratfink scale was contrary to theoretical expectation in both locations; i.e., the greater the boy-parent harmony, the less the likelihood that the boy would tell on others. Thus, this finding raises again the possibility that the norm against telling on others is not exclusively the property of deviants. This finding implies that loyalty to friends is associated with prior family relations that are good, not poor.

Table 5-9

Path Coefficients from School Dropout to Peer Identification

Peer Identification Measure	Los Angeles	Utah
Ace-in-the-Hole	.22	.22
Sociability	.15	.18
Deviance	.13	.18

Table 5-10

Path Coefficients from Boy-Parent Harmony to Peer Identification

Peer Identification Measure	Los Angeles	Utah
Ratfink	−.32*	−.17*
Ace-in-the-Hole	−.21	−.19
Sociability	−.23	−.32
Deviance	−.23	−.31

*Contrary to expectation.

Finally, in both Los Angeles and Utah, having been fired from a job was related to only one peer scale: in Los Angeles to the Deviance scale (.10) and in Utah to the Ratfink scale (-.12). However, since the path coefficients were small and, in the Utah case, contrary to expectations, these findings suggest that the inability to hold a job is far less predictive for these groups than poor school or family adjustment.

The similarities between the two samples on this set of findings is telling, suggesting that common relationships are being tapped. Both the gamma and path analyses suggest that a boy's discernible ties to home and school may be better indicators of his eventual identification with peers than his personal estimates of himself. Again, however, an examination of the squared residual paths in Table 5-11 indicates that much of the variance for the peer scales still remains unexplained by the strain indicators. We would have to conclude, therefore, that while there is some confirmation for the idea that strain encourages peer identification, the strain indicators used here were far from adequate in explaining the greater amount of variance associated with it.

Table 5-11

Effectiveness of Strain as Indicator of Peer Identification

| Peer Identification Measure | Squared Residuals | |
	Los Angeles	Utah
Ratfink	.88	.95
Ace-in-the-Hole	.88	.92
Sociability	.91	.87
Deviance	.90	.86

Source: Table 5-3.
Note: The higher the squared residual, the lower the explanatory power of the measure.

Theorem II. *Decreased achievement results in increased identification with delinquent peers.*
This theorem is an important one because of its relevance for a test of the overall sequence postulated in the theory. It specifies a direct relationship between achievement and peer identification, leaving out the intervening variable of strain. If the relationship should turn out to be a strong one, it would underscore the importance of testing the closed system assumption to determine if strain is a necessary intervening influence between poor achievement and peer identification.

64

Gamma Analysis

As may be seen in Table 5-12, the support for this theorem was mixed. Of the twelve gammas used to test it, 25 per cent in Los Angeles and 42 per cent in Utah possessed signs and magnitudes that were supportive. These proportions were somewhat higher than those found in support of the relation between strain and peer identification (13 per cent in both Los Angeles and Utah). However, when sign alone was considered, these figures rose only to 58 and 67 per cent, respectively—proportions that were lower than on the previous postulate (84 and 71 per cent). Thus, at the outset, the findings suggest the importance of determining whether the relation of achievement to peer identification is mediated by the intervening variable of strain. This task, however, will be undertaken in the next chapter where the whole theory will be carefully scrutinized on this issue.

Table 5-12

Support for Theorem II (Achievement Determines Peer Identification)

Sign Commensu-rate with Theory	Los Angeles		Utah	
	Gamma ⩾ .20	Gamma < .20	Gamma ⩾ .20	Gamma < .20
Yes	3 (25%)	4 (33%)	5 (42%)	3 (25%)
No	2 (17%)	3 (25%)	1 (8%)	3 (25%)

For now, the analysis will concentrate upon a review of those coefficients that were most supportive of the relation between decreased achievement and peer identification. They are listed in Table 5-13.

Two things about these findings deserve attention. First, the importance of school grades is underscored once again. Not only were they predictive of strain, as indicated earlier, but of peer identification as well. Further, the fact that they were associated with peer identification, while such strain indicators as lowered estimates of self were not, once more implies the importance of institutional ties, as contrasted to other kinds of indicators in explaining peer identification. Second, the data reveal an apparently unique tie in Utah between occupational aspiration and both strain and peer identification.

When looking at the relation between achievement and strain in the previous section, we found that lowered aspirations in Utah were predictive of several indicators of strain—school dropout, lowered estimates of self, and lowered estimates of future occupational chances. Now, in testing this theorem, we find

Table 5-13

Supportive Coefficients Between Achievement and Peer Identification

Variables	Los Angeles	Utah
School Grades and Ace-in-the-Hole	−.28	−.37
School Grades and Sociability	−.21	−.35
School Grades and Deviance	−.26	−.24
Occupational Aspirations and Ace-in-the-Hole	(.04)*	−.25
Occupational Aspirations and Sociability	(.04)*	−.23

Source: Tables 5-1 and 5-2.
Note: Parentheses indicate coefficients not exceeding the cutting point.
*Contrary to expectation.

that lowered occupational aspirations are also indicative of peer identification. Apparently, this finding, which is unique to Utah, is contrary to the theoretical supposition that it is high rather than low aspirations which are associated with strain and peer identification. This assumption, often basic to much sociological theory, was definitely not supported by the Utah data.

Path Analysis

As explained earlier, path coefficients were not calculated to test theorems such as this, only the postulates. However, zero-order correlations between achievement and peer indicators strongly support the gamma coefficients just presented. Although success in school, as measured by school awards, was not associated significantly with peer identification, school grades were, as shown in Table 5-14. Both sets of findings, then, suggest a persistent, although not especially large, relationship between lack of achievement and peer identification. A crucial question for subsequent analysis, therefore, is whether the relationship is mediated by strain or not.

Conclusions

In brief, this analysis has indicated that, while evidence supported the postulate that decreased achievement results in increased strain, it did not support the notion that loss of self-esteem is likely to produce identification with delinquent peers. It tended instead to reinforce the idea that strain, as an intervening variable between achievement and peer identification, may not be a necessary

Table 5-14

Zero-Order Correlation of School Grades to Peer Identification

Peer Identification Measure	Los Angeles	Utah
Ratfink	−.13	−.22
Ace-in-the-Hole	−.22	−.24
Sociability	−.22	−.34
Deviance	−.30	−.29

Source: Table 5-3.

one. The analysis also suggested that, of the measures used, poor institutional ties with home and school may be the most effective predictors of peer identification. A key issue for the next chapter, therefore, will be to determine whether this same phenomenon is observed when the relationships of the same sets of variables to delinquency are examined.

6

Relation of Causal Antecedents to Delinquency

In prior chapters we have examined the relationship of social class to all other variables in the theoretical chain, including delinquency, and examined the relationships among the intervening variables of achievement, strain, and peer identification. This chapter is devoted to an examination of the relation of the latter three variables to delinquency. According to the theory, each of them is a causal antecedent whose relationship to delinquency was expressed in the following propositions:

Postulate IV. *Identification with delinquent peers results in delinquency*;
Theorem III. *Increased strain results in delinquency*; and
Theorem V. *Decreased achievement results in delinquency*.

The reader should recall that these propositions were tested using two different kinds of delinquency indicators: (1) a simple dichotomous indicator telling whether the individual has been delinquent or not and (2) twelve multiple indicators, involving interval or near-interval levels of measurement. The multiple indicators were divided into two categories, the first of which was concerned with measuring *degrees* of delinquency, either frequency or seriousness, and the second with *patterns* of delinquency, i.e., the types of delinquency in which different individuals most commonly engaged.

Summarized Findings

All three propositions tested in this chapter received support: identification with delinquent peers was associated with delinquency; strain was associated with delinquency; and lack of achievement was associated with delinquency. As a result, several significant issues were emergent.

The first was the revelation of rather distinctive differences between Los Angeles and Utah relative to the kinds of peer identification associated with delinquency. In Los Angeles, they seemed to reflect a more deviant and sophisticated pattern. The particular peer scales that were most associated with delinquency were those which indicated whether a boy was willing to hide someone from the police or parents and whether he was willing to participate in a variety of different delinquent acts. In Utah, by contrast, the kinds of peer identification associated most with delinquency were of a gregarious and sociable character; i.e., whether the individual was socially inclined or not. Thus, distinctive differences along the peer dimension were delineated.

Second, peer identification in Los Angeles was predictive both of volume and patterns of delinquency. It was associated both with the extent to which an individual would become involved in delinquency and the kinds of offenses he would commit. This was much less true in Utah. Peer identification in that location was much less strongly associated either with the volume or the seriousness of delinquent acts. Instead, it was indicative of certain distinctive kinds of delinquent acts, most notably drinking, truancy, fighting, incorrigibility, and other juvenile-status offenses. In Utah, boys seemed to identify more with those kinds of group activities that were boisterous and gregarious in character than in Los Angeles, suggesting that group-related delinquencies in Utah were less criminalistic in character. This by no means implies that adult-type delinquency did not occur among the Utah group; merely that it may have had less group support than other kinds.

This set of findings seems to illustrate the way in which both peer identification and delinquency may reflect the kinds of communities in which they are found, their metropolitan or nonmetropolitan character, their distinctive kinds of subcultural patterns, or their opportunity structures. It was these kinds of phenomena with which Cloward and Ohlin (1960) were primarily concerned in their theoretical treatise on the relation of illegitimate and legitimate structures. And while these data do little to support or refute their particular formulations, they do seem to support the validity of their approach. These data suggest that an analysis of the relation of community structure to delinquent groups and behavior is an important one. And since this brief review cannot possibly list all of the subtleties that were observed, the reader may wish to give greater attention to them in the analysis that follows.

Third, the fact that both achievement and strain, as well as peer identification, were associated directly with delinquency provided considerable reason to question the adequacy of the causal sequence postulated in the theory. The form in which the theory was stated suggests that the further any antecedent is from delinquency, the weaker its direct association will be. Yet this was not the case. The direct associations of both achievement and strain with delinquency were often stronger and more consistent than the relationship between peer identification and delinquency. Thus, evidence suggests that the theory may be incorrectly formulated, although many of its basic propositions received some confirmation. A new formulation is implied that would posit a direct relation both between achievement and strain and delinquency. And this would include family variables, as well, which were also associated directly with delinquency. The original asymmetric relation implied by the theory may be an incorrect one.

It could be, of course, that the observed associations of achievement, strain, and family variables with delinquency may reflect nothing more than a definitional overlap of our delinquency indicators with their causal antecedents; that is, if a boy is having trouble in school or at home, acts which may themselves result in his being defined as delinquent, then it would come as no surprise if they were associated with delinquency when they were treated as its causal antecedents. Both the antecedents and the delinquency would be the same thing. However, because the achievement and strain indicators were also consistently associated with such measures of delinquency as adult-status offenses and felonious and criminalistic patterns, there is reason to suspect that more than a definitional overlap is involved. The achievement and strain indicators could be causal antecedents to such acts because the likelihood is much less that a definitional overlap is involved.

If so, the data suggest that marginal integration within such major societal institutions as home and school may well be more directly associated with delinquency than peer associations. If that is the case, we should expect more confirmation of it in the next chapter where the causal sequence is examined as a totality, and where the closed system assumption is tested. In any event, better grounds will be discovered upon which to draw some conclusions.

Detailed Findings

The detailed findings from which the foregoing summary was derived are presented below. Each of the three theoretical propositions specifying the bivariate relationships between achievement, strain, and peer identification, on one hand, and delinquency, on the other, are examined one by one. Before turning to them, it should be noted that when a dichotomous indicator of delinquency (delinquent or not delinquent) is utilized, gamma coefficients will be used to measure its relationships to the other variables. But, when the multiple indicators are employed, path or zero-order coefficients will be used because they are commensurate with interval or near-interval levels of measurement. Path coefficients will be used to test the postulate, and zero-order coefficients to test the theorems.

Postulate IV. *Identification with delinquent peers results in delinquency.*

Gamma Analysis

Table 6-1 reveals that, when the dichotomous indicator of delinquency was used, this postulate received a high degree of empirical support. The signs of all the gammas were supportive, with 75 per cent of those for the Los Angeles group and 100 per cent of the Utah group exceeding the .20 cutting point. Of all the propositions examined, this particular postulate may have received the greatest support.

The various coefficients, both for Utah and Los Angeles, are shown in Table 6-2. In addition to the fact that all the coefficients tend to support the postulate, they also hint of possible metropolitan-nonmetropolitan differences. It will be observed that, in Los Angeles, the strongest relationships between peer identification and delinquency involve the Ace-in-the-Hole and Deviance scales, whose items probably reflect a greater commitment to more serious forms of

Table 6-1

Support for Postulate IV (Peer Identification Determines Delinquency)

Sign Commensu-rate with Theory	Los Angeles		Utah	
	Gamma ≥ .20	Gamma < .20	Gamma ≥ .20	Gamma < .20
Yes	3 (75%)	1 (25%)	4 (100%)	0
No	0	0	0	0

Table 6-2

Gamma Coefficients from Peer Identification to Delinquency

Peer Identification Measure	Los Angeles	Utah
Ace-in-the-Hole	.60	.29
Deviance	.49	.37
Sociability	.28	.37
Ratfink	(−.15)	−.48

delinquency than the other two scales. The Ace-in-the-Hole scale reflects a willingness to hide those who are running either from the police or home, while the Deviance scale measures illegal acts exclusively. By contrast, the Ace-in-the-Hole scale in Utah was the least predictive and the Deviance scale had lesser impact. Meanwhile, the Ratfink and Sociability scales, both of which are concerned more with adolescent groupings and activities than serious delinquency, per se, were more predictive. Thus, there is a suggestion of possible subcultural differences that will be explored when the relation of these peer scales to multiple indicators of delinquency are examined.

As has been suggested earlier, the Ratfink scale poses some interesting problems for analysis and interpretation. Although in this case it was associated in Utah with the dichotomous indicator of delinquency, it was not strongly related to the multiple indicators. Findings with respect to it were so mixed and ambiguous that one might be inclined to suggest that it is of little utility in delinquency research. However, as will be seen later, the findings suggest that it may be useful in distinguishing between delinquents and nondelinquents but not in the direction originally anticipated. Instead, it may indicate that *non*delinquents may be as much or more disinclined to tell on others than delinquents.

Path Analysis

In conducting the path analysis, the relationship or peer identification to delinquency was examined using only multiple indicators of delinquency. These indicators, it will be recalled, were of two major kinds. Category 1 indicators measure the extent of an individual's delinquency in terms of both frequency and seriousness. They are most applicable, therefore, to a test of the postulate, since their focus is upon the amounts of different kinds of delinquency. Category 2 indicators, by contrast, provide information on the ratios of different kinds of delinquency—felonies, instrumental acts, conflict behavior, etc.—to the total number of delinquent acts committed by an individual. Thus, they are of greater use in specifying the relation of different patterns of delinquency to different patterns of peer identification than of the extent of delinquent acts.

First, consider the findings for Los Angeles. It will be observed in the listing of Category 1 indicators shown in Table 6-3 that support for the postulate in Los Angeles was not especially strong when *all* of the peer scales were considered. Only 38 per cent of the 24 coefficients were optimally supportive when both sign and magnitude were considered. By contrast, the signs of 41 per cent of the coefficients were contrary to the postulate, although only one of them was of sufficient magnitude to exceed the .10 cutting point. Finally, it will be noted that the residuals (z) reveal that the peer scales, as a whole, did not explain much of the overall variance for the various delinquency indicators, ranging from a low of .88 for average seriousness of offense to a high of .99 for the hell-raising factor.

What is of considerable significance, however, is the fact that, while all of the peer scales were not associated with delinquency, certain of them were consistently predictive. Just as the gamma analysis suggested, the majority of the path coefficients extending from the Ace-in-the-Hole scale (willingness to hide others) and the Deviance scale (willingness to engage in delinquent acts with others) supported the postulate both in terms of sign and magnitude. The greater the peer identification along these dimensions, the greater the frequency or seriousness of delinquent acts. Meanwhile, 83 per cent of the signs for the Ratfink scale (willingness to tell on others) and the Sociability scale (willingness to engage with others in nondelinquent acts) were contrary to the postulate, although in terms of magnitude all of these contrary coefficients, except one, were weak. These findings suggest that the lower the peer identification along these dimensions, the lower the delinquency.

The same configuration may be observed in Table 6-4. This table shows Category 2 indicators in Los Angeles, which are concerned more with offense patterns than with degrees of delinquency. The Ace-in-the-Hole scale was

Table 6-3

Path Coefficients from Peer Identification to Category 1 Delinquency Indicators in Los Angeles

Category 1 Indicators	Peer Identification Measures				
	Ratfink	Ace-in-Hole	Sociability	Deviance	(Z^2)
No. of Offenses	.05*	[.16]	[−.11*]	[.16]	.95
Average Seriousness	.06*	[.21]	−.07*	[.23]	.88
Most Serious	.05*	[.19]	−.07*	[.20]	.90
Theft Factor	.04*	[.12]	−.08*	.09	.97
Hell-Raising Factor	−.06	.01	[.10]	.04	.99
Incorrigibility Factor	.01*	[.11]	−.06*	[.11]	.98

Note: Brackets indicate coefficients equaling or exceeding the cutting point, in this and in subsequent tables.
*Contrary to expectation.

Table 6-4

Path Coefficients from Peer Identification to Category 2 Delinquency Indicators in Los Angeles

Category 2 Indicators	Peer Identification Measures				
	Ratfink	Ace-in-Hole	Sociability	Deviance	(Z)
Adult/Juvenile	.02	[.17]	−.04	[.19]	.92
Felony/Misd.	.01	−.01	−.03	[.25]	.95
Instrumental/ Expressive	.04	[.15]	−.06	[.19]	.93
Retreatism	[.10]	.09	.07	.06	.97
Conflict	.02	.05	−.09	[.23]	.95
Criminalism	.01	[.16]	−.04	[.13]	.95

73

associated directly with adult-status and criminalistic offense patterns, while the Deviance scale was associated directly with adult-status, felonious, instrumental, conflict, and criminalistic patterns. The greater the identification, the greater the inclination to commit these kinds of offenses. Meanwhile, the Ratfink and Sociability scales again were only weakly associated with these or any other patterns, and sometimes in a negative direction.

Although the residuals for both categories of indicators were high, the findings do suggest that, in Los Angeles, those peer scales that were associated significantly with delinquency were those that measured the most deviant forms of peer identification; i.e., a willingness to hide someone in trouble and a willingness to participate with others in committing a variety of deviant acts. Mere gregariousness, as measured by the Sociability scale, or an unwillingness to tell on others, as measured by the Ratfink scale, were not predictive.

In Utah, the story was different, as shown in Table 6-5. In terms of the Category 1 indicators—the measures of degrees of delinquency—the peer scales were less predictive. Only 17 per cent of the 24 coefficients supported the postulate in terms of sign and magnitude. Meanwhile, several coefficients were contrary, although only one of them exceeded the .10 cutting point.

Other than the fact that support was generally weak, it is notable that none of the coefficients extending from the peer identification measures to number of offenses exceeded the .10 cutting point—something that was not true in Los Angeles. Moreover, a really definitive pattern of association does not link certain

Table 6-5

Path Coefficients from Peer Identification to Category 1 Delinquency Indicators in Utah

Category 1 Indicators	Peer Identification Measures				
	Ratfink	Ace-in-Hole	Sociability	Deviance	(Z)
No. of Offenses	.08*	.03	.09	.07	.96
Average Seriousness	[−.17]	−.01*	−.02*	.00	.97
Most Serious	.09*	.05	−.05*	[.23]	.94
Theft Factor	.09*	.01	−.05*	.09	.98
Hell-Raising Factor	.07*	.00	[.30]	−.07*	.91
Incorrigibility Factor	[.19*]	.01	[.14]	−.06*	.94

*Contrary to expectation.

peer measures and these Category 1 delinquency indicators as appeared in Los
Angeles, where the Ace-in-the-Hole and Deviance scales were clearly the most
predictive. However, if one examines concurrently the Category 2 indicators
shown in Table 6-6, a pattern does begin to emerge.

Table 6-6

**Path Coefficients from Peer Identification to Category 2 Delinquency Indicators
in Utah**

Category 2 Indicators	Peer Identification Measures				
	Ratfink	Ace-in-Hole	Sociability	Deviance	(Z)
Adult-Juvenile	.06	[−.16]	−.02	[.12]	.97
Felony/Misd.	.08	.00	[−.14]	[.14]	.97
Instrumental/ Expressive	[.11]	[−.11]	[−.15]	[.21]	.94
Retreatism	.00	.04	[.30]	−.01	.90
Conflict	.03	[−.10]	[.11]	.03	.98
Criminalism	.10	−.08	[−.18]	[−.18]	.95

It is apparent in Utah that peer identification is associated less directly with
degrees of delinquency than with certain patterns of delinquency. If one
examines the Category 1 and 2 indicators in common, he will observe several
things that are distinctive.

First, in sharp contrast with Los Angeles, the Sociability scale in Utah—the
one that measures gregariousness more than anything else—is significantly and
directly associated with hell-raising, incorrigibility, retreatism, and conflict; at
the same time, it is negatively associated with high proportions of felonious,
instrumental, and criminalistic offenses. Thus, in Utah, it seems quite clear that,
while boisterous and gregarious group behavior is associated with drinking,
fighting, truancy, and other juvenile offenses, it is not associated with distinctly
criminal kinds of acts. In Los Angeles, by contrast, the Sociability scale tended
either to be nonpredictive or negatively associated with all kinds of offenses
except hell-raising. Thus, the only peer scale on which there were strong
similarities was the Deviance scale. This scale tended to predict adult-status,
felonious, and instrumental kinds of offenses in both places. However, the
magnitude of the coefficients was not so great in Utah, in addition to which
there was a negative association between the Deviance scale and the delinquency

indicator designed to measure adherence to a "criminal" subcultural pattern. Taken in total context, the findings imply that Utah boys may identify more with group activities that are boisterious and gregarious in character than do boys in Los Angeles. If so, the delinquent subculture in Utah may be one that is more supportive of hell-raising than seriously criminalistic kinds of acts. This does not imply that serious delinquency does not occur there; it does. However, when it does, it may be more of an individualistic than a group phenomenon.

These conclusions are supported in part by comparing the findings for Utah on the Ace-in-the-Hole scale with those in Los Angeles. First, while the Ace-in-the-Hole scale was predictive of degrees of delinquency in Los Angeles— the greater the identification, the greater the delinquency—it was not in Utah. Moreover, while this scale was directly associated with adult-status and criminalistic offense patterns in Los Angeles, it was negatively associated with them in Utah. Instead, where there was an association in Utah, it was with juvenile expressive, and non-conflict types of offense patterns, all of which tended to be juvenile rather than adult kinds of offenses. (That is the meaning of the positive correlations in Los Angeles and the negative ones in Utah for the Category 2 indicators.)

Finally, an examination of the findings for the Ratfink scale for both Los Angeles and Utah confirm a point made earlier—namely, that it is a poor measure of peer identification that is unique to delinquents. Although most of the coefficients did not meet levels of acceptability, they were almost always contrary to expectation in their relationship to the Category 1 indicators, suggesting that the lesser the delinquency, the lesser the willingness to tell on others. Thus, the findings suggest that those boys who had the best homes, were doing best in school, and had the least delinquency were those *least* inclined to tell on others. The finding suggests that where group experiences in the past, in family and school, had been best, loyalty to others on this dimension was the greatest. The finding may imply support for a growing number of studies which suggest that delinquent groups are not always characterized by a high degree of cohesiveness, loyalty, and *esprit de corps* (cf. Bordua, 1962:245-246; Empey, 1967:33-36; Klein and Crawford, 1967:63). For example, as Short and Strodtbeck (1965:Chap. 10) suggest, group loyalty, particularly when personal considerations are at issue, is not a strong trait among gang boys. Instead, their findings, like ours, suggest that boys who are making it in the context of conventional institutions are less likely to tell on others, and to possess other characteristics and skills that enhance group feelings and attractiveness. Boys who had experienced the most satisfying institutional backgrounds were least inclined to "fink."

Finally, before moving to a test of the next proposition, it must be observed that, although distinct evidence favors the postulate that identification with delinquent peers results in delinquency, the amount of variance that can be explained by these measures is small. The findings, therefore, simply do not warrant the attribution of much explanatory power, by itself, to peer identification. This is a potentially important finding in light of the immense popularity that group-related and subcultural theories have enjoyed during the past decade, forming the basis for a great deal of policy formulation as well as research. Yet, in a recent statement, Ohlin (1970:3) suggests that this popularity may have been overdone. Said he:

The origin, location, and persistence of different subcultures constitute an important component of the situational field in which delinquent acts occur, *but cannot be taken as the major determinant of these acts in individual cases* [italics ours].

. . . Their contribution to delinquency must be evaluated in relation to other influences and conditions that create the circumstances for delinquent conduct.

Ohlin's conclusion is highly consistent with these findings. While peer identification has been consistently related to delinquency throughout the analysis, it has not been of overriding importance. Furthermore, as will be seen later, other factors are equally, or more strongly, related to delinquency than it is.

The findings have been of importance, however, in indicating that some rather provocative differences may occur in the nature of delinquent groupings in small-town Utah and metropolitan Los Angeles. While peer identification, overall, did not seem to exert the overriding influence suggested by the theory, it was important and did seem to possess different characteristics in the small town vs. the large city setting. Later on in this chapter, therefore, and in the next, where the causal sequence is studied as a totality, this matter will be treated further.

Theorem III. *Increased strain results in delinquency*.

This is the first of the theoretical statements relating variables other than peer identification directly to delinquency. Therefore, it is of considerable importance in the overall test of the theory, since the theory postulated a sequential chain of antecedents leading to delinquency and suggested that the further any antecedent is from delinquency itself, the lesser its influence will be. Peer identification, for example, should be more highly correlated than lack of achievement and so on.

As may be seen in Table 6-7, the results of the gamma coefficients are rather highly supportive of the theorem (remembering that the relationships being measured are between strain indicators and a dichotomous, either/or indicator of delinquency). Fifty per cent of the six coefficients for the Los Angeles samples were supportive, both in terms of sign and magnitude, while for the Utah samples, the figure was 73 per cent. And, when sign alone is considered, all of the Utah and 88 per cent of the Los Angeles coefficients were supportive.

But while these findings may attest to the validity of the theorem, there are important reasons why they may not be supportive of the overall theory. First, as will be observed in the list of coefficients shown in Table 6-8, the relationships between some of the strain indicators and delinquency—most notably school dropout and being fired from a job—are higher than the relationships between peer identification and delinquency shown above. The

Table 6-7

Support for Theorem III (Strain Determines Delinquency)

Sign Commensu-rate with Theory	Los Angeles		Utah	
	Gamma ≥ .20	Gamma < .20	Gamma ≥ .20	Gamma < .20
Yes	3 (50%)	2 (33%)	5 (73%)	1 (17%)
No	0	1 (17%)	0	0

Table 6-8

Gamma Coefficients from Strain to Delinquency

Strain Measures	Los Angeles	Utah
School dropout	.76	.80
Fired from job	.61	.37
Smartness self-concept	−.26	−.26
Leadership self-concept	(−.04)	−.31
Maturity self-concept	(.07)*	−.26

*Contrary to expectation.

magnitude of the school coefficients, especially, suggest that the relation between strain and delinquency need not always be mediated by peer influence.

This possibility is also suggested by the self-concept indicators, especially in Utah. In chapter 5 we found that lowered self-concept was not significantly related to peer identification. Yet we find here that all three indicators of self-concept in Utah and one in Los Angeles are associated directly with delinquency. Thus, in the nonmetropolitan setting, at least, lowered self-esteem may not be as strongly related to peer identification as it is to delinquency.

Finally, a parallel examination of family variables adds further reason to question the delinquency-generating sequence postulated in the formal theory. In Table 6-9, it will be noted that family strain is associated with delinquency more strongly than it was with peer identification (see Table 5-8). Whereas most of the coefficients relating family strain to peer identification in Los Angeles ranged from .16 to .35, here they range from .42 to .76.

Such findings, of course, could be due as much to the criteria that officials use in deciding to place juveniles under official supervision as to the forces that

Table 6-9

Gamma Coefficients from Family Strain to Delinquency

Family Strain Measure	Los Angeles	Utah
Family separation	.76	.49
Parental harmony	−.51	−.25
Relations with parents	−.42	−.36

lead juveniles to commit delinquent acts in the first place. Officials would be more inclined to use family, school, and work problems than peer relationships as the bases for their decisions. However, we have no way of ascertaining at this point whether or not this is true. About all that can be said is that, so far as the gamma coefficients are concerned, the sequential, asymmetric relations postulated in the theory do not seem to be borne out by the test of the theorem, underscoring again the importance of examining the closed system assumption. It will provide the definitive test.

Zero-Order Analysis

Since the path model dealt exclusively with postulates and did not specify any direct causal relationships between strain and delinquency, no path coefficients were calculated. However, zero-order coefficients were computed. Unfortunately, because complete data were not available on all subjects, the self-concept and some of the family indicators had to be dropped. Nevertheless, the remaining findings confirmed those just presented. In Los Angeles, the measured relationships between strain and the Category 1 delinquency indicators are shown in Table 6-10. Fully two-thirds of these coefficients were optimally supportive of the theorem, with only one coefficient being significantly contradictory, i.e., boys whose relationships with their parents were best also tended to be highest on the hell-raising factor. Otherwise, the data were generally in support of the theorem.

The Category 2 indicators in Table 6-11 paint the same general picture, although dropping out of school and being fired from a job were associated more strongly than poor family relations with high ratios of the several different kinds of delinquency. Not only was dropping out of school associated with high ratios of all kinds of delinquency, but was especially strong in its relation to adult-status offenses, instrumental, and criminalistic patterns. Being fired from a job was also associated with several different patterns of delinquency, but not so

Table 6-10

Zero-Order Correlations Among Strain and Category 1 Delinquency Indicators in Los Angeles

Category 1 Indicators	Strain Measures		
	Boy-Parent Harmony	School Dropout	Fired from Job
No. of Offenses	[−.19]	[.37]	[.15]
Average Seriousness	[−.20]	[.42]	[.18]
Most Serious	[−.18]	[.44]	[.20]
Theft Factor	−.01	[.26]	.01
Hell-Raising Factor	[.13*]	[.16]	−.05*
Incorrigibility Factor	−.05	[.19]	.06

*Contrary to expectation.

Table 6-11

Zero-Order Correlations Among Strain and Category 2 Delinquency Indicators in Los Angeles

Category 2 Indicators	Strain Measures		
	Boy-Parent Harmony	School Dropout	Fired from Job
Adult/Juvenile	−.06	[.38]	[.14]
Felony/Misd.	−.03	[.19]	.04
Instrumental/Expressive	−.01	[.31]	.09
Retreatism	[−.27]	[.17]	[.13]
Conflict	.00	[.17]	[.15]
Criminalism	−.04	[.35]	[.10]

strongly. Poor relations between boy and parent, by contrast, were associated significantly only with retreatism—a tendency to run away, use narcotics and alcohol, or to be truant. Thus, the data reveal two things of considerable importance for the Los Angeles sample. First, different antecedents seem to be associated with different kinds of delinquency. Second, these path findings also imply that strain itself, without the intervening influence of peer identification may be instrumental in leading to delinquency.

In Utah, the same general tendencies were in evidence, but with significant differences as well. Consider in total the Category 1 and Category 2 indicators shown in Table 6-12. It will be observed in Category 1 that general support for the theorem in Utah was about the same in Los Angeles. There was very little difference. With respect to Category 2, however, the strain indicators were considerably less predictive. Dropping out of school was associated much less strongly and less frequently with the various patterns of delinquency. Where it was related, however, it was associated again with felonious, instrumental, and criminalistic patterns as in Los Angeles. Poor family relations, meanwhile, were associated somewhat more frequently with different offense patterns, most notably with retreatism as in Los Angeles, but also with felonious and instrumental activities as well. Finally, being fired from a job was not only not significantly associated with some offense patterns as in Los Angeles, but in many cases tended to be negatively associated with delinquency. The latter trend was not marked, however, since the magnitudes of the coefficients were low.

Overall, then, these findings are both paradoxical and provocative. On one hand, they provide rather strong support for the theorem that increased strain results in delinquency. Yet, on the other, they contradict the asymmetric and sequential chain of events postulated in the formal theory; namely, that the impact of events in the chain is sequential and that the further any antecedent is from delinquency, the lesser its influence will be. Although peer identification, a variable that was adjacent to delinquency in the theoretical chain, was associated with delinquency, strain, which was not adjacent, was even more strongly associated. Thus, the evidence raised questions regarding the fundamental character and accuracy of the theory. Moreover, it suggested that when the ties of boys to basic institutions are weak, when they are no longer on the main track leading from childhood to adulthood, they are more likely to be delinquent. This does not seem to be strictly a definitional problem either (i.e., that because boys are not in school or are getting along poorly with their parents, they will automatically be defined as delinquent by the authorities), because many of the strain measures were associated strongly, especially in Los Angeles, not just with less serious offense patterns but with adult-status, felonious, and criminalistic patterns as well.

Theorem V. *Decreased achievement results in delinquency.*
The overall support this theorem received from the gamma coefficients was moderate, but was higher in Utah than in Los Angeles (Table 6-13). For the Utah sample, two of the three coefficients relating achievement measures to a

Table 6-12

Zero-Order Correlations Among Strain and Delinquency Indicators in Utah

Delinquency Indicator	Strain Measure		
	Boy-Parent Harmony	School Dropout	Fired from Job
Category 1			
No. of Offenses	[−.11]	[.26]	[.14]
Average Seriousness	[−.26]	[.16]	.04
Most Serious	[−.21]	[.22]	.03
Theft Factor	−.03	[.24]	.07
Hell-Raising Factor	−.09	[.15]	[.13]
Incorrigibility Factor	[−.13]	.09	.09
Category 2			
Adult/Juvenile	−.04	.05	.08
Felony/Misdemeanor	[−.10]	[.13]	−.07
Instrumental/Expressive	[−.10]	[.13]	−.05
Retreatism	[−.24]	.04	−.05
Conflict	−.09	.04	.09
Criminalism	−.07	[.17]	−.04

Table 6-13

Support for Theorem V (Achievement Determines Delinquency)

Sign Commensurate with Theory	Los Angeles		Utah	
	Gamma ≥ .20	Gamma < .20	Gamma ≥ .20	Gamma < .20
Yes	1 (33%)	1 (33%)	2 (67%)	1 (33%)
No	0	1 (33%)	0	0

dichotomous indicator of delinquency were supportive, both in terms of sign and magnitude, while only one coefficient was supportive for Los Angeles. When sign alone was considered, all of the coefficients in Utah and two of the three in Los Angeles were consistent with expectation.

The supported relationships tended to be relatively strong, as shown in Table 6-14. Both relationships below the cutting point involved school awards as a measure of achievement, suggesting that it was not an especially good indicator. Its association with the delinquency dichotomy in Utah was only -.05, while in Los Angeles it was .03.

Table 6-14

Gamma Coefficients from Achievement to Delinquency

Achievement Measure	Los Angeles	Utah
School grades	−.71	−.67
Occupational aspirations	(−.07)	−.60
School awards	(*.03)	(−.05)

Overall, then, the gamma coefficients suggest that the best measure of lack of achievement, as it relates to delinquency, is poor school grades followed by a low achievement orientation in Utah. Further, the strong associations between these indicators again raise questions about the asymmetric and sequential relations postulated in the theory.

Zero-Order Analysis

Again, because a theorem is being examined, no path coefficients are presented. The zero-order coefficients, however, bear out the gamma findings. As shown in Table 6-15, virtually all of the correlations between school grades and delinquency in both Los Angeles and Utah exceeded the cutting point and were in the expected direction. No other variable, it might be noted, was as consistently related to all of the multiple indicators of delinquency as this one. Of twenty-four coefficients covering both Los Angeles and Utah, only one did not reach the arbitrary cutting point. Likewise, in both places, poor grades were associated most strongly with the frequency and seriousness of delinquency. Only with respect to Category 2 measures was there much sign of difference: in Los Angeles, poor grades seemed slightly more predictive of high ratios of virtually all kinds of delinquency than in Utah.

Table 6-15

Zero-Order Correlations Among Achievement and Delinquency Indicators

	Delinquency Indicator	Los Angeles		Utah	
		Grades	Awards	Grades	Awards
Category 1	No. of Offenses	[−.30]	−.03	[−.32]	−.03
	Average Seriousness	[−.34]	.07*	[−.29]	.06*
	Most Serious	[−.36]	.05*	[−.36]	.01*
	Theft Factor	[−.16]	.05*	[−.21]	.04*
	Hell-Raising Factor	[−.15]	−.14	[−.24]	.01*
	Incorrigibility Factor	[−.19]	−.09	[−.25]	−.08
Category 2	Adult/Juvenile	[−.31]	.03	−.09	.03
	Felony/Misdemeanor	[−.20]	.02	[−.18]	.02
	Instrumental/Expressive	[−.22]	.04	[−.15]	[.10]
	Retreatism	[−.25]	.03	[−.31]	−.07
	Conflict	[−.11]	−.05	[−.12]	−.03
	Criminalism	[−.22]	[.10]	[−.18]	.08

*Contrary to expectation.

In addition to the fact that school awards were not predictive, it is disappointing that the relation between aspirations in Utah and delinquency could not be measured, but because data were not complete on all offenders, coefficients were not calculated, as in the gamma analysis. However, since there has been a marked degree of correspondence between the gamma and the path and zero-order coefficients, it would seem reasonable to speculate that the latter would be confirmatory.

The importance of this comment is related to the fact that, in chapter 5 as well as in this one, there has been a persistent relationship in Utah between low aspirations and strain, peer identification, and now delinquency. The findings seem to reflect a unique pattern for the small-town boys, one in which a *lack* of support for, rather than an adherence to, the American success dream is associated with adolescent difficulty.

Aside from that issue, these findings, like those for strain, provide further documentation of an apparently strong relationship between poor institutional affiliations and delinquency. Several of the measures of strain and achievement were as strongly, or more strongly, associated with delinquency than the measures of peer identification.

Conclusion

This chapter has provided three findings of significance: (1) support for all three of the propositions being tested; (2) evidence that important subcultural differences may exist in metropolitan Los Angeles and nonmetropolitan Utah which have an important impact on the way key variables in the theory are related; and (3) evidence that the asymmetric relations postulated in the theory may be inappropriate. The fact that achievement, strain, and family variables were all related to delinquency as strongly, if not more strongly, than peer identification suggests that these factors may have direct rather than indirect effects. If so, we should expect more confirmation of it in the next chapter when the causal sequence is examined as a totality, and where the closed system assumption is tested.

7

Test of Closed-System Assumption in Los Angeles

According to the formal structure of the delinquency theory, and the rules that were adopted for testing it, one must assume that the theory constitutes a closed system. There should be no direct causal connections between the variables except for those stated in the postulates. For example, in one segment of the theory, it was postulated that strain is followed by peer identification which, in turn, is followed by delinquency. This implies that strain causes delinquency only through the intervening influence of peer identification. If the closed system assumption were true, then, the associations between the adjacent variables of strain and peer identification, and peer identification and delinquency, should be much higher than the direct association between strain and delinquency. In fact, if the closed system assumption were met completely, we would expect the relationship between strain and delinquency, controlling for the influence of peer identification, to disappear.

In order to lay the groundwork for the test, the overall gamma and path findings for the *postulates* for the Los Angeles sample will be summarized graphically. This summary will serve as a bridge between the analysis of bivariate relationships that was conducted in prior chapters and the test of the closed system assumption to follow. The same procedure will be followed in the next chapter in conducting the test for the Utah sample. It was too cumbersome a task to attempt the test for the two samples in a single chapter.

Causal Sequence for Los Angeles

Figure 7-1 summarizes the gamma findings for the Los Angeles sample on the postulates. It will be observed that only those gamma coefficients are presented whose signs were consistent with theoretical expectation and whose absolute value exceeded the .20 cutting point. Thus, they were those coefficients that provided strongest support for the theory.

The first matter of importance is that social class is excluded from the figure since all of its bivariate relationships to other indicators were so low that not a single one met minimal criteria for inclusion. With class excluded, however, there is some confirmation for the theory. Support is provided for the notion that other major concepts in the chain are related and that delinquency could be the product of a series of events, beginning with lack of achievement and proceeding through strain and peer identification. It is notable, however, that, although several indicators of lack of achievement were related to several indicators of

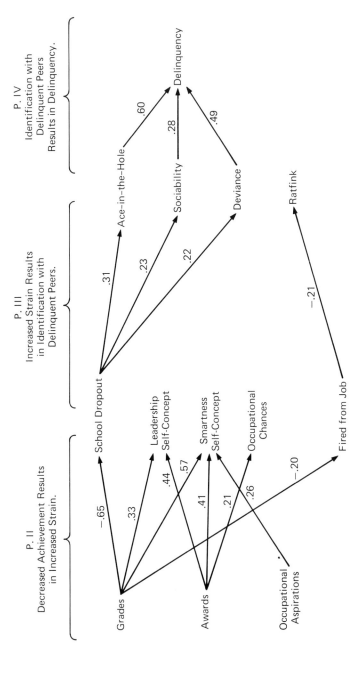

Figure 7–1. Summary of Postulate Findings for Los Angeles (Gamma Coefficients).

strain, all of these strain indicators, especially the self-evaluation measures, were not strongly related, in turn, to peer identification. Only one strain indicator, dropping out of school, served to maintain the chain of relationships. Being fired from a job was also related to peer identification through the Ratfink scale, but that chain did not continue on to delinquency.

The path model presents essentially the same picture (Figure 7-2).[a] Again, class was excluded because its indirect, as well as direct, effects were so low, or so inconsistent, in Los Angeles that class did not seem to warrant inclusion in the model. Although the matter was carefully investigated to determine if it should be retained, even though its effects were slight, we found no grounds for doing so. Thus, the concept will be dropped in all further presentations of data. Beyond class, however, there were other possible paths that called for careful study. As will be noted in Figure 7-2, the major ones are from grades in school, to being a dropout or fired from a job, to peer identification, and from there to delinquency.

In considering the path findings, it should be remembered that certain indicators were omitted from them due to the corrections made for the data loss problem (cf. chapter 3). Nevertheless, it may be that the model represents the basic picture, since many of the indicators omitted from it—e.g., self-concept indicators or estimates of occupational chances—are those in the gamma analysis that did not relate strongly enough to subsequent indicators in the chain to be retained in the gamma analysis (cf. Figure 7-1). Thus, their loss in the path analysis may not be overwhelmingly serious.

It should also be noted that the indicator of boy-parent harmony has been included in the path diagram. In prior chapters, evidence was presented indicating that intrafamily strain may be an important causal variable even though it was not included in the original theoretical statement. Therefore, boy-parent harmony was included as a strain indicator and its effects assessed along with those of the strain measures.

One way in which the path model sheds new light on the entire sequence is its inclusion of multiple indicators of delinquency rather than the dichotomous indicators used in the gamma analysis. As was indicated in chapter 6, the paths between peer identification and delinquency are almost exclusively between the Ace-in-the-Hole and Deviance scales, and most of the multiple indicators. The paths suggest that, in Los Angeles at least, it is these more serious kinds of peer

---

[a]In viewing the path models, the following methodological issues should be kept in mind. First, only those causal paths were retained which exceeded the .10 cutting point. The coefficients for those paths that were retained in the model were recomputed. This step was important, because in many cases the path coefficients were *partial*, normalized regression coefficients. Since certain indicators were dropped because they did not reach the .10 cutting point, the partial coefficients would be expected to change under most circumstances. Thus, in instances where more than one path led into a given indicator, normalized partial regression coefficients were used to estimate the recomputed paths. However, in instances where only a a single path connected two indicators, zero-order correlation coefficients were used as path estimates. It should also be noted that, in some instances, where indicators were dropped, the squared residuals were increased over those reported in Tables 6-3 and 6-4.

88

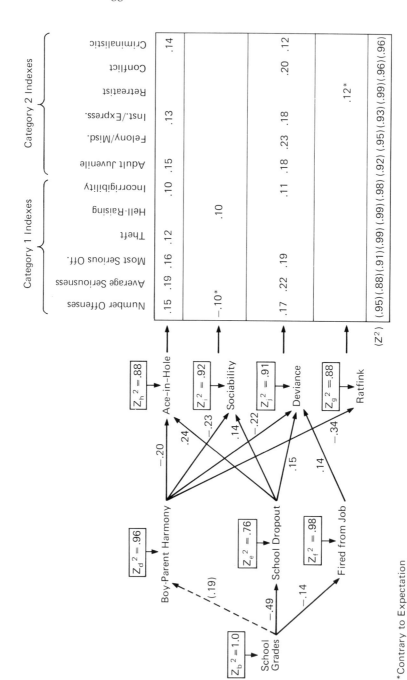

Figure 7-2. General Path Model for Los Angeles (Beta Weights Revised).

*Contrary to Expectation

associations rather than highly social collectivities that are likely to be involved in delinquency.

In summary, both the gamma and path analyses of bivariate relationships in the theory seem to lend some support to the postulated causal sequence. The analyses have tapped some variables which were consistently present in both; namely, poor grades, dropping out of school, identifying with peers, and becoming delinquent. Nevertheless, despite these findings, several hints in prior chapters indicate that the closed system may not hold, that the asymmetric and sequential series of events implicit in the postulates may not be correct. Therefore, the following test of the assumption is of extreme importance.

Summarized Findings

If the closed system assumption were to hold true in Los Angeles, empirical verification for three basic statements would be required:

1. Achievement is related to peer identification only through the intervening variable of strain.
2. Achievement is related to delinquency only through the intervening variables of strain and peer identification.
3. Strain is related to delinquency only through the intervening variable of peer identification.

The analysis, however, failed to confirm any of these statements. For the most part, the total effects of any initial variable (e.g., achievement) upon any subsequent, nonadjacent variable (e.g., peer identification or delinquency) were much greater than their indirect effects. Furthermore, the findings once again affirmed the importance of examining the effects of family variables on delinquency even though they were not included in the original theoretical statement. Their effects were felt upon most other variables, and were often direct rather than indirect.

What is provocative about this particular part of the theoretical test, and why it would seem important to formalize and specify the kinds of relationships expected among basic concepts in any theory is that, although many of the bivariate relationships postulated in the theory did receive support, the closed system assumption did not. While many of the theoretical antecedents may be important, the asymmetric sequence in which they were set forth does not seem to be appropriate. Moreover, it would seem that the role of family variables should somehow be addressed.

To rectify these problems, theoretical revision is implied, revision that may want to take three things into account: (1) the possibility of specifying direct causal effects extending from both lack of achievement and strain to delinquency; (2) the possibility of including family variables somewhere in the chain; and (3) the possibility of reconceptualizing the role of peer identification.

The peer identification issue is not an inconsequential one. Although the test of the closed system assumption suggested that it might have been misplaced in the causal sequence, the test did not indicate that it was unimportant. Except for the Ratfink scale, which was only weakly correlated with delinquency in Los Angeles (-.15), the other relationships were relatively high, especially Ace-in-the-Hole (.60), and Deviance (.49), and to a lesser degree, Sociability (.28). Thus, the issue is not so much that of ruling out the importance of peer identification, but of discovering more precisely what its role is. Rather than exploring the issue further at this point, however, we will consider it after the closed system assumption is tested in Utah. It is possible that the same considerations will apply in both cases.

Detailed Findings

As suggested in the summarized findings, the test of the closed system assumption requires answers to three basic questions. This time, however, they are stated in somewhat different form, taking into account the methodology that will be required to answer them:

1. What are the indirect effects of the achievement indicators on each of the peer scales, via the intervening measures of strain? Are the associations between strain and peer identification greater than those between achievement and peer identification?
2. What are the indirect effects of achievement indicators on the delinquency measures, via the intervening measures of strain and peer identification? Do these effects seem to support the closed system assumption when compared to the total effects of achievement on delinquency?
3. What are the indirect effects of the strain measures on delinquency, via the intervening measures of peer identification? Do they support a closed system assumption?

In attempting to answer these questions, we will use both the gamma coefficients and the path analysis. The gamma coefficients, however, cannot be used to assess the issue of indirect effects in an explicit way, but will only be suggestive of the issues involved. Nevertheless, we include them because none of the indicators will be lost that way and because they provide an excellent complement to the path findings.

In examining direct and indirect effects in the path analysis, we will be referring to variables involved in the test as being one of two types, either as "exogenous" or "endogenous" variables. An exogenous variable is one that appears at the beginning of a causal sequence, such as "achievement," and which functions somewhat like an independent variable. An endogenous variable, by contrast, is like a dependent variable, such as peer identification or delinquency, in that it occurs further along in the causal sequence and is determined by one or more exogenous variables. In other words, the main difference between exogenous and endogenous variables is that endogenous variables are assumed to be wholly caused by variables *within* the theoretical system.

We will examine the closed system assumption by determining whether or not the explained variance between a given exogenous and endogenous variable is totally accounted for by the paths specified within the causal model. For example, consider the hypothetical sequence shown in Figure 7-3. If the closed system assumption for this example were to hold true, we would expect grades to be related to the peer sociability scale *only* through the intervening variables of school dropout and being fired from a job. In operational terms, we would expect the total effect of grades on sociability, as measured by its zero-order correlation, to be equal to the sum of its indirect effects on sociability, as measured by the product of path 1 times path 3, plus the product of path 2 times path 4.

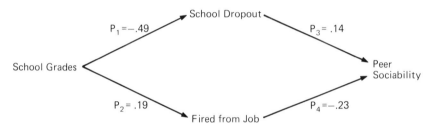

Note: The zero-order r (total effect) between school grades and peer sociability = $-.22$.

Figure 7-3. Accounting for Explained Variance.

When these computations are carried out in the example, however, they question the validity of the closed system assumptions. The zero-order correlations between grades and peer sociability is -.22, while its indirect effects add up to -.11. Thus, the hypothetical findings suggest that only about half of the total effects of grades on sociability are accounted for by the intervening paths through dropout and being fired, and that a sizeable *direct* effect of -.11 may be present even though it is not specified by the causal model. Consequently, if such findings were to be obtained in the actual test of the theory, they would question the validity of the closed system and suggest that a *direct* causal path should be specified between grades and sociability, in addition to the indirect effect originally indicated.

It should be emphasized, however, that this method of subtracting indirect from total effects is not the same thing as computing the direct effects using the path technique. If a direct causal path had been drawn, and examined, leading from grades to sociability, then the direct paths leading from the strain measures to sociability might have changed somewhat. This, in turn, would probably have changed the estimates of the indirect effects. Because of these possibilities, the estimates of differences between total and indirect relationships in the analyses that follow are only approximations of what the direct effects of an exogenous on an endogenous variable might be. With these qualifications in mind, the techniques just described, along with suggestive evidence from the gamma analysis, will be used to examine the three basic questions listed above.

1. Relation of Achievement to Peer Identification via Strain

In examining this relationship, first consider Figure 7-4. It provides summary information, in the form of gamma coefficients, on the relationships of all the achievement indicators to strain, peer identification, and delinquency. These coefficients will help to reflect both upon this and the second question.

It will be noted in the figure that there is some evidence that the relationship between achievement and peer identification is mediated by the influence of strain. While several indicators of achievement—school grades, school awards, and occupational aspirations—were related to several indicators of strain, school grades, alone, were related strongly enough to peer identification to exceed the .20 cutting point. Moreover, the relationships between grades and the peer indicators which did exceed the cutting point were weaker than many of those between grades and indicators of strain.

This conclusion is borne out by the path test, the results of which are provided in Table 7-1. Using the procedures described earlier, it tests the closed system assumption by measuring the total effects of school grades on peer identification, and comparing them with the indirect effects via the strain measures in order to estimate possible direct effects. The table also includes boy-parent harmony as a strain measure and assesses its intervening effects along with the others. In order to keep its indirect effects separate from the others, however, the figures in which they are included along with the effects of other strain measures are enclosed in parentheses. Thus, no attempt is being made to suggest that a measure of family harmony belongs logically at this point in the theoretical chain. Instead, it is included because its presence has obvious impact and therefore has implications for the revision and improvement of theory.

It will be recalled that, for the closed system assumption to hold true in Table 7-1, we would expect zero-order correlation between school grades (which was the only achievement measure used) and a given peer measure to be equal or close to the total indirect effects by way of the strain measures, in the first case, including only school dropout and being fired from a job, or, in the second case, adding boy-parent harmony to the other two. As will be noted, conclusions regarding the validity of the assumption might vary depending upon the strain measures used.

Table 7-1

Relation of Grades to Peer Identification Via Strain (In Los Angeles)

Exogenous Variable (Ex)	Endogenous Variable (En)	Total Effect of Ex on En (Zero Order r)	Total Indirect Effect, Ex on En Via Strain[a]	Total Effect Less Total Indirect Effect[a]
Grades	Ace-in-Hole	−.22	−.12 (−.16)	−.10 (−.06)
Grades	Sociability	−.22	−.07 (−.11)	−.15 (−.11)
Grades	Deviance	−.30	−.09 (−.13)	−.21 (−.17)
Grades	Ratfink	−.13	.00 (−.06)	−.13 (−.07)

[a]Figures *not* in parentheses include only school dropout and being fired from a job as strain indicators. Those in parentheses add the effects of boy-parent harmony to the total.

When only school dropout and work failure indicators of strain were used, the closed system assumption did not hold. The estimated total effects of grades on peer identification were two or three times greater than the indirect effects via strain. The result was that, when indirect effects were subtracted from the total effects, a sizeable amount of variation remained unexplained by intervening effects of the strain indicators. The only possible exception to this general trend involved the Ace-in-the-Hole scale. In this case, the indirect effects of grades did exceed its estimated direct effect, thus lending limited support to a closed system assumption.

In substantive terms, this suggests that poor achievement in school may be sufficient by itself to lead to a deviant peer adjustment without the individual's ever having to experience such additional problems as dropping out or being unable to hold a job. Only in the case of the more sophisticated Ace-in-the-Hole scale was there an indication that the latter experiences are especially important, e.g., that before a boy will be willing to run the risk of hiding a friend from police or parents, he will have experienced even further divorcement from such institutional ties as school and work. Otherwise, poor school performance, by itself, may be sufficient.

By themselves, such findings would be adequate to suggest the need for a revision of the theory. However, an inclusion of family variables in assessing indirect effects adds further complications. The figures in parentheses shown in Table 7-1 indicate that when family harmony is added as a strain measure, the indirect effects of grades on peer identification via strain are heightened on all three measures, and the estimated direct effects are decreased. The findings again suggest the importance of placing family ties somewhere in the chain. They are a force to be reckoned with. Nevertheless, since the estimated direct effects between poor grades and peer identification are sizeable, with the possible exception of the Ace-in-the-Hole scale, the findings do not confirm the assumption that low school achievement is related to peer identification only through stressful experiences that occur later in time. The findings on this particular issue suggest the possible need for a revision of the theory.

2. Relation of Achievement to Delinquency via
Strain and Peer Identification

The second major question had to do with the validity of the sequence suggesting that achievement is related to delinquency only through the intervening effects of strain and peer identification. Does this sequence constitute a closed system?

If the reader will turn once again to Figure 7-4, he will find the results of the analysis using gamma coefficients. Two things of significance will be observed. First, it can be seen that, while several indicators of achievement—school grades, school awards, and future aspirations—were all related to indicators of strain, only school grades were highly related to delinquency. All of the other indicators dropped out. Second, and most significant, the relationship of grades to delinquency (-.71) was the highest of any in the figure, higher even than the relationship of grades to school dropout (-.65). Thus, the magnitude of this relationship raises serious question about the closed system assumption. The size of this coefficient suggests that a direct relationship may exist between lack of achievement in school and delinquency that is not accounted for in the theoretical statements.

This conclusion is strongly supported by the findings shown in Table 7-2. It provides an assessment of the total effects of school grades on the multiple indicators of delinquency as contrasted to its indirect effects via strain and peer identification. First, it will be observed that, while many of the total effects were sizeable, ranging in magnitude from $-.11$ to $-.36$, none of the indirect effects, ranging from $-.01$ to $-.06$, exceeded the .10 cutting point. Second, when the indirect effects were subtracted from the total effects, the differences were large and, in only one instance failed to exceed a magnitude higher in absolute value than .10. Thus, the findings overwhelmingly suggest that the closed system assumption does not hold for this particular segment of the causal sequence. They imply, instead, that the total effects of achievement, as measured by school grades at least, on many different kinds of delinquency are *not* mediated by the intervening effects of strain and peer identification.

These findings may be due in part to a definitional overlap between the forces which lead to law-violating acts, on one hand, and the criteria which authorities use in defining juveniles as delinquent; that is, the findings may reflect the fact that a boy's difficulties in school—truancy and "incorrigibility," as well as poor grades—may be associated with his having been defined as delinquent, quite aside from the possibility that his failures there encouraged him to commit other illegal acts. For example, Elliott (1966) found that juveniles who were experiencing difficulty in school, *and stayed in school*, were more likely to be

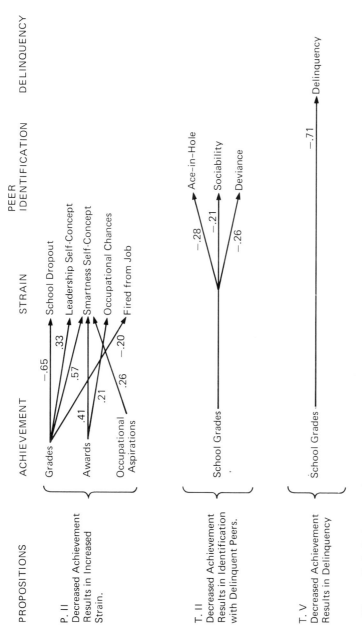

Figure 7-4. Relation of Achievement to Other Indicators in Los Angeles. *Source:* Tables 5-1 and 6-14.

Table 7-2

Relation of Grades to Delinquency Via Strain and Peer Identification (In Los Angeles)

Exogenous Variable (Ex)	Endogenous Variable (En)	Total Effect of Ex on En (Zero Order r)	Total Indirect Effect, Ex on En Via Strain and P.I.	Total Effect Less Total Indirect Effect
	(Category 1)			
Grades	No. Offenses	−.30	−.06	−.24
Grades	Ave. Serious.	−.34	−.06	−.28
Grades	Most Serious	−.36	−.05	−.31
Grades	Theft	−.16	−.01	−.15
Grades	Hell-Raising	−.15	−.01	−.14
Grades	Incorrigi-bility	−.19	−.03	−.16
	(Category 2)			
Grades	Adult/Juvenile	−.31	−.05	−.26
Grades	Felony/Misd.	−.20	−.03	−.17
Grades	Inst./Exp.	−.22	−.05	−.17
Grades	Retreatist	−.25	−.01	−.24
Grades	Conflict	−.11	−.02	−.09
Grades	Criminalistic	−.22	−.05	−.17

officially defined as delinquent than those who dropped out, one ostensible reason being that misbehavior in school is legally definable as a delinquent act. Thus, the chances of being identified as delinquent for the marginal individual are increased over the one who drops out because of the responses of authorities to him.

Our data suggest, however, that this interpretation should not be overdone. A perusal of the kinds of illegal acts that were associated with poor grades included many activities that were not strictly of juvenile status. The degrees of association between poor grades and some of the multiple indicators were quite high: total number of offenses (-.30), average seriousness (-.34), most serious offenses (-.36), high proportion of adult status offenses (-.31), or criminalism (-.22). All of these, and others, were as high or higher than the association between grades and the incorrigibility factor (-.19) which includes truancy among its items. Furthermore, the high association of grades with adult status offenses *directly* counters the argument, because all of the school-related offenses were defined as juvenile in status. Consequently, if grades were related directly to juvenile offenses, the coefficient would have been positive rather than negative. It seems unlikely that the strong relationship between grades and delinquency can be explained solely, or even in large part, by a definitional overlap between antecedents and official criteria.

More pertinent, however, is the fact that the theory was deficient in explaining these relationships, either in terms of the sequence of associations among antecedents or the acts of officials. The findings suggest very strongly the need for a reformulated theory that specifies direct causal effects between achievement and delinquency.

3. Effects of Strain on Delinquency via Peer Identification

The final test of the closed system assumption has to do with the validity of the sequence involving strain, peer identification, and delinquency. When one examines that sequence, he finds the same sorts of theoretical deficiencies that were just described for the relation between achievement and delinquency. It will be observed in Figure 7-5 that, while the gamma analysis supports the postulate that increased strain results in identification with peers, it provides even stronger support for the theorem that increased strain results in delinquency. The relations between nonadjacent variables are the highest. By inference, at least, they question the closed system assumption.

Parallel to these findings are family data that not only paint a similar picture, but raise other questions as well. Figure 7-6 indicates not only that intrafamily problems are related as strongly to peer identification as dropping out of school (and more strongly than being fired from a job), but that their relations to delinquency, per se, are also strong.

The combination of these parallel sets of data are important for three reasons. First, they further, and more seriously, question the adequacy of the causal sequence suggested by the theory. Second, they dramatize the seriousness of the omission of intrafamily tensions from the theory. Family variables, at least for the Los Angeles group, were highly important, and, along with dropping out of school, were highly predictive of delinquency. Third, they are important because of the way they relate to the data on achievement described above. While the prior findings indicated that strain and peer identification were not necessarily intervening influences between poor achievement and delinquency, these findings indicate that strain, whether measured in terms of school, work, or family variables, is important nonetheless. Not only was dropping out of school related rather highly to delinquency (.76) but so was being fired from a job (.61), family separation (.76), poor parental harmony (-.51), and poor boy-parent harmony (-.42). Thus, what these findings imply is that strain, in the

98

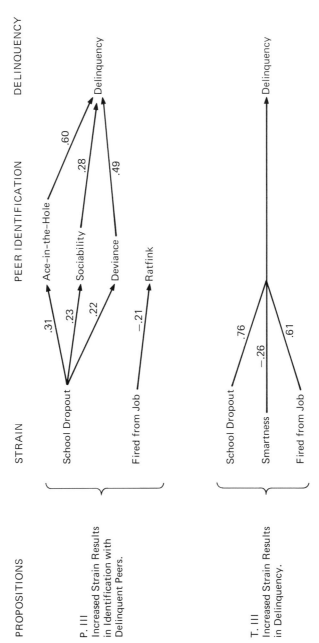

Figure 7-5. Relation of Strain to Other Indicators in Los Angeles. *Source:* Tables 5-1, 6-2, and 6-8.

99

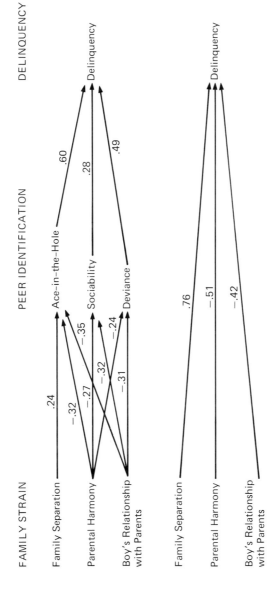

Figure 7-6. Relation of Family Strain to Other Indicators in Los Angeles. *Source:* Tables 5–1, 6–2, and 6–9.

form of broken ties with society's major institutions, as well as poor achievement within them, is directly related to delinquency without the necessary intervening influence of peer identification. However, in order to check the validity of this conclusion even further, let us examine the findings when the more rigorous path test is applied.

In examining the strain-peer identification-delinquency sequence, strain rather than achievement indicators become the exogenous variables. Furthermore, because family indicators have proven to be of importance, a measure of boy-parent harmony was included as one of the strain indicators.[b] The inclusion of this measure, rather than weakening the test of the closed system assumption, only makes it more rigorous. In diagrammatic terms, the causal sequence to be tested appears in Figure 7-7. Notice that, in addition to the causal paths indicated by unidirectional arrows, there are also double-headed arrows drawn among the strain indicators. These arrows represent intercorrelations among the exogenous variables that are of a noncausal nature. Thus, the test must take into account the possibility that, in addition to their indirect effects on delinquency, the strain indicators might also have combined or correlated effects via the peer indicators as well (cf. chapter 3 for a discussion of correlated effects).

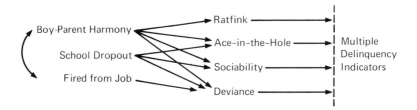

Figure 7-7. Effects of Strain on Delinquency via Peer Identification.

Table 7-3 presents the results of the test taking these factors into account. It is like Tables 7-1 and 7-2 with only one exception: the figures in column four include the correlated effects of the exogenous, strain variables as well as the indirect effects of the peer measures. The results are much like those for the test of the achievement-delinquency sequence. For the most part, the total effects of the strain indicators on delinquency were considerably greater than their indirect effects through peer identification. In only 8 per cent of the 36 relationships tested did the magnitude of the indirect effects reach a .10 level as contrasted

[b]The family separation and parental harmony measures were not included because of the missing data problem.

Table 7-3

Relation of Strain to Delinquency Via Peer Identification (In Los Angeles)

Exogenous Variable (Ex)	Endogenous Variable (En)	Total Effect of Ex on En (Zero Order r)	Total Indirect and Combined Effects of Ex on En via Peer Identification	Total Effect Less Total and Indirect Combined Effects
	(Category 1)			
Boy-Parent Harmony School	Theft Fact.	−.01	−.03	.02
Dropout	Theft Fact.	.26	.03	.23
Fired Job	Theft Fact.	.01	.00	.01
Boy-Parent Harmony School	Hell-Rais.	.13	−.02	.15
Dropout	Hell-Rais.	.16	.02	.14
Fired Job	Hell-Rais.	.05	.00	.05
Boy-Parent Harmony School	Incorrig.	−.05	−.04	−.01
Dropout	Incorrig.	.19	.04	.15
Fired Job	Incorrig.	.06	.02	.04
Boy-Parent Harmony School	Total # Offenses	−.19	−.07	−.12
Dropout	Total # Offenses	.37	.07	.30
Fired Job	Total # Offenses	.15	.02	.13
Boy-Parent Harmony School	Ave. Serious	−.20	−.10	−.10
Dropout	Ave. Serious	.42	.10	.32
Fired Job	Ave. Serious	.18	.04	.14
Boy-Parent Harmony School	Most Serious	−.18	−.10	−.08
Dropout	Most Serious	.44	.08	.36
Fired Job	Most Serious	.20	.05	.15

Table 7-3 (*Cont.*)

Exogenous Variable (*Ex*)	Endogenous Variable (*En*)	Total Effect of *Ex* on *En* (Zero Order *r*)	Total Indirect and Combined Effects of *Ex* on *En* via Peer Identification	Total Effect Less Total and Indirect Combined Effects
	(*Category 2*)			
Boy-Parent Harmony	Adult/Juvenile Offenses	−.06	−.09	.03
School Dropout	Adult/Juvenile Offenses	.38	.09	.29
Fired Job	Adult/Juvenile Offenses	.14	.04	.10
Boy-Parent Harmony	Fel./Misd.	−.03	−.06	.03
School Dropout	Fel./Misd.	.19	.04	.15
Fired Job	Fel./Misd.	.04	.04	.00
Boy-Parent Harmony	Inst./Exp.	−.01	−.09	.08
School Dropout	Inst./Exp.	.31	.07	.24
Fired Job	Inst./Exp.	.09	.04	.05
Boy-Parent Harmony	Retreatism	−.27	−.04	−.23
School Dropout	Retreatism	.17	.00	.17
Fired Job	Retreatism	.13	.00	.13
Boy-Parent Harmony	Conflict	.00	−.05	.05
School Dropout	Conflict	.17	.04	.13
Fired Job	Conflict	.15	.04	.11
Boy-Parent Harmony	Criminalism	−.04	−.07	.03
School Dropout	Criminalism	.35	.07	.28
Fired Job	Criminalism	.10	.02	.08

with fully two-thirds of the estimated total effects. Thus, the conclusion is inescapable that the closed system assumption does not hold for this particular sequence.

As was suggested by the gamma analysis, the effects of strain on delinquency—whether originating in family, school, or work situations—do not appear to be mediated to any significant degree by peer identification. Furthermore, a simple count of the cases in which the effects of school dropout on delinquency were greater than .10 reveals that this was true in 100 per cent of the relationships measured. In contrast, associations of this magnitude were characteristic of less than half of the cases in which boy-parent harmony was involved, and slightly more than half in which being fired from a job was involved. Thus, of the three indicators used, being cut off from the school seems to have had the greater effect on delinquency.

Conclusions

The closed system assumption was not confirmed in Los Angeles for any of the sets of relationships in which confirmation was theoretically desirable. The asymmetric sequence suggested by the theory does not seem to be appropriate. Moreover, the seriousness of omitting family variables was again confirmed.

After testing the closed system in Utah, the implications of these findings will be considered in detail.

8

Test of Closed-System Assumption in Utah

The format for testing the closed system assumption for the Utah sample will be the same as that used for the Los Angeles sample. The overall gamma and path findings for the bivariate test of the postulates will be summarized graphically, followed by a step-by-step test of the assumption. However, since this is the last chapter concerned with testing the theory, it provides the opportunity to summarize some of the major similarities and differences in the findings between Utah and Los Angeles. These similarities and differences have important implications for theoretical reformulation and future inquiry.

Causal Sequence for Utah

The findings for the gamma analysis are presented in Figure 8-1. The coefficients shown meet the same inclusion criteria as the coefficients in Figure 7-1. As may be seen, the general findings for Utah were strikingly similar to those for Los Angeles. One similarity involved the sequential chain that linked poor grades, dropping out of school, peer identification and delinquency. The pattern in both locations was identical. The second similarity involved occupational aspirations as well as school grades. While poor school achievement and lowered aspirations in both locations seemed to lead to lowered self-evaluations (as strain indicators), the latter, in turn, were not related significantly to peer identification. Thus, while a disruption of ties with the school, as exemplified by dropping out, did seem to produce stronger peer ties, poor self-evaluations did not. This seems to be a potentially important finding that warrants attention as the analysis proceeds, especially if it should be found that poor self-evaluations are associated with delinquency, although not with peer identification.

Figure 8-2 provides the summary findings for the path model, with the omission of some of the achievement and strain indicators described earlier. In general, it exhibits the same causal paths suggested by the gamma analysis, and is also much like the path model for Los Angeles (compare Figure 7-2). When one reaches the specific relationships between the peer scales and the multiple delinquency indicators, however, the similarities tend to disappear. Like Los Angeles, there were no direct paths leading into the Ratfink scale in Utah but there were some weak relationships from that point on. Beyond that, the differences far outweigh the similarities. These differences were described in detail in chapter 6 and need only be summarized here:

106

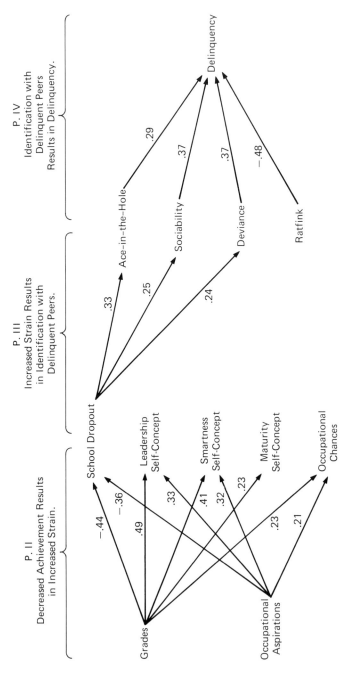

Figure 8–1. Summary of Postulate Findings for Utah. *Source:* Tables 5–2 and 6–2.

107

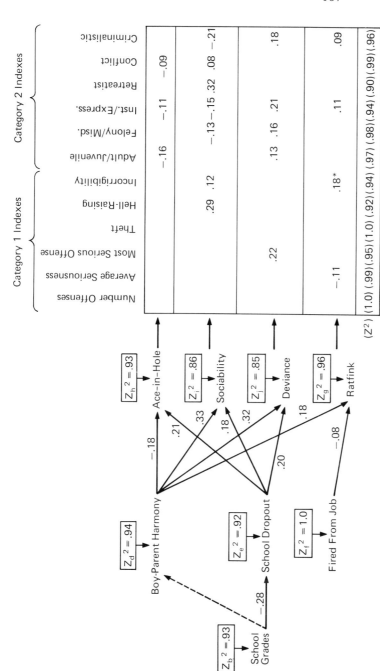

Figure 8-2. General Path Model for Utah (Beta Weights Revised).

*Contrary to Expectation

1. The peer scales in Utah were much less predictive of the Category 1 indicators—the measures of degrees of delinquency. Instead, they were more strongly associated with different kinds of delinquency—Category 2.
2. The Ace-in-the-Hole scale was scarcely associated with delinquency in Utah, whereas it was highly predictive in Los Angeles.
3. The Sociability scale, which was predictive in Utah, was not in Los Angeles.
4. The Deviance scale, which was also highly predictive in Los Angeles, was much less predictive in Utah.

Overall, the peer identification scales that were predictive of delinquency in Utah tended to be associated far more often with juvenile-status and expressive kinds of delinquent acts than in Los Angeles. Thus, by inference, the findings suggest that many of the more serious kinds of delinquent acts committed by the Utah group may not have sprung from learning and associations in the most prevalent subculture found there.

With these similarities and differences noted, the next step is that of determining how the two samples compare when the closed system assumption is tested. This test requires an empirical examination of the same set of questions asked in chapter 7:

1. What are the indirect effects of the achievement indicators on each of the peer scales, via the intervening measures of strain?
2. What are the indirect effects of achievement indicators on the delinquency measures, via the intervening measures of strain and peer identification?
3. What are the indirect effects of the strain measures on delinquency, via the intervening measures of peer identification?

For each question, we need to know whether or not the indirect effects approximate the direct effects. If so, the closed system assumption will have been met; if not it must be rejected.

Summarized Findings

The analysis failed to confirm the closed system assumption for the Utah sample just as it did for the Los Angeles sample. The findings suggest overwhelmingly the need for a drastic revision, either of the causal sequence postulated in the theory or of the entire theory itself. However, before the latter alternative is chosen, it should be remembered that similarities between the two samples were considerably greater than differences, suggesting that some important and common variables were being tapped. A number of indicators in both locations were associated, not only with other indicators directly adjacent to them, but with delinquency itself. It is possible, therefore, that, with some reordering of indicators in the theoretical sequence, greater explanation might be possible.

The analysis also suggested some specific differences between the metropolitan and nonmetropolitan boys which, if taken into account, might add helpful refinements to any theoretical revision: lowered aspirations were associated far more strongly with peer identification and delinquency in Utah than Los Angeles; family disruption seemed to be associated more strongly with difficulty in Los Angeles than in Utah; delinquents may suffer a greater loss of status and self-esteem in Utah than in Los Angeles; and peer identification in Los Angeles seems to have a more sophisticated and seriously deviant character than in Utah, and to be related more consistently with different kinds of delinquency. Since little detail can be gleaned from these summary statements, attention is invited to the longer analysis that follows for specific details.

Detailed Findings

The detailed findings are presented by considering each of the three questions which must be answered in the affirmative if the closed system assumption is to be confirmed. The analysis also includes a summary comparison of the findings for the Los Angeles and Utah groups.

1. Relation of Achievement to Peer
Identification via Strain

In Figure 8-3, the gamma findings for the effects of achievement on peer identification, via strain, are displayed. By comparing this figure with Figure 7-4 for Los Angeles, an important difference will be noted. In addition to the importance of school grades for both groups, the role of a lowered achievement orientation (as measured by occupational aspiration) was of singular importance to the Utah group. Not only were lowered aspirations related about as strongly as school grades to several measures of strain, but were directly related to peer identification as well, possibly without the intervening influence of strain. The same was definitely not true in Los Angeles. The picture that is painted in Utah is one that suggests that lowered aspirations, as well as poor grades, were associated not only with strain—dropping out of school, poor self-evaluations, and lowered estimates of future occupational chances—but with heightened peer identification as well.

Using the more stringent path test, the effects of grades on peer identification via the strain indicator of dropping out of school may be found in Table 8-1. The indirect effects of boy-parent harmony, along with school dropout, are also shown in parentheses so that their effects might be assessed.

The findings are highly similar to those for Los Angeles. When school dropout is used as the sole intervening influence, there is little support for the closed system assumption. The total effects of grades on peer identification are several times greater than the indirect effects through school dropout, suggesting that in Utah, as in Los Angeles, poor performance while still in school seems to enhance

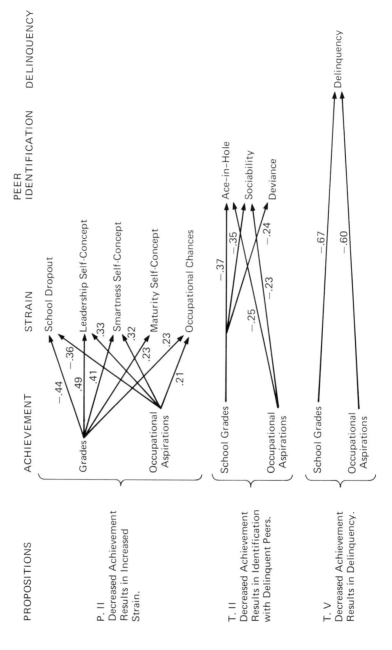

Figure 8–3. Relation of Achievement to Other Indicators in Utah. *Source:* Tables 5-2 and 6-14.

Table 8-1

Relation of Grades to Peer Identification Via Strain (In Utah)

Exogenous Variable (Ex)	Endogenous Variable (En)	Total Effect of Ex on En (Zero Order r)	Total Indirect Effect, Ex on En Via Strain[a]	Total Effect Less Total Indirect Effect[a]
Grades	Ace-in-Hole	−.24	−.06 (−.10)	−.18 (−.14)
Grades	Sociability	−.34	−.05 (−.13)	−.29 (−.21)
Grades	Deviance	−.29	−.06 (−.14)	−.23 (−.15)
Grades	Ratfink	−.22	.00 (−.04)	−.22 (−.18)

[a]Figures *not* in parentheses include only school dropout and being fired from a job as strain indicators. Those in parentheses add the effects of boy-parent harmony to the total.

peer identification. However, when boy-parent harmony is used along with school dropout as a strain indicator, the indirect effects increase somewhat. Just as in Los Angeles, therefore, the inclusion of this family variable suggests that family measures may be of significance in the theoretical chain. If they were included, there would be greater support for the closed system assumption, suggesting the possible need for theory which specifies that achievement has both a direct and an indirect effect on peer identification.

2. Relation of Achievement to Delinquency via Strain and Peer Identification

Refer again to Figure 8-3 for the gamma findings on the effects of achievement on delinquency in Utah. Just as in Los Angeles, there was a strong, inverse relationship between grades and delinquency (-.67 in Utah and -.71 in Los Angeles). This high degree of correspondence between the two strongly suggests that poor performance in school has a strong total effect on delinquency, one that is much stronger than the effects of achievement on other variables in the chain. But, in addition, Figure 8-3 also suggests that, in Utah but not in Los Angeles, lowered aspirations are also highly associated with delinquency (-.60 vs. -.07). It appears that boys in Utah who either do not share, or have discarded, the American tradition of wanting to get ahead, are more likely to become delinquent. This tendency reflects one of the major differences between the metropolitan and nonmetropolitan boys. Furthermore, the findings imply that the effects of poor achievement are direct rather than being mediated by strain and peer identification.

The issue is important because these Utah findings run contrary to empirical findings by Kobrin (1951), Short and Strodtbeck (1965), and Gold (1963) that delinquents evaluate salient features of the middle-class equally as high as nondelinquents. Our research does not address this issue squarely, but it does suggest that the evidence for the Utah delinquents might be to the contrary.

The reason the issue is an important one is that the findings of the investigators cited above, like those for our Los Angeles sample, were obtained largely in metropolitan settings. The Utah culture, by contrast, is considerably more integrated and homogeneous. Given its nonmetropolitan character, and its ties to the conservative fundamentalism of the Mormon Church, it is likely that its effects on the deviant are different and perhaps more pronounced. Norms are more explicit with respect to what a juvenile should not do, such as becoming delinquent, as well as what he should do. Any person who is deviant, moreover, is much more visible. Consequently, an important question raised by the findings has to do with the extent to which the lowered status of the deviant in Utah may tend to bring his aspirations and performance into line with that status. If social control in an integrated culture is increased, then the effects of lowered status will likely reverberate throughout all areas of the deviant's life, social and personal. Not only may his actual achievement in school and community be hindered but he may incorporate a self-image that is reflected in lowered self-evaluations and lowered aspirations. If this is the case, and the next set of findings suggest that it may be, then one might expect that he would not be well-integrated into the social order and that his behavior, his self-evaluations and his aspirations would reflect his position as a peripheral member of the community. More will be said on the subject later in the chapter. First, however, the analysis will concentrate on a more rigorous test of the closed system assumption for this particular sequence.

As may be seen in Table 8-2, the findings do not support the assumption that the effects of achievement on delinquency occur only through strain and peer identification, although the analysis is limited strictly to a test of the effects of grades on delinquency (the aspirations measure was dropped because data on some individuals was incomplete). As in Los Angeles, the indirect, as contrasted to the total effects of grades on delinquency were negligible, strongly suggesting the need for theoretical revision. Moreover, it will be noted in Table 8-2 that the delinquency indicators of number of offenses, the theft factor, and the conflict index are not included in the test of the assumption. This was because the original path analysis indicated that none of the paths leading from peer identification to them exceeded the .10 cutting point. This does not mean, however, that poor grades may not affect these measures directly. The evidence indicates that significant direct effects were present. The zero-order coefficient from grades to number of offenses was -.32, from grades to theft -.21, and from grades to conflict -.12. Thus, these findings question the closed system assumption even more strongly because we did not find the presence of any indirect effects of grades on these three delinquency measures via peer identification; yet significant direct effects were present.

Table 8-2

Relation of Grades to Delinquency Via Strain and Peer Identification (In Utah)

Exogenous Variable (Ex)	Endogenous Variable (En)[a]	Total Effect of Ex on En (Zero Order r)	Total Indirect Effect, Ex on En Via Strain and P.I.	Total Effect Less Total Indirect Effect
	(Category 1)			
Grades	Ave. Serious.	−.29	.00	−.29
Grades	Most Serious	−.36	.01	−.37
Grades	Hell-Raising	−.24	.03	−.27
Grades	Incorrigibility	−.25	−.03	−.22
	(Category 2)			
Grades	Adult/Juvenile	−.09	.00	−.09
Grades	Felony/Misd.	−.18	.00	−.18
Grades	Inst./Exp.	−.15	.00	−.15
Grades	Retreatist	−.31	−.05	−.26
Grades	Criminalistic	−.18	.01	−.19

[a]Three delinquency indicators are not included because they dropped out of the path sequence: no. of offenses, theft and conflict. Their zero-order correlations (total effects) with grades were −.32, −.21 and −.12, respectively, again suggesting the possibility of sizeable direct effects from achievement to delinquency.

3. Relation of Strain to Delinquency via Peer Identification

The gamma analysis of the relation of strain to delinquency in Utah is displayed in Figure 8-4. If one compares this figure with Figure 7-5 for Los Angeles, he will find that both sets of findings imply that the causal sequence suggested by the theory is inappropriate. While only one indicator of strain in both locations—i.e. school dropout—was related consistently to the adjacent peer scales, several strain indicators were related to the non-adjacent delinquency indicator. A direct association is implied. Furthermore, this pattern was more pronounced in Utah than in Los Angeles. Whereas in Los Angeles it was dropping out of school (.76) and being fired from a job (.61) that were linked most strongly to delinquency, these same relationships were not only evident in Utah (.80 and .37), but all three of the self-concept indicators, compared to only

114

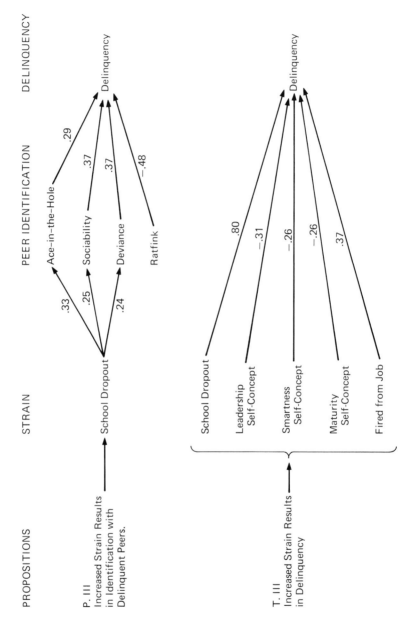

Figure 8–4. Relation of Strain to Other Indicators in Utah. *Source:* Tables 5–2, 6–2, and 6–8.

one in Los Angeles, were linked to delinquency as well: leadership (-.31), smartness (-.26) and maturity (-.26). The relation of a poor self-evaluation to delinquency was more pronounced in the Utah setting. Thus, while both sets of findings question the closed system assumption indirectly, they also seem to support the existence of cross-subcultural differences mentioned earlier. It is the delinquent in the rural environment who seems to suffer the greater loss of self-esteem.

In considering the possibility that this is the case, it is virtually impossible for us to know for certain what is cause and effect in this set of relationships; e.g., whether poor self-evaluation precedes or follows being defined as delinquent. That is the problem of a *post hoc* analysis such as this, rather than a longitudinal study. However, the fact that poor self-evaluations were more pronounced for the Utah group probably illustrates the greater impact on the self of poor achievement, strain, and official labeling in an integrated culture. It seems quite probable that the salience of one's status in such a setting is more vulnerable to threat than in a more impersonal, metropolitan setting, but there is more to the story than has already been presented.

A comparison of the Utah and Los Angeles *family* data also reveals some provocative issues. Again, if Figure 8-5 for Utah is compared with Figure 7-6 for Los Angeles, it will be observed that, while intrafamily problems were related to other variables in the theoretical chain in Utah just as they were in Los Angeles, they may have been of *lesser* importance in Utah. Whereas in Los Angeles, all three family indicators—separation, parental harmony, and boy-parent harmony—were predictive of peer identification, only one indicator, boy-parent harmony, was predictive in Utah. Moreover, the magnitudes of the coefficients expressing the relations between all three family indicators and delinquency were consistently greater in Los Angeles than in Utah: family separation (.76 vs. .49), parental harmony (−.51 vs. −.25), and boy-parent harmony (−.42 vs. −.36).

The data imply that, in the whole constellation of forces, the family unit may be of greater singular importance in Los Angeles than in Utah. When, and if, that unit has difficulty, it will be more likely to result in peer identification and delinquency. Thus, it is possible that greater burdens are placed upon the family unit in an impersonal, metropolitan environment than in a more close-knit, nonmetropolitan community. When the family has internal troubles, they are more likely to result in peer identification and delinquent activities because there are fewer other institutional ties to take up the slack.

If true, the irony of these comparative findings should not go unnoticed. The data have implied, on one hand, that intrafamily problems may be more closely linked to the delinquency of the urban boy simply because the family unit, along with the school, is so uniquely important in an impersonal setting. Yet, on the other hand, the Utah data indicate that a closely knit community in which the family unit shares some of its socializing functions does not provide an unmixed blessing. While the boy who gets into trouble in that setting may not be so dependent upon his family, he may well suffer a more extended loss of status and self-esteem simply because he is so closely linked with the whole

116

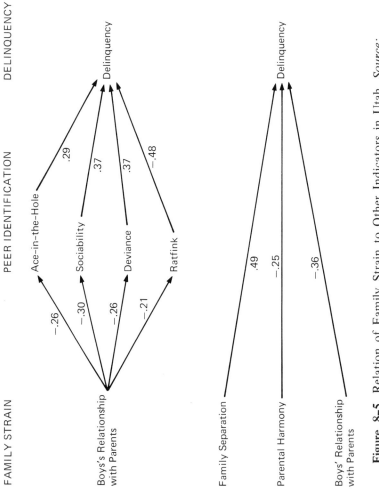

Figure 8-5. Relation of Family Strain to Other Indicators in Utah. *Source:* Tables 5–2, 6–2, and 6–9.

community. The greater integration of the smaller community obviously has its liabilities as well as its strengths, and, thus, affects juveniles in different ways.

The analysis of strain on delinquency in Utah, via peer identification, using the more stringent path analysis, further illustrates the likelihood that peer identification is not a necessary intervening influence. In Table 8-3, it will be

Table 8-3

Relation of Strain to Delinquency Via Peer Identification (In Utah)

Exogenous Variables (Ex)	Endogenous Variables (En)	Total Effect of Ex on En (Zero Order r)	Total Indirect Effect, Ex on En Via P.I.	Total Effect Less Total Indirect Effect
	(Category 1)			
Boy-Parent Harmony	Ave. Serious.	−.26	.02	−.28
School Dropout	Ave. Serious.	.16	.00	.16
Boy-Parent Harmony	Most Serious	−.21	−.07	−.14
School Dropout	Most Serious	.22	.04	−.18
Boy-Parent Harmony	Hell-Raising	−.09	−.10	.04
School Dropout	Hell-Raising	−.05	.05	−.10
Boy-Parent Harmony	Incorrigibility	−.13	.07	−.20
School Dropout	Incorrigibility	.09	.02	.07
	(Category 2)			
Boy-Parent Harmony	Adult/Juvenile	−.04	−.01	−.03
School Dropout	Adult/Juvenile	.05	.00	.05
Boy-Parent Harmony	Felony/Misd.	−.10	−.01	−.09
School Dropout	Felony/Misd.	.13	.01	.12

Table 8-3 *(Cont.)*

Exogenous Variables (Ex)	Endogenous Variables (En)	Total Effect of Ex on En (Zero Order r)	Total Indirect Effect, Ex on En Via P.I.	Total Effect Less Total Indirect Effect
Boy-Parent Harmony	Inst./Exp.	−.10	−.06	−.04
School Dropout	Inst./Exp.	.13	−.01	.14
Boy-Parent Harmony	Retreatism	−.24	−.11	−.13
School Dropout	Retreatism	.04	.06	−.02
Boy-Parent Harmony	Criminalism	−.07	.01	−.08
School Dropout	Criminalism	.17	.00	.17

observed that the total effects of both school dropout and boy-parent harmony on delinquency were much greater in most cases than their indirect effects.[a] There were, however, two exceptional cases in the eighteen shown, and both involved the effects of boy-parent harmony on two specific kinds of delinquency—hell-raising and retreatist behavior. The findings suggest that the indirect effects of peer identification (i.e., the Sociability scale) are important in both cases. Boys whose relations with parents are poor, and who engage in hell-raising or retreatist activities, were those who were high on the sociability peer scale. Otherwise, the closed system assumption does not hold. The effects of strain on delinquency in most cases were direct rather than indirect.

Conclusions

At this point in the analysis, we have been exposed both to the evidence that has tended to confirm the theory and that which has tended to dispute it. Perhaps the most striking thing about the analysis is that, except for social class, the analysis of bivariate relationships tended to confirm many of the propositions of

[a]Two things about this analysis should be noted. First, since the zero-order correlation between school dropout and boy-parent harmony was very low in Utah (−.04), their correlated effects on delinquency were not included. Second, three delinquency indicators—"number of offenses," "theft," and "conflict"—were not included in the test because none of the paths leading from peer identification to them exceeded the .10 cutting point.

the theory. Yet, when the overall causal sequence was examined, taking into account the closed system assumption, the theory was not confirmed. Therefore, building upon the analysis thus far, two things will be done in the remaining chapters.

In chapter 9 the original theory will be reformulated into several alternative models, each of which will then be subjected to empirical assessment. The goal will be to determine whether explanatory power can be increased by any one of them. Chapter 10 will then be concerned with the most productive of these models and their implications for further study.

9 A Test of Alternative Models

Although many of the postulates and theorems in this theory of delinquency received some confirmation, the overall examination revealed several major inadequacies. First, social class proved to be of little explanatory value in Los Angeles, and either contrary to expectation or of questionable utility in Utah. The findings were such as to question the value of the concept in future attempts at theoretical reformulation. Second, the closed system assumption did not hold true for either the Los Angeles or Utah samples. Contrary to theoretical expectation, the achievement and strain measures tended to be more highly related to delinquency than were the indicators of peer identification. Third, the position of peer identification in the causal sequence was found to be ambiguous. The data were unclear as to whether it should be considered as an antecedent to delinquency, a consequence of it, or both. Moreover, the findings hinted that the role of peer identification may be different in Utah and Los Angeles, such that the relationship of peer identification to various kinds of delinquent acts varies in the two locations.

Other investigators have made some observations that are pertinent to these findings, especially as they relate to the fact that achievement and strain were more highly related to delinquency than peer identification. The first has to do with the likelihood that, when young people have weak or nonexistent ties with the traditions and institutions of home and school, they are placed in a particularly vulnerable position. As Matza (1964:51) points out, all juveniles, and especially delinquents, exist within a narrow life space centering around the family, school and peers. Consequently, an especially difficult situation is created for any individual who is cut off from the first two of these three major sources of support. "Stripped of moral guidance . . .," says Matza (1964:89), "he momentarily exists in a stark and frightening isolation."

Our findings provide some support for this point of view. The fact that school and family disruptions were related so strongly to delinquency is testimony to the nature of serious institutional difficulties. What is more, the fact that the relationship of peer identification to delinquency was somewhat weaker than the relationships of school and family indicators to it suggests that the peer group may not have compensated adequately for family and school disruptions. If it had, one might have expected greater evidence that peer identification was a necessary mediatory influence. But, while it was present, it was not sufficient.

Other research findings help, perhaps, to explain why. Short and Strodtbeck (1965:Chaps. 10 and 12), for example, found that gang boys, when compared with non-gang boys of a similar or different class level, were characterized by a long list of disabilities which led to, or were caused by, their lack of effective and rewarding ties with major societal institutions: limited social and technical skills, a low capacity for self-assertion, lower intelligence scores, and even a tendency to hold their own friends, as well as themselves, in low esteem.

It was evidence such as this which led Short and Strodtbeck (1965:231) to depreciate nostalgic references to that "old gang of mine" and to deny the image of the delinquent group as carefree and solidary. They report that such an interpretation may derive more from the projections of middle-class observers than from the realities that dominate delinquent group life.

Similarly Klein and Crawford (1967:231) argue that the internal sources of cohesion in delinquent groups are weak. Group goals which might be unifying are minimal, membership stability is low, and loyalty is questionable. Consequently, it is external threat, not internal cohesion, that holds these groups together. Were it not for the external pressures of police and other officials, the threats of rival groups, or the lack of acceptance by parents, schools and employers, most delinquent groups would have little to unify them. By themselves, such groups do not develop the kinds of group goals and instrumentally oriented activities which might lead to lasting and satisfying kinds of experiences.

Finally, we can ill-afford to forget the possibility that our findings may also reflect the interaction of known delinquents with the official system. One reason the lack of family, school, and work ties may be so highly predictive of official delinquency is that these are the criteria upon which the court and other officials base their decisions. If such ties are lacking for an individual, the likelihood is probably increased that he will be placed in the official custody of the court, adjudicated as a delinquent, and placed under correctional supervision. Only rarely would one expect peer identification to occupy a central position in the decisions that are made. It is readily understandable, therefore, why the predictive efficiency of family separation, dropping out of school, or lack of employment, rather than peer identification, may be increased by official action. A basic question, therefore, is whether peer identification precedes the labeling process, is enhanced by it, or both.

Although our data will not permit an exhaustive examination of this and other issues, they might provide some leads for theoretical reformulation. In the next section of this chapter, several possible models for reformulating the theory are presented and examined. In examining the models, the section will be concerned primarily with three things: (1) determining whether a reordering of variables in the theoretical sequence might increase its ability to explain delinquency; (2) determining whether the capacities of the different models to explain delinquency might vary depending upon the kinds of delinquency involved; and (3) determining the best position for peer identification in the causal sequence. This exploration will be strictly empirical, depending more upon the leads suggested by the findings of prior chapters than upon the introduction of new frames of reference or evidence provided by others.

Alternative Models

Model I

The first model suggests that delinquency may be the direct consequence of poor achievement and strain, and that peer identification results from the labeling process rather than preceding it. In diagrammatic terms, the model would appear as shown in Figure 9-1. It posits a direct causal effect from achievement both to strain and delinquency, a direct causal effect from strain to delinquency, and a direct causal effect from delinquency to peer identification.

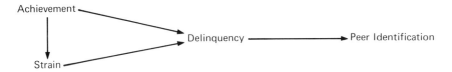

Figure 9–1. Model I.

Model II

The second model, shown in Figure 9-2, makes peer identification a causal antecedent, but places it in a different position in the overall sequence than it had in the original model. In this instance, achievement is said to affect delinquency only through the intervening variables of strain and peer identification; peer identification, in turn, is made a direct consequence of both achievement and strain; and delinquency is made a direct consequence of strain and peer identification.

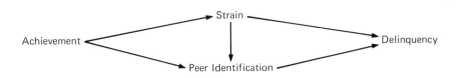

Figure 9–2. Model II.

124

Model III

This model is similar to the model tested originally. However, instead of specifying a simple causal sequence extending from achievement to strain, to peer identification, to delinquency, it adds complexity. Achievement is said to cause strain, and strain to cause peer identification, but, in addition, achievement and strain, as well as peer identification, are treated as direct causal antecedents of delinquency. The model appears in Figure 9-3.

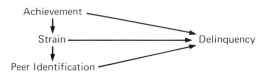

Figure 9-3. Model III.

Model IV

In the fourth and final model, shown in Figure 9-4, only achievement is treated as a causal antecedent of delinquency. Strain and peer identification are moved to the end of the sequence with strain being the product of the labeling process and peer identification the product both of strain and labeling. This model, then, should help to suggest to what degree the labeling process is instrumental in producing both the alienation and peer group relationships heretofore suggested as occurring prior to delinquency.

Although these four models are not exhaustive of the many that might have been formulated, they comprise a reasonable sample of some of the more plausible ones. Thus, they should help to realize the objectives specified above–namely, to determine whether the explanation of delinquency can be increased, whether there are differences in the kinds of delinquency explained by the different models, and whether peer identification should be treated as a causal antecedent or consequence of delinquency.

Figure 9-4. Model IV.

Assessment of the Reformulated Models

All of the models just described were assessed by way of path analysis. The statistical and methodological procedures used were the same as those employed in earlier chapters, with only two exceptions. First, in the interest of simplicity, we did not use gamma coefficients, but relied totally on path coefficients. Since the findings from the two techniques were highly similar, we felt it would be redundant to use both of them again. Furthermore, because path analysis enables us to examine residuals and indirect effects, it provides for a much more sophisticated kind of review than could be derived from the gamma coefficients.

Second, we dropped the Ratfink scale as an indicator of peer identification, and awards in school as a measure of achievement, since they proved to be of minimal explanatory value in the earlier analysis. All other operational measures used in the earlier path model were retained in assessing the reformulated models.

Since a detailed presentation of all the path coefficients for all the models would require too much space and discussion, the models will be assessed only by examining the residuals, first, for the delinquency and, second, for the peer identification measures. Squared residual path coefficients, it will be recalled, indicate the extent to which the variation in a given delinquency or peer measure is *unexplained* by a given path model. By implication, then, the lower the residual the better the explanation. Thus, a squared residual path is like the *obverse* of what we would obtain if we computed a multiple correlation coefficient and squared it. For example, a squared residual path of .84 for a given measure implies that we could explain its variation with an R^2 of about .16. It should be reemphasized that a squared residual indicates the extent to which the variation in a given measure is *not* explained by the path analysis.

Although our examination of the residuals is not excessively elaborate, it will permit some determination of the relative utility of the various models. For those who are interested in reviewing the individual path coefficients, they are presented in Appendix 3.

Explanation of Delinquency

The residuals for the four models, along with those for the original one, are presented in Table 9-1. In reviewing the table, several things should be noted. First, the figures in the table are squared residual path coefficients. Second, the columns of the table indicate the residuals of each model on each of the delinquency measures for both samples. Beneath the heading in each column is a letter designation of the variables used to predict delinquency (A stands for achievement, S for Strain, and P for peer identification). Finally, the bottom row of the table indicates the average of the squared residuals for each model over all of the delinquency measures.

The first thing that will be observed in Table 9-1 is that Model III—the one

Table 9-1

Effectiveness (Squared Residuals) of Theoretical Models in Explaining Delinquency

Delinquency Indicators	Squared Residuals for Los Angeles				
	Original[a] (P)	Model I (AS)	Model II[a] (SP)	Model III[a] (ASP)	Model IV (A)
Category 1					
Number of Offenses	.95	.84	.84	[.83]	.91
Average Seriousness	.88	.78	.77	[.76]	.88
Most Serious	.91	.77	.77	[.75]	.87
Theft	.99	[.93][b]	[.93]	[.93]	.97
Hell-Raising	.99	.93	.94	[.92]	.98
Incorrigibility	.98	[.95]	.96	[.95]	.96
Category 2					
Adult/Juvenile	.92	.83	.82	[.81]	.90
Felony/Misdemeanor	.95	.95	[.92]	[.92]	.96
Instrumental/Expressive	.93	.90	[.86]	[.86]	.95
Retreatism	.98	[.88]	.91	[.88]	.94
Conflict	.96	.95	[.93]	[.93]	.99
Criminalism	.96	.88	[.87]	[.87]	.95
Average	.95	.88	.88	[.87]	.94

Delinquency Indicators	Squared Residuals for Utah				
	Original[a] (P)	Model I (AS)	Model II[a] (SP)	Model III[a] (ASP)	Model IV (A)
Category 1					
Number of Offenses	1.0	[.87]	.91	[.87]	.90
Average Seriousness	.99	.87	.87	[.82]	.92
Most Serious	.95	.84	.89	[.81]	.87
Theft	1.00	[.93]	.94	[.93]	.96
Hell-Raising	.93	.94	.89	[.88]	.94
Incorrigibility	.94	1.00	.95	[.93]	.94

Table 9-1 (*Cont.*)

Delinquency Indicators	Squared Residuals for Utah (*cont.*)				
	Original[a] (P)	Model I (AS)	Model II[a] (SP)	Model III[a] (ASP)	Model IV (A)
Category 2					
Adult/Juvenile	[.97]	1.00	[.97]	[.97]	.99
Felony/Misdemeanor	.98	.96	.94	[.93]	.97
Instrumental/Expressive	.94	.97	.92	[.91]	.98
Retreatism	.90	.87	.88	[.84]	.90
Conflict	.99	.98	.98	[.97]	.99
Criminalism	.96	.96	.92	[.90]	.97
Average	.96	.93	.92	[.90]	.94

Note: A = Achievement, P = Peer Identification, S = Strain

[a]Although the Ratfink scale was used in the original model, it was dropped from Models II and III. This should be taken into account when comparing their residuals with those of the original model.

[b]The lowest residual for each delinquency indicator within both samples is indicated by brackets, [ ]. The higher the residual, the lower the degree of explanation.

that treats achievement, strain, and peer identification as direct causal antecedents of delinquency—yields the lowest residuals for *all* of the delinquency indicators for both samples. It is not only superior to all of the new models but is superior as well to the original model that was the main object of study in this book. Undoubtedly this occurs because Model III makes use of all the variables as direct predictors of delinquency, while the remainder use only one or two subsets. In the interest of parsimony, therefore, any model with fewer predictors that produces residuals that are the *same* as Model III should, since none could be lower, receive preference over Model III, the reason being that the same result would be achieved with less complexity. For example, both models I and III provide the lowest residuals, (.87), for number of offenses in Utah. Since Model III posits this measure to be a function of achievement and strain and peer identification, while Model I posits it to be a function only of achievement and strain, the presence of peer identification in Model III seems to add nothing over the prediction yielded by Model I. Thus, in the interest of parsimony, we would choose Model I as best suited to explaining this measure. With this methodological procedure in mind, let us proceed with the business of matching models to types of delinquency. (Detailed attention to the role of peer identification in the sequence will be treated later.)

128

Model I

The first point of significance that surfaces when the criterion of parsimony is used is that some models predict different kinds of delinquency more efficiently than others (Table 9-1). Moreover, the models do not always predict the same kinds of delinquency in both Los Angeles and Utah. Thus, Model I (Figure 9-1) seems optimally suited to only two delinquency indicators in both Los Angeles and Utah, but they are not the same indicators. In Los Angeles, this model was the best predictor of incorrigibility (.95) and retreatism (.88), while in Utah it predicted number of offenses (.87) and theft (.93). There may have been some overlap between the two locations on the theft scale, since the residual was .93 in both places. However, two other models, II and III, explained this indicator equally well. Since this was the only case in which the residuals were the same on more than two models, it may be an anomaly for which answers are not available. In any event, two conclusions are in order regarding the utility of this particular model. First, poor achievement and strain, by themselves, are not the most efficient predictors of delinquency for either location. Second, the findings suggest that subcultural peculiarities may result in differences in the capacities of the different models to predict delinquency in the Utah and Los Angeles settings. In this case, poor achievement and strain were associated with such juvenile status offenses as incorrigibility and retreatism in Los Angeles, while in Utah they were associated with frequency of offense and theft. Such a finding is one that investigators have suspected for a long time; namely, that different antecedents will be associated with different kinds of delinquent acts. A great deal is lost when delinquency is treated as a single, global concept.

Model II

Model II (Figure 9-2) suggests that delinquency is a joint function of strain and peer identification. Although poor achievement is important, its effects are mediated by the other two intervening variables. In examining this model, it will be necessary not only to determine the capacity of strain and peer identification to explain delinquency, but to test the closed system assumption as well. Although a test of the assumption was not appropriate for Models I, III, and IV, since they specify direct effects from all causal antecedents to delinquency, it was appropriate in this case.

The findings were these. First, the model proved to be of considerable utility in Los Angeles but of little use in Utah. In Los Angeles, it was the most efficient model in explaining the felony/misdemeanor (.92), instrumental/expressive (.86), conflict (.93), and criminalism (.87) indexes. Interestingly, all of these are Category II indicators, describing offense patterns rather than overall amounts of delinquency. Yet, all of these patterns are of a more serious or sophisticated type, suggesting that Model II may be the most appropriate for these kinds of illegal acts in the metropolitan, Los Angeles setting. Such findings lend strength to the idea that not only may alternative theoretical models be needed to explain delinquency in different cultural settings, but that alternative models may be needed within the same single setting. Different models may be needed to explain different patterns of delinquency.

Secondly, the data supported the closed system assumption, lending further credence to the conclusions just stated. Table 9-2 shows the total, total indirect, and estimated direct effects of grades on each of the delinquency measures for which Model II was predictive. As was done in chapters 7 and 8, direct effects were estimated by subtracting the total indirect effects from the total effects for each delinquency measure. Since, in all instances, the total indirect effects closely approximate the total effects, the causal effects of grades on each of the four delinquency measures seem to be almost completely mediated through strain and peer identification. The closed system assumption holds true. Thus, this particular set of findings suggests that, for the study of serious delinquency in urban settings, this model may have utility.

Table 9-2

Assessment of the Closed-System Assumption for Model II in Los Angeles

Exogenous Variable (*Ex*)	Endogenous Variable (*En*)	Total Effect of *Ex* on *En*	Total Indirect Effect *Ex* on *En*, Via Strain and Peer I.D.	Estimated Directed Effect
Grades	Felony/ Misdemeanor	−.20	−.14	−.06
Grades	Instrumental/ Expressive	−.22	−.17	−.05
Grades	Conflict	−.11	−.12	.01
Grades	Criminalism	−.22	−.19	−.03

Model III

Model III (Figure 9-3) was the most efficient predictor of delinquency in both Los Angeles and Utah. It yielded the lowest residuals for five of the twelve delinquency indicators in Los Angeles and nine of the twelve indicators in Utah (Table 9-1). In Los Angeles, this model seemed best suited to the following indicators: number of offenses (.83), average seriousness (.76), most serious (.75), hell-raising (.92), and adult/juvenile offenses (.81). These are mostly Category 1 indicators (the only exception being status offenses), suggesting that

Model III may be most appropriate to explaining those delinquency measures where low values indicate the absence of law violation.

In Utah, Model III was the most important because it also yielded the lowest residuals for three-fourths of the delinquency indicators. The indicators, along with their respective squared residuals are: average seriousness (.82), most serious (.81), hell-raising (.88), incorrigibility (.93), felony/misdemeanor (.93), instrumental/expressive (.91), retreatism (.84), conflict (.97), and criminalism (.90). Thus, in Utah, the prediction of both Category 1 and 2 delinquency indicators seems to be generally maximized by treating them as directly and causally dependent upon all three of the major variables suggested in the original formulation—achievement, strain, and peer identification. In fact, since this model was best suited to Los Angeles as well as Utah, the findings underscore again the inadequacies of the asymmetric, linear sequence posited in the original model and suggest that the effects of major antecedents should be treated as having direct rather than indirect influence. Thus, except for the unique contributions of Model II in explaining serious and sophisticated patterns of delinquency in Los Angeles, this particular model seems to have the greatest universal applicability, being most effective in Los Angeles as well as Utah.

Original Model and Model IV

It is significant that of all the models, neither the original model (Figure 2-1) nor Model IV (Figure 9-4), was the most efficient model for explaining any of the twelve measures of delinquency.

For the Los Angeles sample, neither Model IV nor the original model was most effective in accounting for any given dimension of delinquency. Thus, when peer identification or achievement were treated as causal antecedents, by themselves, they were not optimal predictors. The same was true in Utah, although none of the models, in that location, showed any improvement over the original formulation in accounting for the adult/juvenile index. This measure, with a squared residual of .97, appears to be mainly a function of peer identification in the rural, Utah setting, although the amount of unexplained variation remains large.

Implications for Explaining Delinquency

In the interest of assessing implications, the abilities of the various models to explain delinquency are summarized in Table 9-3. Three matters of significance will be observed.

First, the theoretical model that occupied the primary attention of this book, and the one that has probably best represented sociological thinking in the past decade and a half, proved to be among the least predictive of all the models.

Second, Model III provided the best overall explanation of the several

Table 9-3

Explaining Delinquency: Summary Assessment of the Revised Models

Endogenous Variable	Los Angeles		Utah	
	Model with Lowest Residuals	Closed System Assumption Met?	Model with Lowest Residuals	Closed System Assumption Met?
Category 1				
Number of Offenses	III	N.A.	I	N.A.
Average Seriousness	III	N.A.	III	N.A.
Most Serious	III	N.A.	III	N.A.
Theft	III	N.A.	I	N.A.
Hell-Raising	III	N.A.	III	N.A.
Incorrigibility	I	N.A.	III	N.A.
Category 2				
Adult/Juvenile	III	N.A.	Original	No
Felony/Misdemeanor	II	Yes	III	N.A.
Instrumental/Expressive	II	Yes	III	N.A.
Retreatism	I	N.A.	III	N.A.
Conflict	II	Yes	III	N.A.
Criminalism	II	Yes	III	N.A.

Note: N.A. = not applicable.

delinquency measures. It was best suited to five of the twelve indicators in Los Angeles and nine of the twelve measures in Utah.

Third, there were some significant variations in the capacities of the different models to explain various delinquency measures, not only between but within the two geographical settings under study. In Los Angeles, for example, Model II, which made strain and peer identification direct antecedents of delinquency, provided a high level of prediction for several kinds of serious delinquency—delinquency that was felonious, instrumentally-oriented, criminalistic and conflictive. Yet, in Utah, this model was of little value, suggesting both an important difference across subcultures, and the possible need in Los Angeles for different theoretical models to explain different kinds of delinquency.

This demonstration of delinquency as a differential phenomenon could be one of the major empirical findings of the study. A common weakness in the investigation and treatment of juvenile lawbreaking has been the tendency to treat it as a unitary phenomenon. Yet this indication that different kinds of delinquency may have different antecedents in the same, as well as different, locations suggests that this could be a serious mistake. Along with growing bodies of information that lawbreaking may be a common phenomenon among juveniles from all social strata, these findings suggest that one potentially useful line of investigation might be to determine whether different delinquency patterns exist in such diverse areas as the urban core, in suburbia, in rural areas, or on high school or college campuses. Each has distinctive characteristics, and it would be helpful to determine whether lawbreaking patterns differ within them and whether different antecedents are associated with these patterns. While it is theoretically sensible to suggest that this would be the case, relatively little empirical information is available by which to document what these differences might be.

Explanation of Peer Identification

So much for delinquency. What about the capacity of the several models to explain peer identification? It will be recalled that its role in the causal sequence was found to be an ambiguous one. While it seemed to be an important influence, the findings were unclear as to whether it should be considered as an antecedent to delinquency, a consequence of it, or both.

Table 9-4 indicates the ability of the various models to explain each of the three peer identification measures. For the Los Angeles sample, Model IV (Figure 9-4), which posits peer identification as a causal consequence of both delinquency and strain, yielded the highest degree of explanation.

Under the conditions of this model, the squared residuals for the Ace-in-the-Hole, Sociability, and Deviance scales were .83, .86, and .79, respectively. For the Utah sample, Model IV was also optimally related to the three peer indicators, resulting in squared residuals of .90 for Ace-in-the-Hole, .74 for Sociability, and .83 for Deviance. The residuals of Model II, however, were the same as those of Model IV for the Ace-in-the-Hole and Deviance scales. This raises an important issue, since Model II specifies peer identification to be an antecedent to delinquency, whereas Model IV specifies it as a consequence of delinquency. Thus, although the position of peer identification in the causal sequence in Utah is still very ambiguous, some of that ambiguity may be explained in both cases by the fact that it is preceded in both cases by strain, strain that is induced either by poor achievement, by delinquency, or by both. In Los Angeles, however, where Model IV yields optimal prediction for all three of the peer measures, this concept seems best suited as a joint consequence of delinquency and strain.

Before concerning ourselves with any interpretations of these findings, the closed system assumption for Model IV should be examined. For that model to hold true, we would expect the relationship between achievement and peer identification to be mediated through delinquency alone and delinquency and

Table 9-4

Effectiveness (Squared Residuals) of Theoretical Models in Explaining Peer Identification

Peer Identification Indicators	Squared Residuals for Los Angeles			
	Model I (D)	Model II (AS)	Model III[a] (S)	Model IV (DS)
Ace-in-Hole	.87	.88	.88	[.83][b]
Sociability	.96	.91	.92	[.86]
Deviance	.83	.87	.91	[.79]
Average	.89	.89	.90	[.83]

Peer Identification Indicators	Squared Residuals for Utah			
	Model I (D)	Model II (AS)	Model III[a] (S)	Model IV (DS)
Ace-in-Hole	.94	[.90]	.93	[.90]
Sociability	.84	.81	.96	[.74]
Deviance	.90	[.83]	.96	[.83]
Average	.89	.85	.95	[.82]

[a]Antecedents to peer identification in Model III are the same as those for the original theoretical formulation.

[b]The lowest residual for each measure within both samples is indicated by brackets, [ ].

strain together. As was the case with the earlier tests of this assumption, its validity can be checked by comparing the total effects of grades on peer identification with its indirect effects via the intervening variables. The findings presented in Table 9-5 indicate that, with only one exception, the closed system assumption was *not* met to a very high degree. In most instances the indirect effects were less than half as large as the total effects, thus implying the possibility of relatively large direct effects.

The exception to this general case was the Sociability scale in Utah, which received considerable total indirect effects from grades (−.23, as compared to a total effect of −.34). This exception is of significance, since it was only the Sociability scale in Utah that did not receive low residuals from both Models IV and II. Thus, it seems clearly the case that, although the Sociability scale is the least deviant of the peer scales, it is very likely a causal consequence of

Table 9-5

Assessment of the Closed-System Assumption for Model IV in Los Angeles and Utah

Exogenous Variable (Ex)	Endogenous Variable (En)	Total Effect of Ex on En	Total Indirect Effect, Ex on En, Via Del. and Del. and Strain	Estimated Direct Effect
Los Angeles				
Grades	Ace-in-Hole	−.22	−.11	−.11
Grades	Sociability	−.22	−.05	−.17
Grades	Deviance	−.30	−.11	−.19
Utah				
Grades	Ace-in-Hole	−.24	−.04	−.20
Grades	Sociability	−.34	−.23	−.11
Grades	Deviance	−.29	−.09	−.20

delinquency and strain in Utah. As far as Ace-in-the-Hole and Deviance in Utah and all of the scales in Los Angeles are concerned, any conclusions are difficult to reach. While the peer scales received the lowest residuals from Model IV, the closed system assumption for this model was not met.

Implications for Understanding
Peer Identification

Given the fact that there were some differences between Los Angeles and Utah; that the closed system assumption, with one exception, was not met for Model IV; and that the model (III) which was most efficient in explaining delinquency was not the most efficient for explaining peer identification (Model IV), some perplexing questions are raised.

First, it seems quite possible that the interrelationships of the two concepts have been overplayed in prior theoretical formulations, or that a singular stress upon peer identification as it relates to delinquency has been overdone at the expense of understanding that phenomenon apart from its relation to deviance.

The field is seriously hampered by the fact that we do not even have an adequate baseline of information regarding adolescent groupings in general against which we can measure the characteristics of deviant groupings, and better determine what produces them. Since we know very little about the forces that result in the formation of adolescent groups, about their antecedents, their degrees of cohesiveness, or the gratifications that are inherent in them, it is difficult to generalize about specific delinquent groups or to explain their role in adolescent behavior.

Cloward and Ohlin (1960:19-20) have suggested that delinquents are selective in their withdrawal of support for legitimate norms, consistent with their position in the social structure or the opportunities that are available to them. But is this withdrawal narrowly circumscribed, or is it subject to greater variation than they imply? If role theory is correct, a repertoire of responses, relevant to a wide range of different social circumstances, may better characterize their behavior than adherence to a single pattern. The variety of possible choices is potentially great. For example, Cohen (1969:108) argues that gang and group delinquency are different forms of juvenile deviance and should be treated as separate entities. Gangs, as contrasted to other delinquent groups, are more homogeneous with respect to age, race, sex, background, and their victims; have longer records of delinquency; and are more territorially oriented because of their isolation from conventional institutions and because of all the external pressures that isolation carries with it. By implication, other investigators such as Klein (1970:4) and Short and Strodtbeck (1965:229-234) would seem to agree, noting the extent to which delinquent gangs are without the sponsorship of adults, lack individual and group skills, and suffer continual threat from without.

In drawing an analogy between peer identification and delinquency, we are all too aware that delinquency is not an attribute—something which one either possesses or does not possess, like the measles (Short, 1960:3)—but is a more-or-less thing. By the same token, peer identification should probably be viewed in the same context. If so, we should be cautious regarding the possible inaccuracies of generalizations respecting the fundamental commitment of adolescents either to delinquent or nondelinquent groupings and norms on the basis of their having been defined as delinquent. This in itself is a form of labeling that is often applied without due recognition of the fact that the greater part of all adolescents' time is devoted to conventional relationships and activities. Thus, in seeking to relate peer identification to delinquent behavior, the attribution to certain adolescents of commitments to singularly focused, deviant subcultures or careers may be overly deterministic and inaccurate. It may suggest too much of a dedication on their parts to norms and activities that represent only a minor part of their total cognitive and behavioral repertoires.

Matza (1964:37) reminds us that delinquent subcultures, even if they exist, are manned, after all, by very young and very immature people. It would be surprising, he suggests, if they were to be characterized in highly structured and narrow form. In a more general sense, Eisenstadt (1956) notes that adolescence is a transitional state in which experimentation with a variety of roles is common. Commitment to a particular set of expectations or peers is not to be expected. This does not imply that we should discount, or fail to study, the role of peer identification in its relationship to delinquency, but it does imply that its role should not be overstated.

As mentioned earlier, Ohlin (1970:3) has pointed out that, although delinquent subcultures may be an important component of the situational field in which delinquency occurs, they cannot be taken as the major determinant of individual behavior. This conclusion is certainly well documented in this study. Not only did peer identification appear to be only one of several factors in contributing to delinquency, when individuals were the object of analysis, but some of those factors seemed to play roles that were of equal or greater importance. Thus, until more can be done to place peer identification in some perspective relative to other situational and institutional determinants of behavior, care should be taken not to overemphasize its importance.

Another issue is methodological as well as theoretical. It has to do with the fact that the measurement of peer identification in this case was more attitudinal than behavioral. That is, respondents were asked to indicate how they would react in a variety of situations—some delinquent, some not—in which peers were involved. This is not the same thing as observing how they would actually behave in the same circumstances. Thus, there is a strong possibility that differences in outcome would have occurred had behavioral rather than attitudinal measures been used.

The task of obtaining behavioral indicators, of course, is a difficult one, but some investigators (Klein, 1967; Cartwright, Howard, and Reuterman, 1970) have been successful in doing so. Moreover, although their findings did not always agree (cf. Cartwright et al., 1970:319), these same investigators discovered that the collective behaviors of gang boys did differ depending upon the size, cohesiveness, dispersion, etc., of their various gangs. Thus, in addition to the likelihood that the nature of peer groupings will vary from place to place and group to group, there is also the likelihood that the nature of these groupings will affect actual behavior. Just what these differences will be, and how behavior will differ from attitude, one cannot say at this point in time. However, it is clear that these issues are important ones in attempting to reduce some of the ambiguity associated with peer identification in this study.

Combining the Most Productive Models

Finally, there is the provocative finding that the most efficient model for explaining delinquency (Model III) was not the most efficient model (Model IV) for explaining delinquent peer identification. Thus, without some further exploration of the relation between the two concepts, our inquiry will remain incomplete.

To guide the conduct of further research, it is possible to combine the most productive models described in this chapter. Model III, which was most effective in explaining delinquency, was diagrammed as shown in Figure 9-5(a). Model IV, meanwhile, which was most efficient in explaining peer identification, suggested the causal order shown in Figure 9-5(b). It is possible to combine these two models as shown in Figure 9-5(c). Rather than treating strain and peer

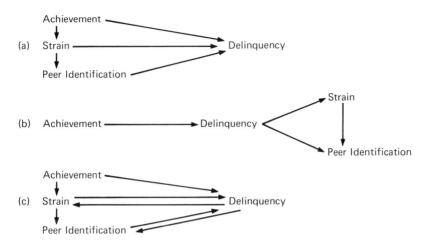

Figure 9-5. Model III(*a*) and Model IV(*b*) Combined (*c*).

identification either as antecedents of delinquency or as consequences of it, this model treats them as interdependent. The double arrows are used to represent such interdependence and to suggest that the concepts are related in cyclical fashion. It is suggested that both strain and peer identification contribute to delinquency, but in turn are enhanced by it. If one wished to pursue the analysis further, he could also look at the cyclical effects involving achievement with other variables.

Such an interpretation closely parallels that of Tannenbaum (1938), who implied a general model of this type. At the outset of a complex process of interaction, boys who are only marginally integrated into the community begin a form of play in which adventure, excitement, and mischief are their chief interests. They play truant, break windows, annoy people, and commit petty thefts—all items of adventure that they do not consider particularly serious. But such activities, especially if they persist, are viewed more seriously by the community. They result in demands for control, chastisement, even court action and punishment.

What emerges is a conflict in definition between the boys and the community, a conflict that is likely to make the problem worse. Boys who are already marginal, but who do not yet define themselves as delinquent, are driven further into deviant group activities by officials, even parents, who do define them as delinquent. Thus, attachment to the peer group is likely to increase so that it becomes a kind of street-corner family for its members. Because they were semidetached from legitimate groups to begin with, increasing conflict only adds to that detachment.

Meanwhile, the attitude of the community continues to harden. More and more, group members—their activities, their hangouts, even their persons—are looked upon with suspicion. All are subject to scrutiny and question.

The final step in the making of delinquents, according to Tannenbaum, occurs when they become enmeshed in society's institutionalized patterns for dealing with them, in their experiences with police, courts, and correctional institutions. This is what Tannenbaum (1938:30) called the "dramatization of evil." As he puts it, "the process of making the criminal is a process of tagging, defining, identifying, segregating, describing, emphasizing, making conscious and self-conscious; it becomes a way of stimulating, suggesting, emphasizing, and evolving the very traits that are complained of." The official process not only tends to isolate the boy from conformist influences, but makes him even more dependent upon the support and encouragement of his deviant peers.

In attempting to relate this formulation to the model suggested above, there is no question that peer identification, as a basic concept, plays a key role. What is not clear, however, is the role played by the concept of strain. Tannenbaum seems to imply its existence in his emphasis upon the notion of escalating conflict between the boys and the community. One might assume that such conflict contributes further to frustration, alienation, and more serious forms of delinquency. Such an assumption was certainly central to the later formulations of such theorists as Cohen (1955) or Cloward and Ohlin (1960). The notion of strain became a key motivating force in their theories both for the formation of peer groups and the committing of delinquent acts.

Hirschi (1969:6-15), by contrast, argues that the concept of strain adds little to delinquency theory, in fact that it is inadequate and misleading.

It suggests that delinquency is a relatively permanent attribute of the person and/or a regularly occurring event; it suggests that delinquency is largely restricted to a single social class; and it suggests that persons accepting legitimate goals are, as a result of this acceptance, more likely to commit delinquent acts [p. 10].

Thus, Hirschi (1969:passim) prefers a control theory of delinquency, instead, in which "strain" is discarded and in which deviant behavior is seen as a function of the attachment of the individual to the social order, his commitment to and involvement in it, and the beliefs he holds. If these things were present, delinquency would be less likely to occur; if they were absent there would be less reason to remain law-abiding.

An interesting aspect of Hirschi's point of view is that it might well be integrated with Tannenbaum's. With little difficulty, the process described by Tannenbaum could be seen as one in which boys were progressively *de*tached from 'legitimate pursuits and associations and progressively *at*tached to deviant ones. If so, a basic question for both theory and research would be that of determining whether strain is a necessary concept in the model sketched above, or whether it might well be dropped.

Unfortunately, our data do not permit us to examine this question. Such an examination would require longitudinal data so that reciprocal causal effects could be studied over a given period. What our data have already suggested, however, is that the attachment of the individual to the home and school is a crucial one, and in its absence delinquency seems more likely to occur. It will be recalled that the effects of such an attachment (or its absence) usually had direct rather than indirect effects on delinquency. Moreover, an examination of the model, both with and without strain included, may be important because, over all others, it seems particularly well suited to the explanation of several measures of delinquency: number of offenses, seriousness, theft, hell-raising and adult-status offenses in Los Angeles; and seriousness, hell-raising, incorrigibility, felonious and instrumental acts, retreatism, conflict, and criminalism in Utah. Moreover, it might help to explain better the role of peer identification in the total picture.

Explaining Other Types of Delinquency

Another issue to be explored has to do with the delinquency measures that were not explained optimally by Model III. It will be recalled that Model II (Figure 9-2) maximized the explanation of several kinds of delinquency in Los Angeles—the felony/misdemeanor, instrumental/expressive, conflict, and criminalism indexes. This model could be combined with Model IV (Figure 9-4) in an attempt to better explain, within the same framework, both these kinds of delinquency and peer identification as well. Their combination is shown in Figure 9-6. In addition to suggesting that peer identification is the product both of achievement and strain, it also treats both strain and peer identification as having reciprocal and interdependent relationships with delinquency. Again, longitudinal data would be required to test the model, but, with it, one could not only determine whether one's ability to explain delinquency and peer identification were increased but whether strain plays a key role.

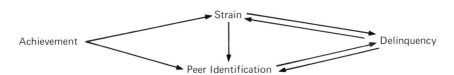

Figure 9-6. The Combination of Models II and IV.

Restructuring Basic Concepts

The model just described might also be of some use in conjunction with a revision and reordering of basic concepts. For example, measures of achievement, such as school grades or awards, or measures of strain, such as school dropout or family disruption, might be treated, as Hirschi's (1969) framework implies, as measures of institutional attachment. If a child comes from a disrupted home or does poorly in school, he is in danger of getting off the institutional track, of losing his ties to two of the most important socializing agencies in society. Therefore, if these indicators were utilized, along with others, as measures of institutional affiliation, and the concepts of achievement and strain eliminated, it might be possible to develop a more parsimonious framework and to determine wherein the new concept is related to, or interdependent with, the concepts of peer identification and delinquency.

Part III
Suggestions for Future Inquiry

10 Theoretical Issues

Many problems relative to the task of constructing theories are appropriate to the explanation of delinquent behavior. The first has to do with the deterministic character of most of them. For example, the basic theme of the literature that gave rise to the theory tested in this study, as Bordua (1961) notes, is irrationalistic and deterministic in its emphasis. Delinquents, especially urban gang boys, are "driven, not attracted." Their lives are characterized by desperation rather than fun. Such theories as those of Cohen (1955), Cloward and Ohlin (1960), and Miller (1958) emphasize the idea that lower-class children are downgraded in both the juvenile and adult hierarchies of our middle-class institutions. They are ill-prepared by family background and cultural heritage to achieve successfully and, as a consequence, their lives are characterized by frustration, negativistic retaliation, alienation, and radical separation from conventional successes and satisfactions.

In taking issue with theory such as this, Matza (1964:21) argues that it is likely

to push criminologists toward a distorted and misleading picture of the delinquent and his enterprise. . . . By assuming constraint and differentiation [from nondelinquents]—by ignoring choice and similarity [with others]— positive criminology leaves unexplained commonplace and consistent features of delinquency life.

In its emphasis upon the disaffection of the delinquent from school, home, and conventional peers, and his attachment to delinquent associates and deviant norms and beliefs, this kind of theory may obscure both the extent to which the delinquent is more like others than different, and the extent to which he either exercises some voluntary choice, or at least is as uncommitted to delinquency as he is to conventional behavior.

Matza (1964:3-11) also reminds us that the metaphysical assumptions about the nature of man upon which any theory is based are extremely important, and that if left unattended, they may return to haunt us. Consequently, he rejects much of contemporary theory and advocates, instead, a return to "soft" rather than "hard" determinism, to a classical conception of the delinquent that would not only consider the element of free will or choice, but would pay closer attention to the ways in which the delinquent is similar to, rather than different from, the nondelinquent.

It is his contention that the delinquent, because of the ambiguities inherent in his adolescent status, "transiently exists in a limbo between convention and crime, responding in turn to the demands of each, flirting now with one, now the other, postponing commitment, evading decision. Thus, he drifts between criminal and conventional action."

Given this state of drift, adolescents may draw upon a repertoire of possible behaviors, some conventional, some deviant. But even in those cases where deviant ones are chosen, there is question whether the choice implies a lasting commitment. American culture, Matza and Sykes (1961) suggest, is not a simple puritanism exemplified by the middle class. Instead, it is a complex and pluralistic culture in which, among other cultural traditions, lies a subterranean tradition—an *infra*culture of delinquency (cf. Empey, 1967:37-38).

This *infra*culture does not represent ignorance of the law nor even repudiation of it; instead, it has a complex relationship to law that is symbiotic rather than wholly oppositional. It is not a separate set of beliefs that distinguish delinquents from other youth, or youth from adults. It is that part of the overall culture that consists of the personal, more deviant, and less-publicized version of officially endorsed values. The two sets of traditions—conventional and deviant—are held simultaneously by almost everyone in the social system and, while certain groups may be influenced more by one than the other, both determine behavior to a considerable degree.

Given the existence of deviant traditions, the potential delinquent has an elaborate set of rationalizations by which to neutralize any delinquent act he may commit. Yet, even with their availability, the adolescent may or may not become delinquent. That depends upon an exercise of "will," and the exercise of "will," in turn, depends upon the presence of two elements: *preparation* (including the skills, courage, and experience needed to commit a delinquent act), and *desperation* (a fatal feeling of having no choice or control over the situation). Thus, Matza seems to view delinquents as flirtatious adolescents who, although they may occasionally "drift" into situations conducive to law-violating behavior, spend most of their time, like others, in conventional pursuits. The factors that might precipitate delinquency are much less definite, much less constraining than the ones suggested by the theory examined in this work.

While there is much that is appealing in Matza's argument, and while it includes many ideas that merit empirical study, there are also some serious problems inherent in it for the scientist. A major one is stated succinctly by Matza (1964:191) in the final paragraph of his work: "Though we may explore and perhaps specify the conditions that activate the will to crime, we cannot definitively state that a crime will be committed." In other words, any switch from a deterministic frame of reference to one that heavily emphasizes the role of individual will can itself create philosophical and methodological problems. To attempt to find out what causes or determines an individual to exercise his will would be a contradiction in terms. In a very real sense, it could be argued that the exercise of will must involve a relatively unconstrained process of human rationality and choice. If so, it would seem that theories based on "soft" determinism would, by their very natures, be concerned more with stating the conditions under which delinquency is *possible* than with making assertions of *probability*. Such an approach would be at odds with the deterministic frameworks within which science usually works. Thus, while theories such as Matza's may provide valuable insights into the nature of delinquency and the types of interactive processes that facilitate its occurrence, they also create serious problems for theory construction and research. It is difficult, if not impossible, to state their propositions in probabilistic terms and, consequently, even more difficult to test them.

The problem inherent in this state of affairs is well put by Rapoport (1968:xxii), who says:

Behavioral scientists can be roughly divided into two groups: those who aspire to the scientific status of physical scientists and, in consequence, tend to select research problems that yield to the analytic method; and those who are moved by a need to "understand man." The former stand in danger of trivializing the study of man and, what is worse, of placing their expertise at the service of groups having the power to manipulate man for their own purposes. The latter stand in danger of obscuring the study of man in free-wheeling speculations without sufficient anchorage in facts or testable hypotheses.

In commenting on this issue at an earlier time, Glaser (1958:686-7) acknowledges that sociological criminologists have tended to be deterministic and to ally themselves with psychiatrists in the struggle against classical legalists and religious leaders over the free will versus determinism issue. However, he labels this struggle a "phony war" involving polemics rather than reality, and maintains that the war is losing its intensity because of a recognition of the importance of voluntaristic rather than reflexive conceptions of human behavior. Contrary to the character of some of their theories, criminologists recognize that humans are aware of alternative courses of behavior and make deliberate choices among them.

While one might like to agree with Glaser, any such agreement would have substance only if it were based upon evidence that better account could be taken both of individual choice and social constraint. Actually, the literature suggests several ways this might be accomplished.

The first is related to a growing recognition of the need to take better account of situation as well as structure in the genesis of delinquent acts. Matza implied their importance in his reference to the ambiguities of an adolescent's status and his tending to flirt, on one hand, with convention and, on the other, with crime. Any drift between the two implies the importance of situational as well as choice factors, in determining the conditions under which delinquency might occur: the opportunity to be delinquent, where it is presented, or the momentary existence of group or institutional constraints.

In a recent treatise on the subject, Lofland (1969) attempts to address some of these issues, to codify, piece together, and interrelate the situational factors that combine to produce the identities and behaviors of deviant individuals, including delinquents.

Lofland's major focus is upon what he calls the "defensive deviant act," which occurs initially as a result of three sequential stages. First, for a normal actor, an event occurs that is defined as a social or physical threat. Second, within the threat situation, a process of psychological "encapsulation" occurs. Encapsulation involves a foreshortening (in social time and space) of the criteria by which an individual judges appropriate social responses. In such a state, individuals have a proclivity for choosing simple, short-term, close-at-hand solutions to their problems, one of which might well be deviant.

Finally, in a process of "closure," an individual selects a response from his repertoire of subjectively available acts. In a manner similar to Matza, Lofland posits a "legitimized public platitude" or set of rationalizations that can be drawn upon to support deviance. Whether or not a deviant act is chosen, however, depends not only upon some choice by the actor, but upon such factors as who else is present in the threat situation, the types of "hardware" (physical objects) present, and the type of place involved.

Although Lofland (1969) does not become heavily involved in the free will versus determinism polemic, his approach suggests some departure from the traditional, deterministic stance. Rather than assuming a "push imagery" of causation in which one searches for anything that might push X (e.g., delinquency) into existence, Lofland focuses upon how X can be "built up, constructed, produced or its occurrence facilitated." His approach to the explanation of deviance is much like that of a chemist in that he attempts to find which elements, combined in which sequence, seem to fabricate deviant acts and identities. The possible virtue of this argument is its emphasis upon understanding acts in addition to actors, and the situational factors that interact to produce them. Such an approach could make a real contribution if it resulted in greater attention to social transactions in which both personal and social factors were key elements.

An interesting aspect of this frame of reference, however, is that it does not imply the necessity to reject all deterministic influences. Rather, it implies that attention be paid to the way in which a number of elements, when combined, interact to form a particular compound, delinquency in this case. Although not much is known at present about the consequence of mixing different elements in varying amounts, the general line of investigation that is suggested is analogous to that which is used in other kinds of scientific endeavor. Moreover, such a stance is compatible with a general theme running throughout this whole work, namely, that delinquency is located not merely in the biographies of individuals but in the biographies of social systems, and in the subsequent interactions between the two (Cohen and Short, 1971). Delinquent acts, like all kinds of social acts, are episodes in an ongoing society that has a long history. They are the consequence of a social process to which different societal institutions and groups, as well as individuals, make contributions. By analyzing this process, and the elements of which it is comprised, it may be possible to gain a better understanding of delinquency (cf. Ohlin, 1970).

Some Conceptual Distinctions

Before any such analysis was conducted, it might be wise to be more explicit than usual about one's dependent variable; i.e., whether one is interested in explaining *law-violating behavior* or *official delinquency*. Law-violating behavior is behavior that is illegal according to existing law but which remains undetected or unacted on by persons in authority. A study of it requires the gathering of data by observation, interview, or some such method rather than relying upon official records as the source of information. Official delinquency, by contrast, is behavior that has been identified and defined by persons in authority as illegal. Official records are usually the source of data in this case.

Although law-violating behavior and official delinquency often overlap, there are some obvious distinctions between them. These differences can be illustrated by reference to the typology shown in Table 10-1.

Table 10-1

Typology of Juveniles and Acts

Types of Juveniles	Types of Acts		
	Law-Abiding Acts	Law-Violating Acts	Officially Labeled Law-Violating Acts
Law Abiders	Yes[a]	No	No
Undetected Law-Violators	Yes	Yes	No
Official Delinquents	Yes	Yes	Yes

[a]Cells in the typology indicate whether or not a given type of act has been committed by a given type of juvenile. It will be noted that five logical combinations have not been included. Four of these combinations (no-yes-no; no-no-yes; no-yes-yes; no-no-no) are empirical impossibilities since they typify juveniles of any type who are not involved in *any* law-abiding acts, an unlikely possibility since it is difficult to conceive of any juvenile whose every act is illegal. Even the most delinquent individual, for example, is engaged in legal acts most of the time. Thus, these four types were not shown above. A fifth type (yes-no-yes), however, does involve an empirical possibility. This type would include juveniles who, although engaged in law-abiding acts, have been caught and labeled for every law-violating act they committed. Since this type is an unlikely possibility, it has also been excluded.

This typology is based upon three distinct types of acts that might be engaged in by adolescents: *law-abiding acts* that do not violate legal norms; *law-violative acts* that violate legal norms but go undetected by juvenile justice officials; and *officially-labeled, law-violative acts* that both violate legal norms and result in negative sanctions from juvenile justice officials. On the basis of these three types of acts, the general population of juveniles could be divided into three subtypes: *law-abiders* who never violate legal norms; *undetected law violators* who engage in both law-abiding acts and law-violative acts; and *official delinquents* who are involved in all three of the types of acts described above. The distinctions among the three types of juveniles help to pinpoint some of the theoretical problems involved in explaining their behavior.

In attempting to explain the law-violating behavior of official delinquents, for example, past research has often compared labeled offenders with non-labeled juveniles on the apparent assumption that the latter fell into the law-abider category. Most likely, however, this assumption was incorrect. Any officially nondelinquent, comparison group probably includes large numbers of un-detected law-violators whose characteristics may not differ very much from those of official delinquents. In fact, it is possible that the smallest and most atypical group of the three are not the official delinquents but the law-abiders, given the present, all-encompassing character of juvenile court law. It is difficult to see how many juveniles could have avoided violating the law, even though their violations were inadvertent. Thus, if we are to improve the explanatory power of existing theory, greater effort must be made to distinguish among the juvenile subtypes shown in the typology, and to conduct research that will draw clearer distinctions among their characteristics and acts.

If our concern is with undetected law-violators, then the task of theory and research is that of explaining why law-violating acts occur, what seems to precipitate them, and whether the population characteristics of undetected law-violators differs from the population of law-abiders, if indeed there are many absolute law-abiders.

By contrast, if our concern is with official delinquents, then investigations must encompass a broader spectrum of phenomena. In addition to indicating whether official delinquents, and their acts, differ from law-abiders and undetected law-violators, and their acts, investigations must take into account the acts and judgments of the agents of juvenile justice. The factors that lead to official labeling, as well as those that lead to law-violating acts, must be explained.

Although most investigators have been vaguely aware of the need to take these complexities into account, research has not always done so. This particular work is an example. In fact, it is only in recent years that much empirical study has been devoted to the analysis of the juvenile justice system, and to the differences in outcome that might be observed if one compared pictures of official delinquents with pictures of undetected law-violators or law-abiders. Moreover, research is hampered not just by a lack of knowledge about the juvenile justice system but by an absence of baseline information on the juvenile population in general and on the three subtypes of which it is comprised. Thus, one important question is how one should proceed with the task of theory construction and empirical research, given current ambiguities.

Assuming that our major concern is with the law-violator and official delinquent types, a traditional approach would be to attempt to explain both in the same theoretical package; that is, to explain why juveniles violate the law and, at the same time, to indicate why some of them are labeled while others are *not* labeled. This traditional approach has been attractive because it avoids many conceptual and operational difficulties. In a simplistic way, investigations have tended to assume a direct correlation between undetected law violations and official delinquency, and have assumed that if official delinquency could be explained, the explanation of law-violating behavior would not be much different. There are grave reasons to question whether this approach adequately addresses the complexities involved. There may be alternative approaches that are superior.

One alternative would be to relate investigations to theoretical frameworks which, for heuristic purposes, separated the study of law-violating behavior from the study of official delinquency. An attempt would be made to explain each of them independent of the other. Obviously, this separation would be, in part, artificial because of the overlap between different populations of acts. Yet, the separation might help to clear up the extent and nature of law-violating behavior, apart from societal response to it, the kinds of juveniles with whom such behavior is most commonly associated, and whether there are distinct differences between undetected law-violators and official delinquents. Moreover, such a separation might help to add important information on adolescent behavior in general, and whether, for example, there even exists a population of complete law-abiders. Practical needs relative to the problems of socializing the young and preventing delinquency, as well as for scientific understanding, require more knowledge in these areas.

By the same token, better theory and more evidence are needed to explain and predict the factors associated with the definition, apprehension, and processing of offenders. This line of investigation might proceed more efficiently if again, for heuristic purposes, it were left unfettered with the need to explain why juveniles break the law, and concentrated instead only on those factors that are associated with their being officially defined as delinquent. Then, once improvements had been made in both domains, their areas of overlap might be more clearly delineated, and the future task facilitated of relating them together into an overarching, theoretical framework. Better grounds might be laid for indicating how the two major components of official delinquency are related.

Methodological Considerations

Methodological considerations also bear on the matter of conducting separate lines of inquiry. In this case, they have to do with the errors introduced into research findings because of the difficulty of measuring one's dependent variable, whether law violation or official delinquency.

As may be observed in Table 10-2, it is possible to classify illegal acts into four conceptually distinct types. Each of the types creates a unique issue pertaining to the construction and testing of delinquency theory.

Table 10-2

A Typology of Delinquent Acts

		Societal Response to Act	
		Not Handled Officially or Undetected	Handled Officially
Type of Act	Juvenile Offenses	Type I	Type III
	Criminal Offenses	Type II	Type IV

On the vertical axis of Table 10-2, it will be noted that the acts for which juveniles might be legally prosecuted can be divided into two major categories. The first category comprises "juvenile offenses" that do not apply to adults and that ostensibly are so designated for the purpose of protecting the welfare of the child. This includes a long list of offenses such as school truancy, incorrigibility, running away from home, curfew violations, smoking, drinking, and many others. The second category comprises what might be called "criminal offenses." Offenses in this category apply to all age levels and may involve victimization or harm to the community. They include such acts as theft, robbery, rape, arson, illicit drug use, and assault and battery.

On the horizontal axis of Table 10-2, delinquent acts can also be categorized along a second, independent dimension, one that is related to official processing. Again, acts can be divided into two mutually exclusive categories. The first category would include law-violating acts, whether they be juvenile or criminal, which do not result in official action either because they are undetected or because police or court officials choose to dismiss them or deal with them informally. The second category includes law violations that result in official processing and labeling.

If one chooses the first approach, and, further, wishes to explain *official* delinquency within a single framework, he must be concerned with the implications of Types III and IV delinquency. Type III involves *juvenile* offenses that have been handled officially. Any test of causal theory that includes acts of this type, especially if that theory also includes such concepts as poor school performance and familial difficulty as causal antecedents to delinquency, must face a difficult problem. The problem stems from the fact that this type of delinquency may be *tautological* with its causal antecedents, since the two may be one and the same. Therefore, to the extent that one's measures of delinquency are comprised of juvenile offenses symptomatic of school trouble or incorrigibility in the home, subsequent correlations between these factors and being officially defined as delinquent may reflect nothing more than a definitional overlap of the delinquency measures with their causal antecedents.

Type IV delinquency, although it involves distinctly criminal offenses and although it is definitionally distinct from juvenile-status acts, is not immune to these same effects. Even if an adolescent is on trial for committing a *criminal* act, the juvenile court may be greatly influenced by such factors as his school performance, family environment, and social class prior to making its disposition. Cicourel (1968:273 ff.) and Emerson (1969:98-99), for example, have found that the parents of higher-class children are better able than those of lower-class children to hire attorneys or guarantee expensive private therapy for their delinquent children. Because of this, higher-class children are more protected against official labeling and severe dispositions from the juvenile court. If social class were posited as a *causal* antecedent to delinquency, any subsequent statistical association between class and official measures of delinquency could be misleading and represent differential handling rather than causation.

Similarly, the courts and police tend to be more lenient toward juveniles who come from intact and well-adjusted families and who are doing well in school. The juvenile court tends to operate on the assumption that such cases are in less need of formal supervision than those who have poor ties with these two basic socializing institutions. Thus, even in those cases that involve only criminal offenses, factors such as family status or institutional ties can affect formal dispositions. As is the case with Type III delinquency, this can confound any attempt to assess causal theory unless the effects of legal processing are somehow accounted for in the theory.

The result is that if official measures are to be used in testing a single theory designed to explain both illegal acts and societal responses, the following two assumptions must be true: (1) that "official delinquency" is positively correlated with the number of illegal acts that are actually committed, and (2) that measurement errors (i.e., regression errors of official delinquency regressed on "delinquent acts") are at most only weakly correlated with the other variables of the theory which reflect official response. If one or both of these assumptions are untrue, then the validity of using official delinquency as an indicator of delinquent acts becomes subject to great doubt.

The first assumption is concerned with the isomorphism, or direct correspondence, between official delinquency and undetected acts of law violation. If an isomorphism can be assumed, then at least one of the problems of using official measures can be discounted. Two groups of empirical findings, however, question the validity of assuming such an isomorphism.

The first group of findings has indicated that most law-violating behavior is not detected (Erickson and Empey, 1963; Short and Nye, 1958; Murphy et al., 1946); and that there is variation with respect to the types of offenses that are detected most frequently. The second group of findings, as suggested earlier, indicates that police and court biases operate in such a manner that certain types of youthful law violators are officially processed while others are not.

Given these problems, it would seem reasonable to suggest that, while official records can be used as an indicator of delinquent acts, they are at best diluted indicators. There is likely to be a positive correlation between number of law-violating acts and number of officially recorded offenses, especially where criminal, as contrasted to age-specific, offenses are concerned. However, there is little evidence to indicate the size of that correlation. In an indirect way, Erickson and Empey (1963) did find that offenders who had been officially processed were the ones who, by their own self-report, were the most delinquent. Even with this finding, however, there was considerable variation from offense to offense, suggesting that the official record was something like the tip of an iceberg whose exact proportions were not well known. While the probability existed that those who had been officially defined were also the most delinquent, the exact size of that probability was not indicated.

The second assumption outlined above has to do with measurement error and whether the possible discrepancy between official and undetected measures is related to other concepts of a theory, especially those that are heavily dependent upon official action (see Costner, 1969:247-248, or Empey and Lubeck, 1971:291-293, for elaborate methodological discussions of this type of error).

This problem might be rectified, in part, by collecting measures of undetected law violation in addition to official measures. By using official and undetected measures in combination, a more complete assessment of causal theories and of the effects of official processing might result. However, this would not exhaust other measurement problems which add further complication to an already complicated picture. Furthermore, the problem might be addressed more efficiently if, as suggested above, two theories were utilized, one to explain law-breaking behavior and the other to describe societal response.

Studies that are limited to law-breaking behavior alone, however, are not without their methodological difficulties, to say nothing of the ethical problems involved in obtaining valid data. Although unofficial lawbreaking, especially that which is juvenile-status in character (Type I in Table 10-2), does not involve official processing, it contains many of the same problems. Since it often involves juvenile statutes that exist for the purpose of protecting the welfare of children and since the acts it comprises are symptomatic of poor institutional ties, Type I delinquency, like Type III, may also be tautological with theoretical variables that are posited as causal antecedents to law-breaking. This is especially true if theory specifies poor school, family, and work ties as important causal factors.

Type II delinquency—that involving unofficially handled criminal acts—is probably the most relevant to the construction and testing of theory concerned with the factors associated with lawbreaking, per se. It involves neither the confounding effects of official processing nor the potentially tautological effects of juvenile offenses. Although serious methodological problems are inherent in obtaining valid measures of this type of act (Clark and Tifft, 1966; Hardt and Bodine, 1965), such measures, if added to those already obtained, might contribute significantly to the development of theories of law-violating behavior—theories that might then be joined fruitfully with theories of societal response.

Assuming that there is some merit in separating the study of law-violating behavior from the study of official response, the next two chapters are devoted to some of the issues inherent in doing so.

11   Law-Violating Behavior

The task of explaining law-violating behavior would seem to require two different levels of analysis. On the organizational level, efforts would have to be made to indicate with greater clarity the institutional, community, and group forces that interact to produce a social context in which law-violating behavior is likely to occur. Then, on a more specific level, the action situation itself would have to be studied. This situation is one in which the potential for delinquency is high, and in which there are usually two or more actors whose motivations and individual strategies are of crucial importance.

In discussing these two levels of analysis, no attempt will be made to cast them into a formal theoretical framework or to develop a set of formal propositions. Rather, the objective will be to sketch a frame of reference that might be productive of further research and theoretical development.

On the organizational level, three major elements seem most likely to set the situational context for delinquent behavior: (1) the system of legal norms that define illegal behavior; (2) the nature of the primary, socializing institutions in any community, most notably its families, schools, and neighborhoods and (3) the presence of illegitimate traditions, structures, and groups. Depending upon the way these elements are interwoven in any particular setting, the chances and nature of law-violating behavior will vary (cf. Ohlin, 1971, and Martin et al., 1968, for parallel but somewhat different formulations).

System of Legal Norms

The system of legal norms is obviously crucial. Becker (1963:8-9) has argued that

social groups create deviance by making the rules whose infractions constitute deviance. . . . From this point of view, deviance is *not* a quality of the act the person commits, but a consequence of the applications by others of rules and sanctions to an 'offender.'

Expanding further on this notion, Quinney (1970) presents both historical and contemporary documentation of the idea that legal definitions of delinquency and crime are derived from the conflicts of various interest groups in society and the relative positions of power they occupy. With respect to the juvenile court, for example, Platt (1969:139) argues that, from the beginning, it has been biased against the urban poor:

155

It was not by accident that the behavior selected for penalizing by the child-savers—drinking, begging, roaming the streets, frequenting dance halls and movies, fighting, sexuality, staying out late at night and incorrigibility—was primarily attributable to the children of lower class and immigrant families.

It is Platt's contention that the underlying premises upon which the court was built were conservative, middle-class oriented, and tended to define as bad those factors most associated with urbanism, industrialization, and the influx of immigrant subcultures. Thus, the very status of delinquent, quite apart from the personal characteristics of those who would occupy that status, was originated by that segment of society then in power.

Other matters of a more subtle nature speak to the same issue. Even the definition of such acts as theft or assault, which on the surface would seem to be acts that everyone could agree upon as being criminal, are affected by interest group pressure. What kinds of theft, and what kinds of assault, committed by whom and under what circumstances, should be considered illegal?

While it is relatively simple to obtain agreement that a boy who knocks down an old woman and steals her purse is guilty of both assault and theft, it is much more difficult to decide whether a particular kind of real estate development is theft, or whether the shooting of a burglary suspect by the police is assault. Consequently, the ways these acts are defined depends very much upon what groups occupy positions of power in society and who the accused are.

If Becker (1963) and Quinney (1970) are correct, then the system of legal norms constitutes a monolithic standard of right and wrong whose effects will vary, depending upon the particular neighborhood, subcultural, or ethnic groups to which it is applied. Since *informal* norms governing conduct in these settings are often at odds with legal norms, it should be possible to document with greater clarity the extent to which the resultant conflict contributes to law-violating behavior without any attempt on the parts of juveniles to be deliberately and consciously delinquent. In any constellation of explanatory variables, the disjunction between official and unofficial norms should contribute significantly to the explained variance.

There is considerable evidence, of course, in support of this conclusion. Referring to the ambiguities of juvenile court law, the President's Commission on Law Enforcement and Administration of Justice (1967:25) noted that legal provisions

are typically vague and all-encompassing: growing up in idleness and crime, engaging in immoral conduct, in danger of leading an immoral life. . . . They establish the judge as arbiter not only of the behavior but also the morals of every child (and to a certain extent the parents of every child). . . . One frequent consequence has been the use of general protective statutes about leading an immoral life and engaging in endangering conduct as a means of enforcing conformity—eliminating long hair, levis, and other transitory foibles so unsettling to adults.

Thus, the system of formal norms provides the general framework within which juvenile behavior is given meaning. Using it as a context for study, knowledge in several areas might be expanded: overall rates of law violation by all juveniles as contrasted to the smaller number that are officially labeled, the extent to which these rates are reflective either of essentially nonharmful and childlike—or criminal-status—violations, and the extent to which acts of both kinds vary from neighborhood to neighborhood and child to child.

As was suggested in Chapter 10 (see Table 10-1), juveniles may be divided into three general types: law-abiders, undetected law-violators, and official delinquents. It could be most helpful if we had something other than vague guesses as to the general parameters of the populations included in all these types (and the acts they engage in), and whether undetected law-violators are more like the law-abiding group or the official delinquents. As will be seen in the next section, existing laws may be such as to define a large proportion of the presently common behaviors of juveniles as delinquent.

The Socializing Institutions

Prior analyses of the primary socializing institutions indicate that they also have marked and differential effects upon law-violating behavior. Beginning with the family, considerable research has indicated that family disorganization is greater among delinquents than nondelinquents. However, greater care should be exercised in indicating what is meant by family "disorganization."

On one hand, some studies, including this one, indicate that intrafamily characteristics, its conflicts and tensions, are differentially productive of law-violating behavior (Schulman, 1949; Monahan, 1957; Toby, 1957; Hirschi, 1969). Their effects, as a result, and their interaction with other situational variables, are factors that require attention in the larger context of sources of illegal acts.

On the other hand, existing evidence suggests that care should be taken to control for the effects of class, ethnic status, and neighborhood in the study of intrafamily characteristics. The reason is that some outcomes that have been attributed to the emotional climate of the home may be due instead to other influences—influences that, while they are related to the home, have roots in the subcultural and other networks of which families are a part. For example, in their analysis of race differentials in gang behavior, Short and Strodtbeck (1965:105-106) found that

... Negro gang delinquency tends *not to be clearly differentiated from non-delinquent behavior*—that participation in the "good" aspects of lower class Negro life (responsibility in domestic chores and organized sports activities) is closely interwoven with "bad" aspects (conflict, illicit sex, drug use, and auto theft).

The literature on lower-class Negro life is rich in detail which supports such a conclusion among adults as well as children and adolescents. As compared with lower-class white communities, delinquency among lower-class Negroes is more of a total life pattern in which delinquent behaviors are not likely to create disjunctures with other types of behavior.

There was evidence throughout their study that family and community life for both adults and children was held much more in common among blacks than in other racial and neighborhood settings.

The same was generally true of the Puerto Rican delinquents that Martin et al. (1968:11-13) studied. Although many of the behaviors in which Puerto Rican children engaged, especially consensual sexual unions, were disavowed and punished by the larger community, they were very much a part of the pattern of life that the Puerto Rican people brought with them to the American city. Thus, a boy who was defined as "vicious" and "immoral" by authorities was seen by his extended family and friends as a likeable, supportive, and courageous friend.

By contrast, *white* gang boys have been found to be more openly at odds with adults in their community (Short and Strodtbeck, 1965:105-112). They were at odds in terms of their activities, which were often seen as rowdy and delinquent, and they were unwelcome in adult hangouts and groups. Much more than among black boys, their delinquent acts represented a protest against, rather than being more nearly a part of, conventional family and community obligations. Thus, the subcultural variations that surround adult-child relations as well as intra-family disruptions, are but one of a number of interdependent variables for which better account might be taken. For example, even within families of the same social class, it is likely that important differences along ethnic and other lines exist. It is little wonder, then, that attempts to explain *individual* delinquent behavior without taking such differences into account, is unlikely to account for much of the variance—why, for example, social class by itself may prove to be of little predictive utility.

Closely related to, and often inseparable from, family influences is the neighborhood as a socializing institution. There has long been a disagreement in the literature whether those neighborhoods with the highest rates of law violations are disorganized or organized. On one hand, Thrasher (1963:20-21) concluded that illegal acts are most likely to occur in "what is often called the 'poverty belt'—a region characterized by deteriorating neighborhoods, shifting populations, and the mobility and disorganization of the slum." On the other hand, it was Whyte's (1955:viii) opinion that the slum may be highly organized, but not in the way that conventional people conceive of social organization. The point is that the degree of organization in any neighborhood may not only vary from place to place, but be characterized by sharply different patterns as well. In some cases, the traditional institutions of socialization and control found in the larger community are ineffective. In others, new patterns are generated or are imported by the particular subcultural or ethnic groups who live there. These patterns are often conducive to behavior that is illegal and disturbing to the larger community. Such behavior may be disturbing to local residents as well, but this will depend upon the extent to which juvenile conduct is well integrated with, or is contrary to, adult expectation. Some of the behavior, as suggested above, may not be especially atypical under certain circumstances.

Given these variations, both in degree *and* kind of neighborhood and family organization, it is not difficult to understand why the school and other conventional institutions become a focal point for adolescent difficulty. The school, for example, usually operates on policies set up and administered by middle-class people whose ways of viewing the world have been shaped by other backgrounds. Operating from a central headquarters, they attempt to impose uniform policies and practices on widely divergent groups who often have little in common. These attempts result in a lack of communication, in conflict, and eventually, in law violation.

In Los Angeles, for example, the Chicano population numbers in the hundreds of thousands. This population, second in size only to Mexico City, has long had a language problem with respect to the schools. Many of the Chicano children do not speak English when they enter school. To the preponderant majority of teachers and administrators, who neither speak Spanish nor know the customs of the Chicano, this has traditionally been labeled a singular disability.

Whereas in other schools in Los Angeles, parents and teachers are urging their children to learn a second language (which may well be Spanish), and considering them brilliant if they do, the Chicano children have suffered because although they already know one language, it is not English. Consequently, rather than communicating initially with their students in Spanish, and then teaching them English, teachers have disavowed the use of Spanish only to see many children fall progressively further behind in all their subjects. The result has been the highest dropout rate in the city, along with which have emerged some of the most delinquent and persistently stable gangs in the country (cf. Klein, 1971).

What these examples indicate, then, is that the relationship of the primary institutions to law-violating behavior cannot be treated as social structures that have the same socializing impact in all settings. Rather, the nature of the institutions and their impact will vary from place to place. In attempting to develop theoretical and research models, therefore, it will be necessary to account for the ways different kinds of organizations contribute to the commission of illegal acts. But rather than suggesting that illegal acts are essentially unpredictable, the evidence implies that what we lack are adequate typologies by which various kinds of institutional networks can be taken into account, and their differential effects assessed. This conclusion is no less true of the *illegitimate* networks that are the subject of analysis in the next section.

Illegitimate Traditions and Structures

Virtually equal in impact to, and often inseparable from, the family, neighborhood, and school are illegitimate structures in the community. A number of different investigators have observed that a great deal of illegal behavior results from the transmission to the juvenile of local traditions of group-supported delinquency, some of it criminally and career-oriented (Cressey, 1964; Kobrin, 1951; McKay, 1949; Thrasher, 1963).

By way of illustration, Short (1963) refers to a question posed for the staff of a YMCA gang program in Chicago: "What are the most significant institutions for your boys?" The answer from a detached worker was revealing. "I guess," he said, "I'd have to say the gang, the hangouts, drinking, parties in the area, and the police." While these would scarcely be acknowledged as "institutions" in the conventional sense, there was agreement among other workers that the answer of the first worker was correct. One of them would have added the boys' families to the list, but the overall conclusion was that the most viable places for the boys were the street corners, the pool halls, taverns, and "quarter parties" in which adults as well as juveniles often participated. Relating this back to the system of formal norms, it is easy to see why law violations would be high in such an area. Many of the regular activities of these juveniles, although a normal part of daily life, were officially illegal. Without any deliberate intent on their parts to be delinquent, they were law violators by definition. Because of this fact, problems of social organization for the larger society as well as the juvenile are created, problems regarding the definition of what behaviors shall and shall not be tolerated. The potential for conflict is high.

Information regarding the network of informal "institutions" for middle- and upper-class juveniles is not so readily available, documenting a serious omission in the literature. But with the advent of the drug scene, pot parties, underground protest, and changes in sexual mores, it is undoubtedly the case that there are parallel associations on these social strata as well. Illegal structures, very much a part of the lives of juveniles, undoubtedly contribute to what is officially defined as illegal.

Other kinds of illegitimate structures are harder to describe and detect. In their study of groups in an Italian neighborhood, for example, Kobrin, Puntil, and Peluso (1967) located six groups whose access to illegitimate structures varied considerably. Four of the groups were clearly delinquent, while the remaining two were described as "unconventional" (but not especially delinquent) and "respectable."

Of particular interest are the contrasting characteristics of the two groups on opposite ends of the delinquency continuum—the *sophisticated* delinquents on one extreme and the *respectable* nondelinquents on the other. The sophisticated delinquents

were highly knowledgeable of channels for the disposal of stolen goods and the resources available for protection in the event of detection. . . . They came from well-connected families, had 'plenty of clout,' commanded good jobs through politics and the rackets when they worked, were well supplied with money, and were first in their age group to own new automobiles [p. 103].

The respectable nondelinquents, by contrast, were the best educated in the neighborhood, participated in the social activities of the local parish church, and occasionally engaged in such conventional civic activities as collecting for the Red Cross.

What is perhaps most significant about the findings were the prestige rankings of these two groups by representatives from each of the six delinquent and nondelinquent groups. There was a surprising consensus that the prestige of the sophisticated delinquents in the neighborhood was the highest, and that of the respectables the lowest. There was a touch of disdain for the respectables as "do-nothing" kids. The sources of this disdain, moreover, stemmed not only from the adolescent perspectives of the informants, but from the nature of the neighborhood as a whole.

According to the authors (p.101), "there had existed for some time a firmly established integration of the legitimate and illegitimate elements of the community, manifested in a locally acknowledged alliance between the political leadership and that of the city's gambling, vice, and other rackets." Furthermore, the prestige of the respectable group may have suffered because their fathers tended to be civil servants in local government who had moved out of local, social circles because they enjoyed some independence from the control of local politicians. Thus, this particular neighborhood seemed to be characterized, at the very least, by an ambivalence toward law-abiding and conventional structures, or, at the very most, by stronger ties to illegitimate than legitimate ones. Without doubt, the perceptions and behaviors of juveniles were influenced by these conflicting elements.

While this may well be an atypical community, much about it is familiar. As Daniel Bell (1959) has noted, Americans generally are characterized by an "extremism" in morality; yet they also have an "extraordinary" talent for compromise in politics and a "brawling" economic history. These contradictory features form the basis for an intimate and symbiotic relationship between crime and politics, crime and economic growth, and crime and social change—not an oppositional relationship. The tradition of wanting to get ahead by the shortest possible route is no less an ethic than wanting to observe the law.

Adult crime, not just delinquency, has been a major means by which a variety of people have achieved the American success ideal and obtained respectability, if not for themselves, for their children. The basic question, therefore, is whether this deviant tradition contributes more than we realize to the behavior of younger, as well as older, people—to adolescents from all strata and communities as well as those from lower-status and deprived communities. Rather than delinquent subculture being uniquely the property of young people, it may have roots in the broader culture (cf. Empey, 1967).

These roots have recently come to the attention of the powerful and respectable in society. With the advent of extensive drug use among their own as well as other children, and the indirect support for that use by powerful and legitimate, as well as illegitimate groups, they are more conscious of the problem than ever before. It becomes increasingly difficult for them to maintain that there is not a close and symbiotic tie between legitimate and illegitimate structures, involving the technology and economics of drug production and supply, on one hand, and political corruption and organized crime on the other.

In summary, our review thus far has suggested that, although the system of legal rules is intended to provide a monolithic backdrop against which all childhood behavior should be judged, that system may, itself, create conflict, a conflict that is as old as classical criminology. Hypothetically, the primary institutions in society are supposed to socialize all children in much the same way, such that they and their parents can be judged by the same legal standard. The existing literature suggests, however, that this is not the case. Not only does socialization vary from place to place, but apparently deviant traditions and structures throughout society also make formal and informal expectation less than consistent.

In attempting to provide a framework within which to analyze these forces, social scientists have used two contrasting models, a "consensus" model and a "conflict" model. Of the two, the consensus model has enjoyed the greater popularity, emphasizing the idea that all of the elements of social organization are a highly integrated and closely-knit whole. Drawing upon Dahrendorf's analysis (1959:161-162), Quinney (1970:8) has summarized the main assumptions of this model as follows:

(1) society is a relatively persistent, stable structure; (2) it is well-integrated; (3) every element has a function—it helps maintain the system; and (4) a functioning social structure is based on a consensus on values.

In other words, the consensus model suggests that most people share the same general objectives, agree on basic definitions of right and wrong, and engage in a mutually supporting set of activities. Thus, by definition, a young person who violates the law is one who rejects the basic consensus and threatens the stability of the whole.

By contrast, the conflict model assumes that: (1) at every point society is subject to change, (2) it displays at every point dissension and conflict, (3) every element contributes to change, and (4) it is based on the coercion of some of its members by others [Quinney, 1970:8].

In this case, one would assume that society is characterized by diversity and change, and that is held together, not by consensus, but by force and constraint, and that, although certain values predominate, they do so more by the fact that they are supported by dominant groups and interests than by the members of society as a whole (Dahrendorf, 1958:127).

While space does not permit a detailed assessment of all the implications of these contrasting perspectives, it is probably accurate to conclude that there is much in the conflict model that might be added to the consensus model in the analysis of law-violating behavior. In terms of what we have seen, there are significant indications that large differences do exist in American society over the ways its subcultures and communities are organized, and over the effects these variations have on childhood behavior. In their studies of juvenile law violation, however, sociologists have probably not devoted enough attention to an *empirical* cataloging of the extent and nature of differences as well as similarities. We have been aware of their existence, in a somewhat subjective way, for a long time. But to say, for example, that specialized argots and expectations exist, or that relationships between adults and children vary considerably, is to be very unspecific. As Short (1965:157) suggests, these kinds of things do not really define the characteristics of different subcultural, group, and neighborhood settings, nor do they guarantee that children growing up in these settings automatically become carriers of their traditions. Thus, if the relationship between law-violating behavior and different kinds of social settings is to be better understood, typologies along several different dimensions are needed—typologies by which the effects of differential organization could first be catalogued, and then related to behaviors in some empirical way.

For example, a neighborhood typology could specify how neighborhoods are ordered along one or more dimensions, what factors determine this ordering, and the ways in which these factors are related. Were this done, it might be possible to incorporate in a typology such things as racial, subcultural, and structural variables which heretofore have been analyzed separately in relation to delinquency. If so, such a framework might indicate with greater clarity the kinds of neighborhoods which typify those, on one extreme, in which law violations are likely to be the highest and those, on the other extreme, in which they would be the lowest. Thus, the most immediate consequence would be the lending of greater form, in operational terms, to existing impressions and insights. Research might then be forthcoming that could lend greater substance to the sociological argument that, by taking kinds of systems into account, the explanation of law-violating behavior could be improved.

Equally important would be research concerned with determining how much variation and departure from a consensus model a society can tolerate before that departure becomes dysfunctional and threatening to the welfare of the whole. Although there is a great deal of speculation on the matter, few have taken the trouble to treat it empirically. Yet a concern with deviance and sub-group variation is as old as human society. Until more is known about it, little can be done to add substance to conflicting demands for the imposition of strong controls, on one hand, and pleas for greater toleration and pluralism on the other.

Typologies are also an aid to the development of theory. Since the primary function of a typology is to present a set of types that identify, simplify, and order concrete phenomena, it is, in a real sense, an embryonic theory. With further refinement, therefore, it might stimulate a clearer definition of concepts and the development of a more rigorous deductive system. Efforts that are turned in this direction could help to answer the question whether the methods of science, and its search for regularities, are appropriate for the understanding of law-violating behavior on organizational and societal levels.

The Action Situation

While the use of new approaches might lead to a more definitive understanding of the way differential community organization might lead to differential rates of law violation, the most challenging task would be that of relating such findings to individual behavior. The focus of analysis would shift from the level of organization to the level of the actor in an action situation. This shift in level of analysis has been characterized historically by a curious disjunction between what is found on an organizational level and what people consider important when they look at the individual.

Paradoxically, the most common approach has been to see the law violator as a disturbed person who would be delinquent no matter what the setting. Despite the movement of social scientists away from this perspective for some time now, the belief that the roots of law violation are in the personality of the violator is a persistent one. Yet after decades of research, personality disturbance has thus far proven to be a weak predictor. As Hathaway, Monachesi, and Young (1960:439) put it, personality measures "are much less powerful and apply to fewer cases among total samples than would be expected if one read the literature on the subject." Summaries of other studies on adult criminals, the majority of whom are young, suggest (1) that offenders are more like than different from the general population, and (2) that measures of personality which yield deviancy variations reliably still do not distinguish criminal behavior types (cf. Schussler and Cressey, 1950; Lagache, 1950; Mensch, 1963).

But whereas there seem to be reasonably good grounds for rejecting personality as a primary cause for the preponderant majority of law violators, the more difficult question has to do with Matza's challenges mentioned earlier in chapter 10. His position, it will be recalled, was that delinquents tend to be flirtatious adolescents who, although they may occasionally "drift" into situations conducive to law-violating behavior, are not really wedded to any consistent patterns of illegal behavior and, thus, such behavior cannot be predicted within a deterministic framework. The factors that might precipitate individual delinquency are too indefinite and too subject to chance.

At present, no conclusive evidence either substantiates or disproves Matza's position. However, some clues indicate where one might begin in attempting to resolve the issue. First of all, the findings of this study have tended to confirm the findings of a long list of other studies (cf. chapter 1) that *known* delinquents do not possess the requisite cognitive nor social skills to cope with the school environment. They tend to score lower on intelligence tests when social class is held constant, and their interpersonal and organizational skills are less than nondelinquents. Thus, very early in their lives, they are sidetracked from the major institutional avenues leading from childhood to adulthood. They find themselves without the institutional activities that provide the kinds of supports that make conventional activities more highly appealing than deviant ones. They are socially "defrocked," as it were.

One basic research question, therefore, is whether the same is true of the larger population of law violators who are not officially known to be delinquent. How much more might be known if samples from the general childhood population were chosen and studied to determine the effects of their institutional affiliations upon their individual behaviors? Would some of the same patterns be observed? Could individual law-violating behavior be predicted with any greater certainty if good measures of institutional affiliation were available?

There is also evidence that, in the absence of institutional affiliations, many "defrocked" adolescents turn to each other in search of social gratification. Delinquent gangs and groups and delinquent subcultures often result. However, several questions regarding these groups are unresolved. On one hand, there are findings which suggest that these collectivities become reference groups. The fact that they exist, and often persist over long periods of time, suggest that some individual needs are being met. Moreover, such groups become the carriers of deviant traditions.

Earlier, in describing the Provo Experiment (Empey and Rabow, 1961), we observed, for example, that despite the fact that the location of the experiment was not in a highly urbanized area,

the concept of a 'parent' delinquent subculture has real meaning for it. While there are no clear-cut gangs, per se, it is surprising to observe the extent to which boys from the entire county, who have never met, know each other by reputation, go with the same girls, use the same language, or can seek each other out when they change high schools. About half of them are permanently out of school, do not participate in any regular institutional activities, and are reliant almost entirely upon the delinquent system for social acceptance and participation.

In further study of the same boys (Erickson and Empey, 1965), it was found that boys who had been the most delinquent were those most inclined to have delinquent associates. The thing that is significant about these findings is that they are consistent with the much larger body of data on delinquency gathered in urban areas.

On the other hand, a growing number of investigators seriously question the rewards to be gained from deviant group membership. Short and Strodtbeck (1965:231) depreciate nostalgic references to that "old gang of mine" and question the image of the group as carefree and cohesive. Matza (1964:53-55) uses the term "sounding" to refer to the incessant plumbing and testing through insult by group members of one another's status and commitment to delinquency. Miller (1958:519) implies that members are under constant pressure to protect status and assert masculinity. And Klein and Crawford (1967:63) suggest that the internal sources of group cohesion may be weak. Were it not for the external pressures of police, rival gangs, parents and teachers, such groups would have nothing to unify them. Thus, such findings raise perplexing questions regarding the orientations and inclinations of individuals in the action situation. If they are not strongly tied to conventional institutions, and if their ties to delinquent groups are tenuous, then how will they be inclined to behave when the risks of law violation and further trouble are imminent? Such questions cannot be resolved until several kinds of information are available, information that could be useful in helping to indicate something more about adolescent populations and law-violating behavior in general, not just the behaviors of known offenders.

Need for Baseline Information

As pointed out in chapter 9, the field is seriously hampered by the fact that we do not even have an adequate baseline of information regarding adolescent groupings in general against which we can measure the cohesiveness of deviant groupings, and better determine what produces them. Since we know very little about the forces that result in the formation of adolescent groups, their antecedents, their degrees of cohesiveness, or the gratifications inherent in them, it is difficult to generalize about specific, deviant groups or to explain their place in the whole constellation of adolescent behavior. Moreover, such information is important as it relates to the connection between personal disability—low interpersonal and cognitive skills, or low school status—and group behavior in middle- and upper-class groups. Most of our studies have been of lower-class boys; yet the mounting evidence suggests that law violations and deviant groups are very much a part of the lives of adolescents on other strata as well. Thus, attempts to understand deviance require that we study adolescent populations in general, and conforming as well as deviant behaviors.

Rules of the Game

An analysis of the action situation also suggests that we must be aware of the motivations and strategies of the individual actor. But while there has always been a tendency to look at motivations apart from social context, little in contemporary social science would suggest that that this approach is adequate. Instead, there are better ways to formulate the basic questions: (1) What is there about the individual in a given social context that might motivate him to want to participate in a deviant game? and (2) Assuming that he is inclined to play such a game, in what position, and under what circumstances, would he be inclined to play it?

Attempts to answer such questions would form a better bridge to the earlier discussion having to do with legal rules, socializing institutions, and illegitimate structures on an organizational level than would a concern with intrapsychic phenomena apart from social context. Cohen (1960) and Cohen and Short (1971) have noted, for example, that most human life is organized in terms of social games. Thus, if baseball is the game being played, we can often make better sense out of the behaviors of the different players if we know the rules of the game than if we know only the more general skills of each of the players. If we do not, we may only see a meaningless collection of disconnected acts with the players, at times, appearing to be demented.

For example, a stranger to baseball, observing the wild antics of the third and first basemen when they are expecting a bunt, would have good reason to question their sanity. They charge wildly toward the plate and the man with the club every time the ball is thrown. From a strictly objective point of view, as well as that of the stranger, they stand a good chance of having their teeth knocked out by a line drive. Yet, from the viewpoint of anyone who is acquainted with the game, the behavior is sensible, not stupid. The third or first baseman who *does not* charge the plate is the one who is deviant, the one who might be considered to be out of his mind, the one who will not be kept on the team.

The same might be said for a variety of other activities. If different individuals contribute to some social enterprise in different ways, the participants see their contributions as hanging together and constituting an entity in its own right: "A baseball game," "a geography class," "a church service," "a shoe store," "a prison racket."

Each activity operates according to a set of rules, some informal, some formal. These rules specify a set of positions or roles—third baseman, teacher, minister, clerk, or con politician—and indicate what the player of each position is supposed to do in relation to the players of other positions. They also include criteria for evaluating the success of the total enterprise or the contributions of individual players.

In order to "fit in," as Cohen (1960:000) puts it,

you have to know the rules; you have to 'have a program,' so that you may know what position each man, including yourself, is playing; and you have to know how to keep score. You cannot make sense out of what is going on, either as a participant or as an observer, unless you know the rules that define this particular sort of collective enterprise.

The point is that one's very self is constituted not just of characteristics peculiar to him but of the positions he plays in various games. Others are able to place him and have successful relations with him in terms of the positions he plays and the positons they play. His public reputation, his self-respect, depend upon how well he plays his position and, if he is a part of a team game, how well his team as a whole does.

Our prior description of the general elements contributing to law violation have suggested that too little attention has been paid to game phenomena in the specific situation. On one hand, we have not been cognizant enough of the variations in rules operative among juveniles in different kinds of communities within the overall society. Thus, if one's own, or an official and conventional, definition of the situation were imposed upon them, one might not only fail to understand the games being played but would miss much that is significant. The same body of interaction occurring in different settings might have much different meaning. Behavior that might be disavowed by adults in a middle-class neighborhood might well be a part of the subcultural fabric of a black or Italian neighborhood. Behavior that might represent a disruption of ties between youth and adults in one might be just the opposite in another. For example, "It often shocks the unsophisticated to find that many *professional* criminals . . . are graduates of loving homes, who are successfully identifying with their fathers [Glaser et al., undated:20]." Thus, in addition to the need for better information on the characteristics of different subcultures, neighborhoods, and communities, we need to know how those characteristics are translated into action on the microsociological level (Cohen and Short, 1971).

In the Italian neighborhood discussed above, the sophisticated delinquents were apparently tuned in to illegitimate as well as legitimate structures as a method of realizing their goals, while the "respectables," the children of civil servants, were oriented to the more conventional expectations of the larger community. The interesting thing about both sets of juveniles, however, is that there was not a serious disjunction between parents and children in either case. Rather, both groups were reflecting conflicting sets of expectations that existed side-by-side in the same neighborhood, expectations that were carried not only by juveniles but by parents.

In a black neighborhood, by contrast, Short and Strodtbeck (1965:275) suggest that reasonably common patterns between adults and children have relatively less meaning simply because neither adults nor children were tied very effectively either to legitimate or illegitimate structures.

We firmly believe that need dispositions which are requited by gang membership arise in the interaction between the lack of preparation for school-type achievement in the home and in the absence of access to alternative adaptions to failure in the schools. . . . By the time boys acquire the identity associated with gang membership, a police record, or dropping out of school, the process of selectivity for failure is established.

Thus, the understanding and prediction of individual behavior in either case would rest not only upon some delineation of differences on a general level, but the way these differences were translated into action on the level of the child.

With regard to the more difficult question of what position a given individual will play in the games open to him, we know relatively little. However, two things in general can be noted. First, it is obvious that, judged by the system of legal norms, the sheer number of opportunities to commit illegal acts in some neighborhoods will be greater than others. In some settings, for example, such activities as public drinking, shifting sexual liaisons, truancy, and even drug use are so common that virtually every adolescent will be involved at one time or another without the necessity for him to be wedded to a role that, in his neighborhood, is distinctively deviant. This is likely to be true in many middle- and upper-, as well as lower-class neighborhoods, but in the absence of definitive studies, it is difficult to be sure.

Second, in assessing the calculus of individual decision-making, it is probably safe to assume that little risk of official punishment is run by the person who engages in illegal acts. Commenting on this issue, Strodtbeck and Short (1964:135-139) conclude that the disposition by an individual to "join the action" is not satisfactorily explained by uniquely deviant values or irrational tendencies. Even gang violence—which from the perspective either of the individual or the larger society is very serious—actually erupts in not more than one out of five potential instances. And when serious consequences do arise, they are discovered by the authorities in only about 20 per cent of the cases. The result is that "for average Negro gang boys the probability of arrest for involvement in instances of potential violence is probably no greater than .04, and for the very skillful this figure might fall to .02."

These estimates receive confirmation from a number of other studies of undetected delinquency in which the acts of adolescents from all social strata, not just black gangs, were the objects of analysis. The degree of apprehension was extremely low, somewhere between 3 and 5 per cent of all self-reported offenses (Erickson and Empey, 1963; Gold, 1966; Murphy, Shirley, and Witmer, 1946; and Porterfield, 1946). Thus, "however estimated, the probability of avoiding serious outcome appears to be sufficiently large to make the option of joining the action quite attractive" (Strodtbeck and Short, 1964:135). Greater payoff for explaining many individual adolescent acts may come, therefore, from a better understanding of adolescent norms in general, and from local rules in particular, than from personally neurotic or irrational forces.

Another reason for paying attention to the rules of different games has to do with the likelihood that young people, like their parents, possess a repertory of possible behaviors, some conformist, some deviant, that are applied in different contexts. In conventional settings, they can, and usually do, behave conventionally; in delinquent settings they behave illegally. Matza (1964:27-30) suggests, however, that the range of possible behaviors open to young people makes them highly susceptible to "shared misunderstanding"—a tendency to attribute greater commitment to delinquency to each other than any one of them actually feels. This may well be true and has many ramifications for a legal system that often makes the same assumption and treats individuals accordingly. The key question, however, is not how the legal system responds but how consistently this "shared misunderstanding" results in acts that are delinquent. Given a knowledge of certain social pre-conditions, it may be possible to predict with some accuracy how individuals will respond, with "shared misunderstanding" a contributor, not a deterrent, to the outcome.

For some individuals the motivation to join the action is inherent in the positions they customarily play (Short, 1965:163):

As obvious examples, a leader may be *required* to 'join the action,' or even precipitate it if the situation involves *group threat*. A 'War Counselor' is required to perform when gang conflict appears imminent or is engaged.

For others, motivation is related to self-concept;

boys who describe themselves in 'scoutlike' terms (loyal, polite, helpful, religious, obedient) are *more* involved in conflict behavior than are boys who describe themselves as 'cool aggressives' (mean, tough, troublesome, cool).

Because they see themselves as loyal and helpful, "scouts" are more willing to accept and discharge obligations to the collective welfare, even if delinquent, than boys who play it cool. As a consequence, they often find themselves in situations in which role expectations, threats to present status, and rewards make their involvement in delinquent acts more likely. The striking thing about this possibility is that, for some kinds of illegal acts, the most loyal and constructive individuals, not the more irresponsible and less socially motivated ones would be the most likely to be involved.

Finally, it should be observed that, even in individual acts of violence, evidence indicates that if more concerted effort were made to document certain key elements in the action situation, it might be possible to be more definitive about the conditions under which law violation will occur. Consider the behavior of the murderer (Glaser et al., undated):

Most often, he is a good example of a product of the 'culture of violence.' The murderer frequently lives in a milieu where passionate assault, under certain circumstances, is not only excused but even expected. 'Premeditation,' when it exists, is usually some activity like staggering out of a barroom to find a convenient weapon. In a large number of cases, the person he murders on return is a friend. Both are drinking, both are trying to prove their masculinity, both know the survivor will not be severely condemned by the people that matter (their other friends) even if the police and courts take a dim view of the outcome. The quick-triggered male who assaults (and kills, occasionally) is often responding to an affront to his maleness, doubly intolerable because it comes from another male.

One reason we may not have more empirical, as contrasted to impressionistic, evidence on acts such as this is because we have not devoted much attention to explaining individual behavior. For example, Ohlin (1971:2) notes in a recent publication that his and Cloward's theoretical treatise *Delinquency and Opportunity* (1960) was not intended to explain individual acts of law violation. Instead, like other theoretical formulations,

it sought to account for the social distribution of delinquent norms embodied in four different types of delinquent subcultures. It tried to build on the pioneer work of Albert Cohen who first raised to critical attention questions concerning the persistence and sources of delinquent subcultures.

In other words, their level of analysis was on the more general, organizational level. But while it is imperative that such analyses be conducted, it is equally imperative that the behavior of the actor on a different level be studied. Our ability to explain law-violating behavior in the long run depends upon both kinds of analysis and an adequate bridging between them.

12 The Juvenile Justice System

Our review to this point lends some credence to the idea that there might be merit in attempting to formulate theory and conduct research on law-violating behavior, separate and apart from official response to it. The analysis has suggested that, when law violation is considered apart from official response, it appears to be an extremely common phenomenon. In many cases, it can be viewed as a more-or-less "normal" response to the way American society in general, and neighborhoods in particular, are organized. Thus, by focusing upon law violation as an inseparable, rather than uniquely pathological, part of the life experiences of most juveniles, it may be possible not only to increase understanding, but to provide better guidelines for the redefinition of our formal system of legal norms and ways to both protect the welfare of children and society.

At the same time, one must be concerned with the overlap between juvenile behavior and official response to it. Christensen (1967:221) estimated in his report for the President's Commission on Law Enforcement and Administration of Justice that the probabilities of arrest for American males sometime during their lives was 52 per cent, and for females was 13 per cent. It was also estimated in 1964 that about 1 in 6 boys and 1 in 23 girls would be brought before the juvenile court for delinquency sometime before 18 years of age (cf. Perlman, 1965:1), an estimate that might be low in light of current trends. Yet, no matter where he looks, one finds evidence of confusion, even bewilderment, regarding the goals and methods of juvenile and criminal justice systems.

The President's Commission on Law Enforcement (1967:53) noted that although police, courts, and correctional agencies all share the same major objective of reducing crime, they usually use conflicting methods and focus upon conflicting subobjectives. Despite the subjectivity of their operations, they rarely, if ever, make their systems the object of systematic study.

One result has been a suggestion by Wheeler and Cottrell (1966:44) that "no responsible business concern would operate with as little information regarding its success or failure as do nearly all of our delinquency prevention and control programs." And Cicourel (1968:331) notes that "for years, sociologists have complained about 'bad' statistics and distorted bureaucratic recordkeeping, but have not made the procedures producing the 'bad' materials . . . an object of study."

Despite the overwhelming feeling that greater understanding of the system of juvenile justice is needed, our problems stem not only from a lack of data but a lack of defensible theoretical frameworks within which the collection of data makes sense. With reference to the juvenile court, for example, Matza (1964:118) points out that adjudicative criteria are so broad and all-encompassing that the nature of court operations becomes very obscure. Thus, he was led to conclude that "the great variation from court to court is one of the most important and revealing generalizations one can make about the type of juvenile justice regularly dispensed."

Because of problems like these, it was suggested in chapter 10 that attempts be made to develop theory and conduct studies on the system of juvenile justice apart from the study of law-violating acts. Emergent findings might then provide a more definitive understanding of both the uniqueness and overlap of *official* delinquency with law violating behavior. Space does not permit a complete review of all the relevant literature, but since the law enforcement and court segments of the juvenile justice system are of the greatest importance in defining who, and who shall not, be officially defined as delinquent, greatest attention will be paid to them.

The Police and Community

Existing studies suggest that at least four general factors are likely to affect police decisions about whether juvenile lawbreakers should be processed or not. The first factor is *structural* by nature and has to do with the organization of police departments and the communities in which they are located. Goldman's (1969) study of four municipalities in Pennsylvania, for example, revealed wide variations in the manner in which police dealt with juveniles. He found that police were very sensitive to such factors as general community sentiment and pressures from political or special interest groups. In fact, the proportion of juvenile arrests referred to court varied from a low of 8.6 per cent for one municipality to a high of 71.2 per cent for another. Similarly, in a study of forty-six independent police departments in California, representing cities ranging in population from 1,068 to 2,682,381 inhabitants, Klein (1970) found that the range of juvenile arrestees counseled and released rather than being referred to court or other official agencies ranged from 2 per cent in one department to 82 per cent in another. Obviously, if one wanted to learn much about why some juveniles become official delinquents, and others do not, he would want to know much more about the determinants of such widely discrepant rates.

In the Pennsylvania communities, Goldman (1969) found that the highest arrest rates occurred in the community with the highest socio-economic level. Yet, this community also had the lowest rate of court referrals. By contrast, the lowest arrest rate was found in a relatively lower-class, commercial community which not only had the highest rate of serious crimes, but which also had the highest court referral rate of those who were arrested.

In a similar vein, Wilson (1970) studied the operations of juvenile officers in two different metropolitan locales which he called "Eastern City" and "Western

City." Western City's police force was highly professionalized and centralized, and most of its officers were from other parts of the country. Eastern City, by contrast, did not have a professionalized police force. It was highly decentralized (operating from several distinct precincts), juvenile officers worked alone with a minimum of supervision, and officers were often locals who came from the neighborhoods under their jurisdictions.

The manner in which the two departments dealt with juveniles differed widely. Western City police treated juvenile offenders strictly according to rule. It arrested a higher proportion of its city's juvenile population and its dealings with youth were impersonal. Eastern City's police, by contrast, dealt with youth with a much higher degree of tolerance and personalization. In fact, "bringing a *kid* in" was considered to be a low-status arrest in the eyes of other officers, unless the offense involved was very serious. Furthermore, Eastern City Policemen had often been raised in the neighborhoods of their precincts, had gotten in trouble themselves as youths, and were more likely to handle juveniles in an individualized and understanding manner. Thus, these findings would suggest that the structure of police departments, as determined both by the external communities in which they operate and by their own internal arrangements, have a significant impact upon the ultimate determination as to whether juveniles become officially delinquent or not.

A second factor affecting police decision-making is the nature of the *situation* surrounding their contact with juveniles. Piliavin and Briar (1964) contend that police exercise an immense latitude of response in dealing with juveniles. Like Goldman (1969), they found that the demeanor of the youths involved in potential arrest situations is a critical determinant of who is arrested and who is not. Youths who are uncooperative or who act tough are more likely to be arrested than youths who are cooperative and play the role of the contrite and repentant wrongdoer. This led Piliavin and Briar (1964) to conclude that the official delinquent

is the product of social judgment. He is a delinquent because someone in authority has defined him as one, often on the basis of the public face he has presented to officials than of the kind of offense he has committed.

Black and Reiss (1970), like Piliavin and Briar, also found demeanor to be an important factor in the processing of juvenile offenders, although they found the relationship between arrest and demeanor to be curvilinear. That is, delinquents who acted overly-deferential toward police were as likely to be arrested as those who acted antagonistic, while those who acted "civil" had the lowest probability of arrest. However, Black and Reiss also found that other situational factors were equally, if not more, important. First, they found that about 78 per cent of the complaints registered against juveniles were reactive (citizen-initiated) rather than proactive (police-initiated). This suggested very strongly that the moral standards of citizens have more to do with who is defined as delinquent than the standards of the police. Second, they found that the presence of a citizen complainant in a potential arrest situation was of extreme importance. Police usually complied when complainants demanded the arrests of juveniles. Black and Reiss did not find a single instance in which police arrested a juvenile when the complainant asked for leniency. Furthermore, in situations where no complainant was present, police were very unlikely to arrest juveniles, and were more likely to release them without formal sanction.

A third factor is *behavioral*, and has to do with the *type of crime* involved in a police-juvenile contact situation. Some findings suggest that serious offenses are more likely to result in arrest or court referral than less serious offenses (McEachern and Bauzer, 1967; Terry, 1967; Goldman, 1969), but precise information concerning the probability of arrest for different categories of offenses is largely unavailable.

Goldman (1969), however, found that the juvenile offenses most frequently referred for court action were robbery, larceny, riding in a stolen car, sex offenses, and incorrigibility. Offenses least likely to result in court action were gambling, traffic offenses, mischief, property damage, and drunkenness. Thus, offenses involving crimes against persons were most likely to be reported.

A final factor has to do with the *personal attributes* of both police officers and juveniles. Piliavin and Briar (1964) and Goldman (1969) found that black youths are more likely to be arrested or referred to court than whites, but Black and Reiss (1970) found no evidence of racial discrimination on the part of the police officers. The disparity could be due to regional differences between the studies, but could also be due to the complainants present in arrest situations. Black and Reiss (1970), for example, found that black complainants were far less tolerant toward juvenile suspects than white complainants and were thus more likely to convince police of the need for arrest. Other factors, such as sex, age, prior record, and family status (McEachern and Bauzer, 1967; Goldman, 1969; Terry, 1967) have also been found to be related to dispositions in police-juvenile contacts.

The personal attributes of police—their ethnic backgrounds, degrees of tolerance, levels of education, and personalities—undoubtedly also affect the complex processes involved in the handling of juvenile suspects. Both Goldman (1969) and Wilson (1970) found that the tolerance and attitude of police toward juveniles had a lot to do with the rate of official processing and, further, that police might fail to report juvenile cases that could result in their own embarrassment. Skolnick (1966) also suggests that occupational pressures can affect the "working personalities" of policemen. Police are continually confronted by the possibility of danger and must also assert their authority. Skolnick points out that danger can lead to self-defensive conduct and that the assertion of authority can be used to reduce threats. Westly (1953) has also pointed out that police may resort to defensive and violent conduct in order to defend and preserve their status and self-esteem in the face of depreciatory conduct.

Thus, findings on police-juvenile contacts have suggested that a whole series of factors at four different levels—structural, situational, personal, and behavioral—can impinge upon the process through which some juveniles, but not others, are officially defined as delinquent. While many different kinds of studies might be conducted, one that might be especially helpful would be that in which typologies of police response were first constructed, and then related to the gathering of data in different neighborhoods. Such typologies might help to bridge the gap between different patterns of juvenile behavior and the way the legal system responds. Empirical data could be gathered that would help to provide a context for understanding the differentials in police response, and to pin down those factors that seem to be most crucial in determining arrest under a variety of different community and situational circumstances, as well as those that are strictly legal and formal in character.

The Juvenile Court

If, due to the complex interaction of the factors just discussed, the police decide to file charges against a juvenile, or if he has been referred to court by school or other officials, he then becomes subject to the equally complex operations of the juvenile court. On a general level, the court is of crucial importance because it is the instrument by which society formally inducts the individual into a deviant status. As Erikson (1964:16) points out,

The community's decision to bring deviant sanctions against an individual is not a simple act of censure. It is a sharp rite of transition, at once moving him out of his normal position in society and transferring him into a distinct deviant role. . . . Perhaps the most obvious example of a commitment ceremony is the criminal trial, with its elaborate formality and ritual pageantry. . . .

Now an important feature of these ceremonies in our own culture is that they are almost irreversible. Most provisional roles conferred by society—like those of the student or conscripted soldier, for example—include some kind of terminal ceremony to mark the individual's movement back out of the role once its temporary advantages have been exhausted. But the roles allotted to the deviant seldom make allowance for this type of passage. He is ushered into the deviant position by a decisive and often dramatic ceremony, yet is retired from it with hardly a word of public notice. . . . Nothing has happened to cancel out the stigmas imposed upon him by earlier commitment ceremonies. . . .

Although Erikson's remarks apply most directly to the adult offender, and the "ritual pageantry" of the criminal court, they have some relevance here. Juvenile proceedings, in large part, are insulated from public view. Yet, as Lemert (1970:142) suggests, the official processing of juveniles is problematic because the "insight and social stamina to manage stigma are not given to many people—least of all to the kind of children most likely to come to the juvenile court."

As Erikson (1964) suggests, the transition from a nondelinquent to a delinquent status is much like passing through a one-way door. Once entered, the task of cancelling out the stigma imposed by the court ceremony is not a simple one. Certainly, there are no equivalent rites-of-passage to signify the individual's movement back out of the status, and if such a transition does occur it is usually due much more to the vagaries of such things as maturational reform than to the formal acts of the legal system and community.

It has been theorized (Lemert, 1951:70-71) that this process can lead to a cyclical escalation of both delinquent activity and severity of sanctioning. Upon being defined as delinquent, the individual may tend to adopt a deviant self-image and thus to commit more illegal acts. These, in turn, could lead to further sanctioning which, again, might precipitate further delinquency. The process might continue until the delinquent fully accepts his status and the role behavior associated with it.

To determine whether this and similar consequences actually occur, analyses on two levels are needed. First, on a structural level, attention could be paid to the guiding philosophy of the juvenile court and whether, in actual operation, this philosophy is implemented. There may be countervailing forces that make such implementation difficult. Second, at an action level, there is an interplay of structural and situational factors between juveniles and officials about which little is known. This interplay is also in need of attention.

Structural Level

Since the inception of the juvenile court in Cook County, Illinois, in 1899, a philosophy has emerged which emphasizes the particular needs of juvenile law-violators. Unlike adult courts, the juvenile court is supposedly less concerned with determining guilt and meting out punishment than with diagnosing and treating the causes of juvenile misbehavior. Constructed on a medical model, the prevailing philosophy emphasizes the use of clinicians and case workers in the discovery of personal ills and the prescription of remedial solutions. It is intended to combine scientific, legal, and humanistic resources rather than to be punitive in its orientation.

Criticisms of the court, as most people know, are increasingly common, both with respect to its philosophy (Platt, 1969) and because its philosophy is inconsistent with actual practice (Dunham, 1958; Lemert, 1970). The omnibus nature of juvenile statutes results in such a wide latitude of discretion that the court is placed in the position of sitting in judgment, not only on the behavior of the child but on his morals, and those of his parents as well (President's Commission on Law Enforcement, 1967:25). Cases in court are often poorly prepared and presented, and the personal idiosyncracies of judges often make decision-making anything but consistent (George, 1968). Reflecting these problems, recent Supreme Court decisions would suggest that the juvenile may have gotten the worst of two possible worlds: he has received neither the constitutional protections afforded the adult relative to the establishment of guilt and sanction, nor has he received the help supposedly inherent in the special provisions of the juvenile court (George, 1968).

In noting these limitations, critics often assume that they are due primarily to inadequacies in the training of juvenile judges, to excessive case loads, or to the imposition of codes of juvenile conduct by "moral entrepreneurs" that are more harmful than helpful. While these factors are, in part, at fault, there are other considerations on a cultural level to which little attention has been given.

A major one has to do with the social functions of punishment. In our preoccupation with the more obvious factors that impinge upon court practices and decision-making, especially those that are punitive in character and harmful to the individual, we have tended to ignore the possible social functions that such practices may play. A number of theorists over the years have noted that punishment may serve as a means of maintaining social solidarity by setting the normative boundaries of society.

The delinquent, like the criminal, is a means of dramatizing the threat of crime to the stability of society. Coser (1962:72) points out that just "as bodily pain serves as a danger signal, calling for the mobilization of energies against the source of disease, so crime . . . alerts the body social and leads to the mobilization of otherwise inactive defense mechanisms." As Durkheim (1947:102) put it, "Crime brings together upright consciences and concentrates them." Or, as Mead (1928:591) says, "The criminal . . . is responsible for a sense of solidarity. . . . The attitude of hostility toward the lawbreaker has the unique advantage of uniting all members of the community." By using punishment as a reaction to crime, society tries to neutralize the offender as a potential source of infection for others.

Put in social system terms, punishment serves a boundary-maintaining function for society. "The only material," says Erikson (1964:13-14)

found in a system for marking boundaries is the behavior of its participants; and the kinds of behavior which best perform this function are often deviant, since they represent the most extreme variety of conduct to be found within the experience of the group. . . . Each time the group censures some act of deviation, then, it sharpens the authority of the violated norms and declares again where the boundaries of the group are located."

In a very real sense, therefore, the community may have greater investment in keeping the offender in a deviant status than in changing that status. That may be why we have elaborate rites of passage leading into the deviant role but none leading out of it. The offender, in one sense, may be of greater worth to society as a deviant than as a conformist.

Generally, such remarks have greater reference to adult rather than juvenile lawbreakers. However, an important empirical question is how much they may be applicable to juveniles as well. Obviously, the question is a difficult one to study, but there are some clues. In a national opinion poll, the Joint Commission on Correctional Manpower and Training (1968) discovered that the public was not only highly ambivalent regarding the administration of justice but unable to recognize the contradictions inherent in their own opinions. "One must conclude," says the report, ". . . that the public feels the system is currently inadequate. At the same time, the public is not eager to bring about change."

While it is difficult to be certain, it is possible that the public's ambivalence is rooted, in part, in the cultural tradition that punishment as well as treatment are useful societal goals. If true, strong forces are still at work in support of a punitive reaction by the juvenile court.

Juvenile court reforms and philosophy, with their emphasis upon individualized treatment, were supposed to be an antedote to such punishment traditions. Yet, paradoxically, they may have reinforced, not weakened them. The reason, as Toby (1964) notes, is that the treatment, like the punishment philosophy, still tends to place the primary source of difficulty within the offender. As a consequence, it has never seriously challenged the social functions of punishment. Whether the offender's behavior is defined as wicked, and in need of punishment, or pathological and in need of treatment, the result is much the same. Removing the offender for purposes of "treatment" has the same social function as removing him for purposes of punishment: it validates the diagnosis of undesirability and excuses basic institutions—school, church, work, and community—from responsibility. The notion of some kind of relatively permanent malignancy is reaffirmed.

In an effort to outline and understand the structural parameters within which the juvenile court must work, it would seem wise to consider such factors as these as well as those that are more concrete and easily documented. One cannot give substance to the character of the legal system until its relationships to the broader culture are more clearly delineated.

On the operational level, Matza (1964) has suggested that juvenile court judges are caught in the midst of a variety of societal cross-pressures which in turn put the juvenile court in a state of delicate equilibrium. One of the judge's major problems is to decide which clients are to be dismissed or "rendered unto probation," thus satisfying the demands for mercy by humanitarians and professional underlings, and which are to be "rendered unto prison," thus satisfying the demands of those indignant groups in society who demand punishment. In the context of such pressures, Matza (1964:124-126) suggests that the court employs at least three criteria in making its dispositions. The principle of offense (e.g., the more serious the crime, the more severe the disposition); the doctrine of parental sponsorship (e.g., children who lack a stable home environment are in need of protection by the state); and considerations of residential availability (e.g., the bedspace available in different types of correctional alternatives)—all have a bearing on dispositions.

Thus, if a juvenile has committed a serious offense, and risk of public scandal is high, he is liable to be incarcerated. If, however, the risk of scandal is moderate, the decision will depend upon the nature of his parental sponsorship. If his sponsorship is adequate, then he will probably receive probation; if it is inadequate, then the chances are increased that he will be incarcerated. Finally, if the risk of public scandal is low, then only those offenders with virtually no parental sponsorship will go to an institution—providing, of course, that bedspace is available.

Action Level

The relatively small body of available research on the juvenile court at the action level suggests that the decisions of the court are constrained both by its ties to the larger community and culture, and by a series of situational and personal factors as well. Terry (1967), for example, found that the severity of disposition meted out by the juvenile court is most strongly a function of the amount of deviance engaged in by offenders. However, he also found slight positive associations between severity of disposition and unfavorability of social biography, age, and involvement with adult offenders, and slight negative associations with the seriousness of the offense and the number of individuals involved in that offense.

Emerson's (1969) research has suggested that the nature of courtroom ceremony and demeanor have a great deal to do with whether or not juveniles are labeled as delinquents. He found that in the courtroom setting, juveniles are faced with a very rigid set of behavioral expectations. They must stand only when appropriate, use honorary terms of address, speak politely and in complete sentences, and convey a properly deferential and remorseful attitude. Deviation from these expectations increases the probability of a youth's incurring a judge's wrath and of being formally labeled delinquent. Accordingly, the courtroom situation creates the following dilemma:

A youth who has any reservations about the role of contrite wrongdoer in which he finds himself encounters a basic dilemma. In adopting the penitant stance in order to protect character and save face from the full implications of his misconduct, he must become personally involved in his own discrediting; but if he tries to maintain a sense of personal dignity by showing distance from this role he is apt to face severe sanctioning and perhaps more fundamental discrediting at the hands of the court [Emerson, 1969:197].

Lines for Further Inquiry

Given these few examples, it is clear that empirical study along three dimensions might be useful. The first has to do with the major functions of the juvenile court. Besides some effort to determine whether the actual operation of the court is consistent with its avowed philosophy, insofar as the individual child is concerned, attention might be paid to its social functions as well. Regardless of imperfections on the level of the individual, it would be important to learn to what extent the court performs functions essential to the existence of society as an organized entity. Does the court have a boundary-maintaining function, as some theorists have suggested? To what extent is there public and cultural support for a court model favoring punishment and deterrence as well as treatment and help? Part of our failure to explain why actual juvenile court operation seems to be so much at odds with its humanitarian philosophy may be due, in part, to the fact that it is attempting to incorporate and perform several functions that are inherently contradictory.

The second dimension has to do with the legal and conceptual frameworks within which the court operates. Does juvenile court law represent a biased middle-class morality legislated and implemented by middle-class persons to the detriment of less powerful subgroups and classes? If this seems to be the case, what are the implications for making changes that might seriously affect the possible boundary-maintaining functions of current legal rules and court practices?

On the conceptual level—the level at which childhood problems are defined by court personnel—serious questions have been raised. Does the medical model upon which court adjudication is based—with its elaborate diagnostic frameworks, assumed causalities, and treatment alternatives—provide a logically and empirically validated set of guidelines for decision-making? Many critics would answer no, but that answer scarcely provides viable alternatives. Besides the need to document current inadequacies, there is the more difficult problem of identifying and testing approaches that might be more successful.

A third dimension has to do with the courtroom itself, broadly conceived, as an arena for action. Which characteristics of juveniles and officials seem to be crucial in producing certain kinds of outcome? To what extent do the social biographies and personal attributes of the principal actors enter into the picture? To what extent do situational factors, within the context of courtroom ceremonies, affect outcomes? Finally, to what extent are the pressures of outside factors—cultural traditions, current fads, and social pressures—discernible in the actions that are taken? All of these are vital components of a setting in which personal and social factors come together in a way that is unique and potentially productive of a great deal of information.

Consequences of Labeling

The final arena requiring attention has to do with the role of official action and labeling in the generation of new delinquent acts. Once an individual has been officially labeled, there are distinct possibilities that he will be further socialized in such a way that his violations will increase. Without going into the voluminous literature on this subject, especially that having to do with the correctional experience, it may be sufficient to note that once a deviant act has been committed, and once an individual has been defined socially as a delinquent, then escalation to a deviant identity becomes possible. As Lofland (1969) points out, the escalation situation par excellence is one in which the individual encounters both conventionals and deviants on a day-to-day basis, and in which there are unanimous imputations of deviance from both types of persons. Research evidence indicates that this occurs.

Schwartz and Skolnick (1962) found that the further offenders had been involved in the legal process (even though these offenders were actually hypothetical), the less inclined employers were to hire them. The employers were imputing a deviant identity to persons whom they had never seen, and thus would not offer them employment. Similarly, among peers a delinquent is subjected to considerable "masculinity" and "membership" anxiety, as Matza (1964:53-58) puts it, over the role he should play. When in the company of other delinquent boys, he may not only feel that he has to live up to minimal delinquent expectations but to appear more delinquent than he actually is, just as people in church often feel they have to appear more holy than they actually are. In other words, the possibility is strong among delinquents that a mutual misconception predisposes the individual to exhibit, even adopt a deviant identity, that, in part, he does not believe in. In a sense, he may become increasingly delinquent more in response to role expectations than to a strong, personal conviction that he is, and should remain, criminal.

As a final line of investigation, therefore, it would be important to be more precise about the extent to which court processing initiates and perpetuates the development of delinquent careers and identities. Are such processes essentially irreversible, or are there rites-of-passage in a reverse direction—from the status of delinquent to nondelinquent? Surprisingly little systematic attention has been paid to this matter, either to isolate those factors that might now be in operation, to see whether others might be developed, or to learn what types of persons might be most in need of them.

Conclusion

To sum up, two general lines of investigation have been suggested in this and preceding chapters. The first would be concerned with law-violating behavior which could be studied on two levels of analysis. One would be organizational. A series of studies could be devoted to an identification of the way the primary socializing institutions and illegitimate structures in neighborhoods of different types interact with the monolithic system of formal norms to set the stage for the commission of illegal acts. Many studies along this line have been conducted, but what is lacking are definitive means for relating them in some typological system that would provide empirical rather than impressionistic criteria for predicting differential rates and patterns of law violation in different neighborhoods, communities, and subcultures.

A second level of analysis could be concerned with the action situation. This situation is one in which the potential for law violation is high, and in which there are usually two or more actors whose individual motivations and strategies are of crucial importance. While these motivations and strategies are undoubtedly affected by the nature of societal and local organization, social scientists, as yet, have not been able to build adequate bridges between the two. The actor's motivations constitute an intervening variable between social organization, on one hand, and actual behavior on the other. Consequently, research on the action level, despite its difficulty, might be most valuable because of its concern with linking these sets of variables. The prediction of individual behavior depends upon it.

Then, as this chapter has suggested, more study of the juvenile justice system itself is required if official delinquency is to be understood. Because official delinquents comprise only a fraction of all law violators, far more empirical information is required on the traditions, practices, and policies that lead to official labeling. The factors that combine to produce official delinquents are obviously different and more complex than those that combine to produce law violators.

Until greater substance is acquired in both arenas, it will be difficult to determine whether deterministic frameworks can be applied to the under-standing of delinquency, and whether general theory in the area is possible.

Appendixes

Appendix 1: Construction of Delinquency Indexes

This appendix describes the twelve different indexes of delinquency that were developed for this study, and briefly summarizes the literature that is pertinent to them. Generally, the indexes can be divided into two major categories. Category 1 indexes are those that measure degrees of delinquency, either in terms of frequency or seriousness. A high score on these scales indicates a high degree of delinquency, while a low score indicates the opposite. Category 2 indexes, by contrast, are designed to reflect offense patterns. A high score on one of them indicates a high proportion of the types of offenses in question. The way in which these scales were constructed, along with some pertinent literature references are described below.

Category 1 Indexes

In all, six indexes in this category were constructed.

Number of Offenses. The first was a simple measure of number of delinquent acts. An enumeration of all offenses appearing on each subject's record was used as a delinquency indicator. Besides its utility for summarizing total number of official acts, such an indicator has proven useful to other investigators. Martin and Klein (1965), for example, discovered that, for the purpose of discriminating between "core" and "fringe" members of black gangs in Los Angeles, frequency was a better measure than such measures of seriousness as the indexes developed by Sellin and Wolfgang (1964), Robin (1967), McEachern and Bauzer (1967) or the Uniform Crime Reports.

Seriousness. Two indicators of seriousness were derived. They were based upon a scale developed in the following manner: official records of juvenile offense behavior were studied and thirty-one of the most common offenses were selected. A list of these offenses was then submitted to officers in the juvenile divisions of the Los Angeles City Police Department and the Los Angeles County Sheriff's Department, and to thirteen judges and referees in the Los Angeles Juvenile Court. Each official was then asked to rate the seriousness of each offense on a five-point scale, ranging from 0 (least serious) to 5 (most serious). The resulting ratings are displayed in Table A1-1. Although court officials tended to rate offenses as somewhat less serious than officers, there was a rather high degree of similarity with respect to ranking.

On the basis of this scale, the two seriousness indicators were developed. The first measures the *average* seriousness of all offenses for which an individual was charged as shown in the formula

$$\sum_{i=1}^{N} \frac{F_i \times S_i}{N}$$

Table A1-1

Offenses Arrayed by Average Seriousness Rating

Offenses	Judgments			
	LAPD	Sheriff	Juvenile Court	Total
	$N=17$	$N=20$	$N=13$	$N=50$
Aggravated assault; possibility of great harm; use of weapons	4.9	4.8	4.5	4.7
Child Molesting	5.0	4.7	4.5	4.7
Forceable rape	5.0	4.6	4.6	4.7
Arson	4.9	4.6	4.5	4.7
Narcotics use (excluding glue)	4.8	4.5	4.5	4.6
Robbery	4.7	4.8	4.5	4.6
Drunk driving	4.0	3.6	3.8	3.7
Possession of dangerous weapons	3.9	3.6	3.5	3.7
Breaking and entering; burglary	4.4	3.7	2.7	3.7
Glue sniffing	4.0	3.5	2.8	3.5
Association with known users	3.9	3.4	2.9	3.4
Automobile theft	4.1	3.4	2.8	3.4
Non-forceable homosexual behavior	3.7	3.6	2.7	3.4
Probation violation; i.e., "ineffective rehabilitation	3.7	3.6	2.5	3.3
Grand theft (greater than $50 and excluding auto)	3.7	3.4	2.5	3.3
Forgery (fictitious checks)	3.6	2.9	3.0	3.1
Runaway from correctional program	3.5	3.0	2.8	3.0
Assault and battery	3.5	2.7	2.9	3.0
Incorrigibility: defiance of teachers, parents and others	3.7	2.7	2.7	3.0
Damaging property; malicious mischief	2.8	2.4	2.3	2.5
Non-forceable heterosexual behavior	2.1	2.6	1.8	2.2

Table A1-1 *(Cont.)*

Offenses	Judgments			
	LAPD	Sheriff	Juvenile Court	Total
	N=17	N=20	N=13	N=50
Liquor violations (possession drinking)	2.4	2.2	2.2	2.2
Fighting; disturbing peace	2.6	2.0	2.0	2.1
Runaway from home	2.6	1.8	1.8	2.1
Petty theft	2.8	1.7	1.9	2.1
Truancy from school	2.3	1.6	2.0	2.0
Gambling, loitering, improper companions	2.2	2.0	1.5	1.9
Driving without a license	1.5	1.8	1.8	1.7
Other traffic violations	1.8	1.2	1.6	1.5
Curfew violations	1.7	1.2	1.1	1.4
Smoking	1.1	.5	.3	.7

where F_i = frequency of ith offense
S_i = seriousness of ith offense
N = number of offenses

The second measure simply took account of the scale ranking of the *most serious* offense in his record, which was then used as a separate index.

While space does not permit a detailed description of all the seriousness measures that have been developed by others, the reader may wish to compare our two simple indicators with some of the more prominent ones: (1) the Sellin and Wolfgang index (1964), which was conceived as an alternative to the Uniform Crime Report index and thus was administratively oriented; (2) the Robin (1967) and McEachern and Bauzer (1967) indexes, which utilized the probability of official response to an act (arrest or court hearing) as a measure of its seriousness—i.e., the greater the probability of response, the greater the seriousness; or (3) the Shannon index (1968), which ranks offenses in geometric progression based upon the frequency with which police contact for each offense occurred in the community, the assumption being that the less frequency the greater the seriousness.

Factor-Analysis Scales. An effort was made to derive additional empirical scales using factor analysis techniques. Before describing the results of that effort, however, a brief review of the literature will indicate the prior difficulties that have been encountered, not only in the use of factor analysis but scaling techniques as well.

Since they occurred first, consider scaling techniques. The most successful endeavors have occurred using self-reported delinquency data. Scales along two general dimensions have been developed, the first involving juvenile-status offenses and the second, theft offenses. Both Nye and Short (1957; 1958) and Erickson and Empey (1965) developed independent scales involving such offenses as petty theft, truancy, defying authority, and destroying property. Erickson and Empey (1965) also developed two theft scales, one a *general* theft scale and the second a *seriousness* theft scale. This development was corroborated in part by Scott (1956) who developed a theft scale for college students.

By contrast, Shannon (1968) considered his efforts to develop an acceptable scale, using official data, a failure. He could not obtain acceptable levels of reproducibility. Thus, it is questionable whether official data will lend themselves to this task.

Efforts using factor-analysis techniques have also been somewhat contradictory. Short and Strodtbeck (1965: 87-89) were successful in extracting and rotating five factors from the self-reported behaviors of members of delinquent gangs. Quay and Blumer (1963) were also successful, although they used the official records of delinquents who had been committed at least once to a correctional institution. However, if one examines the two sets of factors, he discovers little overlap between them. The Short and Strodtbeck (1965:87-89) factors included the following:

1. "Conflict": individual and gang fighting, carrying concealed weapons, and assault.
2. "Stable Corner Activities": individual and team sports, social activities, and gambling.
3. "Stable Sex": sexual intercourse, statutory rape, signifying, hanging out, alcohol.
4. "Retreatism": homosexuality, fathering a bastard, common-law marriage.
5. "Authority Protest": auto theft, driving without a license, public nuisance, theft, alcohol, runaway.

By contrast, the Quay-Blumer (1963:275-276) factors were:

1. "Truancy": truancy, bi-polar with auto theft.
2. "Impulsive thrill seeking": driving without a license, reckless driving, alcohol.
3. "Personal aggression": assault, disorderly conduct, alcohol.
4. "Impersonal Aggression": assault, disorderly conduct alcohol.
5. "Youthful": runaway, bicycle theft, bi-polar with possessing dangerous weapons, and stolen goods.

Thus, although both groups of investigators were successful in extracting empirical factors, it is not clear why the factors differed so much, i.e., whether differences were due to the methods involved, to a sampling of different populations, or to the fact that the factors were based, in one case, upon self-reported data and in the other, upon official data. As a consequence, progress to date is not reassuring. Many questions remain unanswered.

Even so, the compelling need to isolate valid and useful measures of delinquency remains so great that effort was made in this case to derive additional factor analysis scales. It was hoped that some similarities with previous efforts might be discovered, especially since we were using official data.

The principal component method of factor extraction was utilized with a varimax solution for orthogonal rotation. Communality estimates were based upon the multiple correlations of each offense predicted from all others. We extracted and rotated two, three, four, five, and six factors in separate runs and arbitrarily selected the six factor set shown in Table A1-2 as most representative of the patterns that were involved. Only those items loading .30 or higher were utilized in assigning factor scores. Furthermore, only the first three of the six factors were utilized for measurement purposes, since they seemed to have the clearest and most relevant meanings.

It will be observed in Table A1-2 that the first factor seems to represent a general *theft* trait: burglary, petty theft, auto theft, and grand theft, all with factor loadings higher than .30. What is significant about this trait is that it is one that both Short and Strodtbeck (1965:90) and Quay and Blumer (1963:276) failed to isolate in their analyses but that seemed important with these samples of official offenders.

The second factor we have called the *hell-raising* factor because it includes disturbing the peace, alcohol, assault, gambling, and curfew violations, all of which had factor loadings in excess of .30. While this factor does not overlap to any extent with any of the Short-Strodtbeck factors that were based on self-report data, it is similar to Quay and Blumer's "personal aggression" factor—assault, disorderly conduct, and alcohol—which was also based on official data.

The third factor, containing only two offense loadings greater than .30, we have called the *incorrigibility* factor, since those two were truancy and malicious mischief. This, again, bears little relation to the Short and Strodtbeck factors, but may be similar to Quay and Blumer's "truancy" factor. Thus, although our factors were far from confirmatory of previous ones, there were enough similarities to suggest the possibility that empirically derived measures of this type may have some predictive utility.

In order to utilize the factors in our analyses, factor scores for each individual were calculated according to the following formula:

$$\sum_{i=1}^{N} F_{ij} X_i$$

where X_i is the frequency of occurrence of the ith offense and F_{ij} is the factor

Table A1-2

Factor Matrices

Offense	Factor Loadings					
	I Theft	II Hell-Raising	III Incorrigibility	IV	V	VI
Burglary	.51	−.03	.10	−.03	−.09	−.02
Petty theft	.48	.04	.28	.14	.07	.02
Auto theft	.36	.08	−.15	.11	.19	−.07
Grand theft	.33	.07	.11	−.03	.05	.07
Disturbing peace	−.07	.39	.14	−.07	.06	.01
Liquor	−.02	.38	.25	.05	.14	−.18
Assault/Battery	.00	.36	−.06	.02	−.10	.05
Gambling, etc.[a]	.13	.32	.06	−.24	−.02	−.06
Curfew	.18	.32	.16	.21	.07	−.14
Malicious mischief	.15	.13	.34	−.02	.11	−.15
Truancy	.02	.11	.30	.02	.05	.00
Traffic	−.04	.07	.10	−.38	.19	.06
Runaway (home)	.02	.03	.07	.31	.02	.01
Hit-run	.04	−.03	−.04	−.04	.31	.00
Arson	−.01	−.06	.00	−.01	−.02	−.33
Sex Offenses	−.01	.10	−.03	−.08	−.13	−.27
Narcotics	.15	.27	−.11	.09	−.09	.04
Probation violation	.05	−.04	.06	.11	−.11	.11
Dangerous weapon	.04	−.04	.01	.05	.26	.12
Incorrigible	−.19	.01	.09	.26	−.06	.09
Runaway (Institution)	.15	.06	−.02	.12	−.09	.08
W.I.C.	−.01	.01	−.04	.10	.02	.02
Destitute	−.06	−.05	−.08	.02	.03	−.02
Robbery	.07	.11	−.24	.04	.08	.09

Table A1-2 *(Cont.)*

Offense	Factor Loadings					
	I Theft	II Hell-Raising	III Incorrigibility	IV	V	VI
Forgery	.06	.01	.18	.00	−.06	.02
Defiance	−.03	.05	.01	.09	.26	.01
Smoking	.10	−.05	.21	.06	.19	−.01
Murder	−.03	−.02	−.02	−.01	−.01	.00

aAlso includes loitering and improper companions.

loading of the ith offense on the jth factor. Recalling that only those items loading .30 or higher were utilized, the following is an example of the way the scoring was applied. On the theft scale, an individual committing a single petty theft (.48), a single burglary (.51), and a single auto theft (.36) would receive a score of .48 +.51 +.36, or 1.35. Or, on the hell-raising scale, a person with a record of disturbing the peace (.39) and gambling (.32) would receive a score of .71.

The three factor indexes, along with our index of offense frequency and the two indexes of seriousness, constituted the Category 1 indicators that we used in our test of theory.

Category 2 Indexes

Adult/Juvenile Index. The first of the Category 2 indexes, we have labeled a adult/juvenile index. Adult-status offenses comprise all offenses that, whether engaged in by juvenile or adult, would constitute violations of the law. Juvenile-status offenses, by contrast, are those that are proscribed *only for juveniles*—i.e., incorrigibility, truancy, running away, alcohol, etc (cf. Sellin and Wolfgang, 1964:72).

The grounds for developing such an index are inherent in a growing body of writings, all of which argue that juveniles should not be prosecuted for offenses for which adults could not be prosecuted (cf. Kvaraceus, 1964; Morris, 1966). Such offenses should be defined as nonlegal in character and handled in other ways by educational and welfare agencies. Consequently, there seemed to be merit in attempting to assess, in this test of theory, whether the antecedents associated with adult-status offenses might differ in some substantive way from juvenile offenses. Despite the fact that any such analysis would be beclouded by the possible overlap between causal antecedents and official decision-making, especially with respect to juvenile status offenses, the existence of significant differences would provide better grounds for assessing findings.

In dealing with repeat offenders, as this study did, it is rare that one finds an individual whose official offenses are totally juvenile in nature. Consequently, the score for any individual on the adult/juvenile index was obtained as follows:

$$\frac{A}{A + J}$$

where A indicates the sum of adult status offenses and J indicates the sum of juvenile status offenses only. In other words, his score would be interpreted simply as the proportion of all his offenses that are adult in status. A high score would indicate that they were largely of adult status, while a low score would indicate that they were juvenile. It was our hope that emergent scores would enable us to determine whether different antecedents were associated with adult-status or juvenile-status patterns.

Felony/Misdemeanor Index. The second Category 2 index is designed to shed further light upon the universalistic end of the offense continuum. As its name implies, it provides a measure of offenses according to their legal classification in the California Penal Code.

It is operationalized as follows:

$$\frac{F}{F + M}$$

where F indicates the sum of felonies and M the sum of misdemeanors. The score for any individual is represented by the proportion of all legally classifiable crimes (in the prima facie sense) that are felonies. Thus, this index is interpreted in the same way as the adult/juvenile index.

Subcultural Indexes. Three subcultural indexes were devised according to which delinquent offenses were classified as either criminal, conflict, or retreatist. The construction of these indexes was given impetus by the work of Cloward and Ohlin (1960:9), who theorized that delinquent acts might be classified according to the subcultures that give them meaning. Thus, according to their scheme, such acts as theft, extortion, and other illegal means of securing income would characterize a *criminal* subculture; a *retreatist* subculture would be characterized largely by drug consumption; and a *conflict* subculture by the manipulation of violence.[a]

Following the lead provided by Cloward and Ohlin, we developed three

---

[a]Attempts to locate gangs which devote themselves primarily to one or the other of these orientations have not proven universally successful. Short and Strodtbeck (1965:10-13, 90) had difficulty in locating such singularly focused gangs, while Spergel (1964), and Kobrin, Puntil, and Peluso (1967) had somewhat better success. Nevertheless, the fact that gangs are not readily classified according to subculture does not necessarily preclude the possibility that individuals and their acts may be so classified.

subcultural indexes. However, the offenses included in them may differ somewhat from what they would have envisioned, especially the *retreatist* index that included, in addition to drug-related offenses, such things as running away and truancy. The *criminal* index, however, included only criminal offenses like burglary, theft of various kinds, robbery, and forgery, while the *conflict* index included such things as defiance of authority, assault, disturbing the peace, arson, and murder. A complete list of the items included in all three indexes may be found in Table A1-3.

These indexes, like those described previously, indicate the proportion of an individual's offenses that fell under one of the three types; i.e.,

$$\frac{X}{A + B + C}$$

where A, B, C indicate the sum of either criminal, conflict, or retreatist offenses and X either A, B, or C.

Instrumental-Expressive Index. The final Category 2 index is closely related to, and overlaps, the subcultural index and perhaps other indexes as well. It was suggested by Chambliss (1967) who postulated a single continuum according to which delinquent acts may be classified either as instrumental (i.e., crimes for profit) or expressive (apparently including both the retreatist and conflict orientations). Thus, the instrumental-expressive index is a simple measure of the proportion of all offenses that are crimes for profit, i.e.,

$$\frac{I}{N}$$

where I indicates the sum of instrumental offenses and N the total number of an individual's offenses.

In all, the Category 2 indexes include a adult/juvenile index, a felony/ misdemeanor index, three subcultural indexes, and an instrumental/expressive index. The kinds of offenses included in each of these indexes are summarized in Table A1-3 (page 194).

Table A1-3

Designation of Offenses Included in Category 2 Indexes

Offense	Adult/ Juv.	Fel./Misd.	Inst./Exp.	Subcult.
Burglary	Adult	Felony	Inst.	Crim.
Auto theft	Adult	—[a]	Inst.	Crim.
Petty theft	Adult	Misd.	Inst.	Crim.
Heterosexual behavior	Adult	—	Exp.	—
Narcotics	Adult	Felony	Exp.	Retreat.
Traffic	Adult	Misd.	Exp.	—
Probation violation	Adult	Felony	Exp.	—
Possessing weapon	Adult	Felony	Exp.	Conf.
Incorrigibility	Juvenile	—	Exp.	—
Runaway-home	Juvenile	—	Exp.	Retreat.
Runaway-Institution	Adult	Felony	Exp.	—
Truancy	Juvenile	—	Exp.	Retreat.
Alcohol	Juvenile	—	Exp.	Retreat.
Curfew	Juvenile	—	Exp.	—
Destitute	Juvenile	—	Exp.	—
Robbery	Adult	Felony	Inst.	Crim.
Grand theft	Adult	Felony	Inst.	Crim.
Forgery	Adult	Felony	Inst.	Crim.
Defiance	Juvenile	—	Exp.	Conf.
Smoking	Juvenile	—	Exp.	—
Hit-run	Adult	—	Exp.	—
Assault	Adult	Misd.	Exp.	Conf.
Disturbing peace	Adult	Misd.	Exp.	Conf.
Malicious mischief	Adult	Misd.	Exp.	Conf.
Gambling	Adult	Misd.	Exp.	—
Arson	Adult	Felony	Exp.	Conf.
Murder	Adult	Felony	Exp.	Conf.

[a]Offenses not classifiable on their "face" are indicated by —.

Appendix 2
Descriptive Characteristics
of Samples

Appendix 2

Table A2-1

Family Intact (Percentage of Samples)

	Los Angeles		Utah	
	Delinquents	Non-Delinquents	Delinquents	Non-Delinquents
Yes	36.0	81.2	65.3	84.0
No	58.4	17.6	32.9	15.0
No information	5.5	1.2	1.9	1.0
Total	99.9	100.0	100.1	100.0
N	233	85	213	100

Table A2-2

Rank of Father's Occupation (Percentage of Samples)

	Los Angeles		Utah	
	Delinquents	Non-Delinquents	Delinquents	Non-Delinquents
1	3.0	1.2	1.9	11.0
2	3.9	8.2	10.3	18.0
3	18.9	14.1	9.4	13.0
4	15.5	12.9	23.0	32.0
5	13.7	20.0	30.5	14.0
6	13.7	22.4	8.5	2.0
7	5.6	3.5	2.3	0.0
8–10	15.0	14.1	0.5	0.0
No information	10.7	3.5	13.6	10.0
Total	100.0	99.9	100.0	100.0
N	233	85	213	100

Table A2-3

Parents Get Along Together (Percentage of Samples)

	Los Angeles		Utah	
	Delinquents	Non-Delinquents	Delinquents	Non-Delinquents
Very well	20.2	45.9	39.4	53.0
Quite well	14.6	22.4	23.5	23.0
Average	20.6	24.7	16.4	16.0
Not so well	15.5	3.5	7.0	3.0
Not at all well	18.0	2.4	5.2	3.0
No information	11.2	1.2	8.5	2.0
Total	100.1	100.1	100.0	100.0
N	233	85	213	100

Table A2-4

Boy Gets Along with Parents (Percentage of Samples)

	Los Angeles		Utah	
	Delinquents	Non-Delinquents	Delinquents	Non-Delinquents
Very well	17.2	28.2	16.9	32.0
Quite well	18.9	25.9	33.3	41.0
Average	27.0	42.4	28.2	19.0
Not so well	28.3	3.5	13.1	5.0
Not at all well	7.7	0.0	5.2	1.0
No information	0.9	0.0	3.3	2.0
Total	100.0	100.0	100.0	100.0
N	233	85	213	100

Table A2-5

Left High School (Percentage of Samples)

	Los Angeles		Utah	
	Delinquents	Non-Delinquents	Delinquents	Non-Delinquents
Yes	68.2	25.9	62.4	6.0
No	29.6	74.1	35.7	93.0
No information	2.1	0.0	1.9	1.0
Total	99.9	100.0	100.0	100.0
N	233	85	213	100

Note: Utah subjects were asked, "Are you attending school now?; Los Angeles subjects were asked, "Did you leave school at anytime prior to now?" The Utah answers were thus reversed for this table.

Table A2-6

Grades in School (Percentage of Samples)

	Los Angeles		Utah	
	Delinquents	Non-Delinquents	Delinquents	Non-Delinquents
Mostly A's	0.9	10.6	1.9	13.0
Mostly B's	10.7	34.1	13.1	37.0
Mostly C's	45.1	45.9	37.1	41.0
Mostly D's	27.9	8.2	32.4	7.0
Mostly F's	7.3	0.0	8.0	1.0
No information	8.2	1.2	7.5	1.0
Total	100.1	100.0	100.0	100.0
N	233	85	213	100

Table A2-7

Won Award at School (Percentage of Samples)

	Los Angeles		Utah	
	Delinquents	Non-Delinquents	Delinquents	Non-Delinquents
Yes	47.6	45.9	25.8	30.0
No	49.8	50.6	65.7	67.0
No information	2.6	3.5	8.5	3.0
Total	100.0	100.0	100.0	100.0
N	233	85	213	100

Table A2-8

Boy Considers Self a Leader (Percentage of Samples)

	Los Angeles		Utah	
	Delinquents	Non-Delinquents	Delinquents	Non-Delinquents
Yes	21.9	21.2	11.7	19.0
No	42.1	35.3	45.1	29.0
Not sure	35.2	41.2	29.6	40.0
No information	0.9	2.4	13.6	12.0
Total	100.1	100.1	100.0	100.0
N	233	85	213	100

Table A2-9

Smartness Compared to Others (Percentage of Samples)

	Los Angeles		Utah	
	Delinquents	Non-Delinquents	Delinquents	Non-Delinquents
Smarter	18.9	28.2	10.3	9.0
About same	56.7	63.5	54.9	84.0
Inferior	6.9	2.5	15.0	4.0
No information	17.6	5.9	19.7	3.0
Total	100.1	100.1	99.9	100.0
N	233	85	213	100

Table A2-10

Rank of Occupational Aspiration (Percentage of Samples)

	Los Angeles		Utah	
	Delinquents	Non-Delinquents	Delinquents	Non-Delinquents
1	0.4	0.0	0.0	0.0
2	3.0	0.0	1.4	0.0
3	9.0	5.9	10.3	0.0
4	18.0	5.9	32.4	7.0
5	5.6	18.8	6.6	3.0
6	8.2	9.4	12.7	13.0
7	3.9	16.5	9.9	29.0
8-10	30.9	41.2	10.8	31.0
No information	21.0	2.4	16.0	17.0
Total	100.0	100.1	100.1	100.0
N	233	85	213	100

Table A2-11

Chances of Getting Aspired Occupation (Percentage of Samples)

	Los Angeles		Utah	
	Delinquents	Non-Delinquents	Delinquents	Non-Delinquents
Almost certain	22.3	23.5	16.0	18.0
Probably will	17.6	36.5	27.7	31.0
50-50 chance	37.3	29.4	37.1	31.0
Probably won't	8.2	5.9	6.6	7.0
Almost certainly won't	2.6	2.4	2.3	3.0
No information	12.0	2.4	10.3	10.0
Total	100.0	100.1	100.0	100.0
N	233	85	213	100

Table A2-12

Ever Fired from a Job (Percentage of Samples)

	Los Angeles		Utah	
	Delinquents	Non-Delinquents	Delinquents	Non-Delinquents
Yes	23.6	7.1	23.0	12.0
No	72.1	92.9	70.9	82.0
No information	4.3	0.0	6.1	6.0
Total	100.0	100.0	100.0	100.0
N	233	85	213	100

**Appendix 3
Path Coefficients for
Models I, II, III, and IV**

Table A3-1

Model I for the Los Angeles Sample

	(Strain and Achievement Treated as Exogenous, Delinquency as Endogenous)				(Delinquency Treated as Exogenous, Peer Identification as Endogenous)		
	Boy-Parent Harmony	Dropout	Grades	Fired from Job	Ace-in-the Hole	Sociability	Deviance
Average Seriousness	-.10 (.10)[a]	.30 (.30)	-.16 (-.16)	.10 (.10)	.68 (.65)	.40 (.47)	.47 (.41)
Most Serious	-.08	.32 (.33)	-.17 (-.18)	.12 (.12)	-.48 (-.41)	-.29 (-.37)	-.54 (-.44)
Adult/Juvenile	.04	.31 (.30)	-.16 (-.16)	.07	.20 (.22)	.09	-.08
Felony/Misd.	.02	.13 (.13)	-.14 (-.14)	.00	-.24 (-.25)	-.03	.14 (.10)
Instr./Express.	.07	.27 (.31)	-.09	.04	.00	.13 (.05)	.42 (.28)
Retreatism	-.22 (-.23)	.02	-.18 (-.21)	.08	.04	-.02	.07
Conflict	.05	.15 (.15)	-.02	.13 (.13)	.01	-.01	.26 (.24)
Criminalism	.04	.32 (.35)	-.06	.04	.05	-.09	-.08
Theft	.05	.25 (.26)	-.06	-.03	-.01	-.09	-.12 (-.09)
Hell-Raising	-.20 (-.20)	.13 (.13)	-.11 (-.11)	.09	.13 (.14)	.11 (.11)	.14 (.20)
Incorrigibility	.00	.13 (.13)	-.13 (-.13)	.04	.09	.05	.07
Number of Offenses	-.10 (-.10)	-.27 (.28)	-.13 (-.14)	.08	-.02	.02	.04

Note: The paths between achievement and strain are described in chapter 8.

[a]Figures in parentheses indicate revised paths computed after dropping those paths less than .10 in absolute value.

Table A3-2

Model I for the Utah Sample

	(Strain and Achievement Treated as Exogenous, Delinquency as Endogenous)				(Delinquency Treated as Exogenous, Peer Identification as Endogenous)		
	Boy-Parent Harmony	Dropout	Grades	Fired from Job	Ace-in-the Hole	Sociability	Deviance
Average Seriousness	-.21 (-.21)[a]	.10 (.10)	-.21 (-.21)	.04	.23 (.22)	-.06	.38 (.33)
Most Serious	-.15 (-.15)	.14 (.14)	-.28 (-.28)	.01	-.07	-.01	-.02
Adult/Juvenile	-.03	.01	-.08	.07	-.15 (-.16)	.10 (.10)	-.19 (-.21)
Felony/Misd.	-.07	.11 (.09)	-.13 (-.15)	-.09	.03	-.03	-.08
Inst./Express.	-.07	.10 (.08)	-.11 (-.13)	-.06	-.15 (-.24)	.37 (.20)	.49 (.47)
Retreatism	-.17 (-.18)	.01	-.28 (-.27)	-.04	.06	.31 (.22)	.05
Conflict	-.06	.09	-.12 (-.11)	.11 (.09)	-.10 (-.12)	.09	-.01
Criminalism	-.04	.13 (.12)	-.13 (-.14)	-.06	-.08	-.42 (-.32)	-.42 (-.41)
Theft	.00	.16 (.17)	-.15 (-.16)	.03	.04	-.01	-.18 (-.20)
Hell-Raising	-.04	.05	-.02 (-.20)	-.03	-.04	(.21)	-.14 (-.14)
Incorrigibility	-.08	.01	-.22 (-.25)	.08	.03	-.03	-.06
Number of Offenses	-.07	.16 (.15)	-.25 (-.27)	.10 (.10)	.13 (.17)	.19 (.09)	.25 (.25)

Note: The paths between achievement and strain are described in chapter 9.

[a] Figures in parentheses indicate revised paths computed after dropping those paths less than .10 in absolute value.

Table A3-3
Model II for the Los Angeles Sample

(Strain and Peer Identification Treated as Exogenous, Delinquency as Endogenous)

	Boy-Parent Harmony	Dropout	Fired from Job	Ace-in-the Hole	Sociability	Deviance
Average Seriousness	-.06	.33 (.35)	.09	.12 (.10)	-.07	.19 (.18)
Most Serious	-.06	.36 (.39)	.11 (.11)	.09	-.06	.15 (.16)
Adult/Juvenile	.07	.33 (.33)	.06	.10	-.04	.16 (.14)
Felony/Misd.	.05	.18 (.16)	-.02	-.04	-.03	.24 (.20)
Inst./Express.	.11 (.11)[a]	.27 (.28)	.02	.10 (.08)	-.06	.20 (.18)
Retreatism	-.25 (-.25)	.10 (.12)	.09	.05	-.06	.01
Conflict	.09	.14 (.12)	.10 (.11)	.03	-.07	.21 (.16)
Criminalism	.06	.32 (.33)	.03	.09	-.05	.11 (.10)
Theft	.06	.26 (.25)	-.04	.07	-.09	.11 (.06)
Hell-Raising	-.25 (.19)	.18 (.18)	.09	.07	.11 (.12)	.09
Incorrigibility	.01	.17 (.19)	.02	.06	-.05	.08
Number of Offenses	-.10 (-.11)	.32 (.34)	.07	.06	-.11 (-.11)	.11 (.14)

(Strain and Achievement Treated as Exogenous, Peer Identification as Endogenous)

	Boy-Parent Harmony	Dropout	Grades	Fired from Job
Ace-in-Hole	-.20 (-.20)	.20 (.24)	-.09	-.05
Sociability	-.21 (-.22)	.08	-.14 (-.17)	-.08
Deviance	-.20 (-.20)	.03	-.23 (-.26)	.09

Note: The paths between achievement and strain are described in chapter 8.
[a]Figures in parentheses indicate revised paths computed after dropping those paths less than .10 in absolute value.

208

Table A3-4
Model II for the Utah Sample

(Strain and Peer Identification Treated as Exogenous, Delinquency as Endogenous)

	Boy-Parent Harmony	Dropout	Fired from Job	Ace-in-the Hole	Sociability	Deviance
Average Seriousness	-.25 (-.25)[a]	.15 (.16)	.02	-.10 (-.11)	-.10 (-.10)	.21 (.21)
Most Serious	-.21 (-.18)	.21 (.19)	.00	-.09	-.08	.18 (.13)
Adult/Juvenile	-.05	.04	.06	-.17 (-.17)	.00	.12 (.14)
Felony/Misd.	-.11 (-.11)	.15 (.15)	-.10 (-.10)	-.02	-.16 (-.17)	.13 (.13)
Inst./Express.	-.11 (-.12)	.15 (.14)	-.08	-.14 (-.14)	-.17 (-.16)	.21 (.20)
Retreatism	-.16 (-.16)	.02	-.02	.05	.22 (.26)	-.04
Conflict	-.07	-.06	.11 (.10)	-.09	.11 (.10)	.02
Criminalism	-.10 (-.10)	.19 (.18)	-.08	-.12 (-.11)	-.19 (-.18)	.18 (.17)
Theft	-.03	.20 (.24)	-.03	.03	.04	.09
Hell-Raising	-.05	-.05	-.15 (-.15)	-.03	.30 (.30)	.01
Incorrigibility	-.10 (-.09)	.05	.10 (.10)	.00	.16 (.15)	-.04
Number of Offenses	-.08	.20 (.20)	.11 (.11)	.00	.10 (.15)	.05

(Strain and Achievement Treated as Exogenous, Peer Identification as Endogenous)

	Boy-Parent Harmony	Dropout	Grades	Fired from Job
Ace-in-Hole	-.14 (-.14)	.17 (.16)	-.17 (-.17)	-.06
Sociability	-.26 (-.27)	.12 (.11)	-.25 (-.25)	-.05
Deviance	-.28 (-.28)	.17 (.17)	-.17 (-.17)	.03

Note: The paths between achievement and strain are described in chapter 9.
[a]Figures in parentheses indicate revised paths computed after dropping those paths less than .10 in absolute value.

Table A3-5

Model III for the Los Angeles Sample

	(Achievement and Strain and Peer Identification Treated as Exogenous, Delinquency as Endogenous)						
	Boy-Parent Harmony	Dropout	Grades	Fired from Job	Ace-in-the Hole	Sociability	Deviance
Average							
Seriousness	−.06	.28 (.29)	−.12 (−.13)	.09	.12 (.10)	−.07	.17 (.16)
Most Serious	−.05	.30 (.32)	−.14 (−.15)	.10 (.10)	.09	−.07	.12 (.13)
Adult/Juvenile	.08	.30 (.28)	−.12 (−.12)	.06	.10 (.07)	−.04	.14 (.12)
Felony/Misd.	.05	.14 (.16)	−.09	−.02	−.05	−.04	.23 (.20)
Inst./Express.	.11 (.11)[a]	.25 (.28)	−.05	.02	.10	−.07	.19 (.18)
Retreatism	−.24 (−.23)	.03	−.19 (−.21)	.09	.05	−.06	−.02
Conflict	.08	.14 (.12)	.02	.10 (.11)	.03	−.07	.21 (.16)
Criminalism	.06	.30 (.33)	−.04	.03	.09	−.06	.10 (.10)
Theft	.06	.24 (.25)	−.04	−.05	.07	−.09	.10 (.06)
Hell-Raising	.21 (.21)	.13 (.13)	−.10 (−.10)	.09	.07	.11 (.10)	.09
Incorrigibility	.02	.12 (.13)	−.12 (−.13)	.01	.06	−.06	.06
Number of Offenses	−.10 (−.11)	.27 (.29)	−.12 (−.15)	.07	.06	−.12 (−.05)	.09

Note: The paths between achievement and strain, and strain and peer identification are described in chapter 9.

[a]Figures in parentheses indicate revised paths computed after dropping those paths less than .10 in absolute value.

Table A3-6

Model III for the Utah Sample

	(Achievement and Strain and Peer Identification Treated as Exogenous, Delinquency as Endogenous)						
	Boy-Parent Harmony	Dropout	Grades	Fired from Job	Ace-in-the Hole	Sociability	Deviance
Average Seriousness	-.21 (-.21)[a]	.11 (.11)	-.24 (-.24)	.02	-.12 (-.12)	-.15 (-.15)	.19 (.19)
Most Serious	-.16 (-.16)	.15 (.15)	-.30 (-.30)	-.01	-.11 (-.11)	-.14 (-.14)	.16 (.16)
Adult/Juvenile	-.03	.02	-.09	.06	-.18 (-.17)	-.02	.11 (.14)
Felony/Misd.	-.09	.12 (.10)	-.17 (-.18)	-.11 (-.11)	-.04	-.19 (-.19)	.12 (.13)
Inst./Express.	-.09	.12 (.09)	-.15 (-.16)	-.09	-.15 (-.14)	-.19 (-.17)	.20 (.21)
Retreatism	-.13 (-.13)	-.03	-.23 (-.22)	-.02	.04	.27 (.20)	-.06
Conflict	-.05	-.08	-.11 (-.13)	.10 (.08)	-.10 (-.07)	.09	.02
Criminalism	-.07	.16 (.13)	-.18 (-.19)	-.09	-.13 (-.12)	-.22 (-.20)	.16 (.17)
Theft	-.01	.17 (.17)	-.17 (-.16)	.02	-.04	-.07	.08
Hell-Raising	-.04	-.06	.14 (.14)	-.14 (-.14)	.03	.25 (.25)	-.01
Incorrigibility	-.07	.01	-.20 (-.21)	.09	-.01	.13 (.11)	-.05
Number of Offenses	-.05	.15 (.15)	-.24 (-.27)	.11 (.10)	-.02	.05	.03

Note: The paths between achievement and strain, and strain and peer identification are described in chapter 9.
[a]Figures in parentheses indicate revised paths computed after dropping those paths less than .10 in absolute value.

Table A3-7
Model IV for the Los Angeles Sample

	(Strain Treated as Endogenous, Delinquency as Exogenous)			(Peer Identification Treated as Endogenous with Delinquency and Strain as Exogenous)		
	Boy-Parent Harmony	Dropout	Fired from Job	Ace-in-the Hole	Sociability	Deviance
Average Seriousness	-.52 (-.51)[a]	.06	-.14 (-.09)	.61 (.55)	.28 (.28)	.40 (.41)
Most Serious	.37 (.32)	.19 (.26)	.19 (.18)	-.51 (-.39)	-.23 (-.30)	-.55 (-.42)
Adult/Juvenile	-.23 (-.14)	-.01	-.00	.11 (.12)	-.07	-.23 (-.23)
Felony/Misd.	.31 (.29)	-.16 (-.15)	-.14 (-.14)	-.16 (-.17)	.11 (.11)	.27 (.22)
Inst./Express.	.01	-.16 (-.06)	.18 (.22)	.14 (.03)	.15 (.11)	.51 (.47)
Retreatism	-.09	.19 (.20)	.12 (.10)	.04	-.02	.08
Conflict	.09	.13 (.15)	.17 (.14)	.01	.01	.26 (.24)
Criminalism	.16 (.16)	.45 (.37)	.07	-.06	-.02	-.10 (-.17)
Theft	.29 (.29)	.08	-.22 (-.23)	-.05	.00	-.08
Hell-Raising	.40 (.42)	.05	-.10 (-.10)	.03	.26 (.25)	.14 (.11)
Incorrigibility	.10 (.11)	.08	-.06	.07	.10 (.10)	.09
Number of Offenses	-.61 (-.64)	-.07	.17 (.17)	.02	-.24 (-.24)	-.05
Boy-Parent Harmony				-.18 (-.18)	-.30 (-.30)	-.27 (-.28)
Dropout				.16 (.16)	.12 (.11)	.06
Fired from Job				-.07	-.06	.08

Note: The paths between achievement and delinquency may be found in chapter 7. They are comparable to the zero-order r's reported therein.
[a]Figures in parentheses indicate revised paths computed after dropping those paths less than .10 in absolute value.

Table A3-8
Model IV for the Utah Sample

	(Strain Treated as Endogenous Delinquency as Exogenous)			(Peer Identification Treated as Endogenous, with Delinquency and Strain as Exogenous)		
	Boy-Parent Harmony	Dropout	Fired from Job	Ace-in-the-Hole	Sociability	Deviance
Average Seriousness	-.63 (-.59)ᵃ	.04	.76 (.78)	.12 (.01)	-.29 (-.21)	.09
Most Serious	.21 (.22)	.23 (.25)	-.41 (-.41)	-.08	.03	.04
Adult/Juvenile	.19 (.23)	-.13 (-.09)	.04	-.05	.21 (.22)	-.03
Felony/Misd.	.09	.01	-.20 (-.21)	.03	.00	-.06
Inst./Express.	-.23 (-.19)	-.27 (-.23)	-.32 (-.23)	-.22 (-.24)	.16 (.15)	.44 (.43)
Retreatism	-.09	-.08	-.23 (-.24)	.05	.29 (.26)	.04
Conflict	.02	-.14 (-.13)	-.18 (-.13)	-.09	.09	.02
Criminalism	.17 (.14)	.21 (.27)	-.10 (-.18)	-.04	-.26 (-.30)	-.37 (-.32)
Theft	.35 (.38)	.07	.06	.12 (.14)	.27 (.22)	-.17 (-.18)
Hell-Raising	.09	.13 (.14)	.05	.05	.23 (.23)	-.04
Incorrigibility	.00	.02	.04	.03	.01	-.09
Number of Offenses	-.34 (-.32)	.05	.22	.02	-.19 (-.13)	.24 (.21)
Boy-Parent Harmony				-.17 (-.20)	-.30 (-.30)	-.26 (-.28)
Dropout				.20 (.20)	.18 (.18)	.20 (.20)
Fired from Job				-.07	-.08	-.02

Note: The paths between achievement and delinquency may be found in chapter 7. They are comparable to the zero-order *r*'s reported therein.

ᵃFigures in parentheses indicate revised paths computed after dropping those paths less than .10 in absolute value.

References

Becker, Howard S.
  1963 *Outsiders: Studies in the sociology of deviance.* New York: The Free
        Press of Glencoe.

Bell, Daniel
  1959 *The end of ideology.* Glencoe: The Free Press.

Black, Donald J., and Albert J. Reiss
  1970 Police control of juveniles. *American sociological review* 35
        (February):63-77.

Bordua, David J.
  1961 A critique of sociological interpretations of gang delinquency. *Annals
        of the American academy of political and social science* 338
        (November):120-136.
  1962 Some comments on theories of group delinquency. *Sociological inquiry*
        (Spring):245-246.

Boyle, Richard P.
  1968 On the diffusion of path analysis to sociologists. Unpublished
        manuscript.
  1970 Path analysis and ordinal data. *American journal of sociology* 75
        (January):461-480.

Burgess, Ernest W.
  1952 The economic factor in juvenile delinquency. *Journal of criminal law,
        criminology, and police science* 43 (May-June):29-42.

Call, Donald J.
  1965 Frustration and noncommitment. Ph.D. dissertation. Eugene,
        Ore.: Department of Sociology, University of Oregon.

Cartwright, Desmond, Kenneth I. Howard, and Nicholas A. Reuterman.
  1970 Multivariate analysis of gang delinquency: II. structural and dynamic
        properties of gangs. *Multivariate behavioral research* 5 (July):303-323.

Catton, William R., Jr.
  1961 The functions and dysfunctions of ethnocentrism: a theory. *Social
        problems* 8 (Winter):201-211.

Chambliss, William J.
  1967 Types of deviance and the effectiveness of legal sanctions. *Wisconsin
        law review*: 703-719.

Christensen, Ronald
  1967 *Projected percentage of U.S. population with criminal arrest and
        conviction records.* Task Force Report: Science and
        Technology:216-228. Washington, D.C.: U.S. Government Printing
        Office.

214

Cicourel, Aaron V.
1968 *The social organization of juvenile justice.* New York: John Wiley.

Clark, John P., and Larry S. Tifft
1966 Polygraph and interview validation of self-reported deviant behavior. *American sociological review* 31 (August):516-523.

Clark, John P., and Eugene P. Wenninger
1962 Socio-economic class and areas as correlates of illegal behavior among juveniles. *American sociological review* 26 (December):826-834.

Cloward, Richard A., and Lloyd E. Ohlin
1960 *Delinquency and opportunity: A theory of delinquent gangs.* New York: The Free Press.

Cohen, Albert K.
1955 *Delinquent boys: The culture of the gang.* Glencoe: The Free Press.
1959 The study of social disorganization and deviant behavior. In Robert K. Merton, Leonard Broom, and Leonard Cottrell, Jr. (eds.), *Sociology today.* New York: Basic Books.
1960 Delinquency as culturally patterned and group-supported behavior. Address to the 12th Annual Training Institute for Probation, Parole and Institutional Staff, San Francisco: Mimeographed.

Cohen, Albert K., and James F. Short, Jr.
1971 Juvenile delinquency. In Robert K. Merton and Robert A. Nisbet (eds.), *Contemporary social problems.* New York: Harcourt, Brace and World.

Cohen, Bernard
1969 The delinquency of gangs and spontaneous groups in delinquency. In Thorsten Sellin and Marvin Wolfgang (eds.), *Delinquency: Selected studies,* p. 61-111. New York: John Wiley.

Coser, Lewis A.
1962 Some functions of deviant behavior and normative flexibility. *American journal of sociology* 68 (September):172-181.

Costner, Herbert L.
1965 Criteria for measures of association. *American sociological review* 30 (June):341-353.
1969 Theory, deduction and rules of correspondence. *American journal of sociology* 75 (September):245-263.

Costner, Herbert L., and Robert K. Leik
1964 Deductions from axiomatic theory. *American sociological review* 29 (December):819-835.

Cressey, Donald R.
1964 *Delinquency, crime and differential Association.* The Hague: Martinus Nijhoff.

Dahrendorf, Rolf
1958 Out of Utopia: toward a reorientation in sociological analysis. *American journal of sociology* 67 (September):115-127.
1959 *Class and class conflict in industrial society.* Stanford: Stanford University Press.

DeFleur, Lois B.
1969 Alternative strategies for the development of delinquency theories applicable to other cultures. *Social problems* 17 (Summer):30-39.

Dennis, W.
1960 Causes of retardation among institutional children. *Journal of Genetic psychology* 19:47-59.

Dentler, Robert, and Lawrence J. Monroe
1961 Early adolescent theft. *American sociological review* 26 (October):733-743.

Deutsch, Martin, and Associates
1967 *The disadvantaged child.* New York: Basic Books.

Dirksen, Cletus
1948 *Economic factors in delinquency.* Milwaukee: Bruce Publishing Co.

Duncan, Otis Dudley
1966 Path analysis: sociological examples. *American journal of sociology* 72 (July):1-16.
1970 Path analysis: sociological examples (1970 Addenda). In H.M. Blalock (ed.), *Reader on causal models.* Chicago: Aldine Publishing Company.

Dunham, Warren H.
1958 The juvenile court: contradictory orientations in processing offenders. *Law and contemporary problems* 23 (Summer):508-527.

Durkheim, Emile
1947 *Division of labor in society.* Glencoe: The Free Press.

Eaton, Joseph W., and Kenneth Polk
1961 *Measuring delinquency: A study of probation department referrals.* Pittsburgh: University of Pittsburgh Press.

Eisenstadt, S.N.
1956 *From generation to generation.* Glencoe: The Free Press.

Elliott, Delbert S.
1966 Delinquency, school attendance and dropout. *Social problems* 13 (Winter):312.

Emerson, Robert M.
1969 *Judging delinquents: Context and process in the juvenile court.* Chicago: Aldine Publishing Co.

Empey, LaMar T.
1956 Social class and occupational aspiration: A comparison of absolute and relative measurement. *American sociological review* 21 (December):703-709.
1967 Delinquency theory and recent research. *Journal of research in crime and delinquency* 3 (January):28-41.

Empey, LaMar T., and Maynard L. Erickson
1966 Hidden delinquency and social status. *Social forces* 44 (June):546-554.

Empey, LaMar T., and Steven G. Lubeck
1968 Conformity and deviance in the "situation of company." *American sociological review* 33 (October):760-774.
1971 *The Silverlake experiment: Testing delinquency theory and community intervention.* Chicago: Aldine Publishing Co.

Empey, LaMar T., and Jerome Rabow
1961 The Provo experiment in delinquency rehabilitation. *American sociological review* 26 (October):679-696.

Erikson, Kai T.
1964 Notes on the sociology of deviance. In Howard S. Becker (ed.), *The other side*. New York: The Free Press.

Erickson, Maynard L., and LaMar T. Empey
1963 Court records, undetected delinquency and decision-making. *Journal of criminal law, criminology, and police science* 54 (December):456-469.

Erickson, Maynard L., and LaMar T. Empey
1965 Class position, peers and delinquency. *Sociology and social research* 49 (April):268-282.

Erickson, Maynard L., LaMar T. Empey, and Max L. Scott
1965 *School experiences and delinquency*. Washington D.C.: President's Commission on Juvenile Delinquency and Youth Crime.

Eynon, Thomas G., and Walter C. Reckless
1961 Companionship at delinquency onset. *The British journal of criminology* (October):167.

Fenton, Norman
1935 *The delinquent boy and the correctional school*. Claremont: Claremont Colleges Guidance Center.

Geis, Gilbert
1965 *Juvenile gangs*. President's Committee on Juvenile Delinquency. Washington, D.C.: U.S. Government Printing Office.

George, B. James
1968 *Gault and the juvenile court revolution*. Ann Arbor: Institute of Continuing Legal Education.

Gibbs, Jack
 1967 Identification of statements in theory construction. *Sociology and social research* 52 (October):72-87.

Glaser, Daniel
 1958 The sociological approach to crime and corrections. *Law and contemporary problems* 23 (Autumn):685-697.

Glaser, Daniel, Donald Kenefick, and Vincent O'Leary
 (undated) *The violent offender*. Washington, D.C.: U.S. Government Printing Office.

Glueck, Sheldon, and Eleanor T. Glueck
 1950 *Unravelling juvenile delinquency*. Cambridge: Harvard University Press.

Gold, Martin
 1963 *Status forces in delinquent boys*. Ann Arbor: University of Michigan.
 1966 Undetected delinquent behavior. *Journal of research in crime and delinquency* 3 (January):27-46.

Goldfarb, W.
 1953 The effects of early institutional care on adolescent personality. *Journal of experimental education* 12:106-129.

Goldman, Nathan
 1969 The differential selection of juvenile offenders for court appearance. In William J. Chambliss (ed.), *Crime and the legal process*, p. 264-290. New York: McGraw-Hill.

Goodman, Leo A., and William H. Kruskal
 1954 Measures of association for cross classifications. *Journal of the American statistical association*, 49 (December):732-764.

Gordon, Robert A., et al.
 1963 Values and gang delinquency. *American journal of sociology* (September):109-128.

Gould, Leroy C., and Clarence Schrag
 1962 Theory construction and prediction in juvenile delinquency. In *Proceedings of the social statistics section of the American statistical association*, p. 68-73.

Gould, R.
 1941 Some sociological determinants of goal striving. *Journal of social psychology* 13 (May):461-473.

Hardt, Robert H., and George E. Bodine
 1965 *Development of self-report instruments in delinquency research*. New York: Syracuse University Youth Development Center.

Hathaway, Starke R., Elio D. Monachesi, and Laurence A. Young
 1960 Delinquency rates and personality. *Journal of criminal law, criminology, and police science* 50 (February):439.

Healy, William, and Augusta F. Bronner
  1936 *New light on delinquency and its treatment.* New Haven: Yale University Press.

Heise, David R.
  1969 Problems in path analysis and causal inference. In Edgar F. Borgatta (ed.), *Sociological methodology*, p. 38-74. San Francisco: Jossey Bass, Inc.

Hirschi, Travis
  1969 *Causes of delinquency.* Berkeley: University of California Press.

Hollingshead, A.B.
  1949 *Elmtown's youth.* New York: John Wiley and Sons.

Hunt, J.M.
  1961 *Intelligence and experience.* New York: Ronald Press.

Joint Commission on Correctional Manpower and Training
  1968 *The public looks at crime and corrections.* Washington, D.C.: U.S. Government Printing Office.

Klein, Malcolm W.
  1970 *Police processing of juvenile offenders: toward the development of juvenile system rates.* Criminal Justice Planning Projects. Los Angeles County Sub-Regional Board, California Council on Criminal Justice. Part III.
  1971 *Street gangs and street workers.* New York: Prentice-Hall.

Klein, Malcolm W. (ed.)
  1967 *Juvenile gangs in context.* Englewood Cliffs: Prentice-Hall.
  1970 *Some remarks on gangs.* Delinquency Prevention Report:3-6. Washington, D.C.: U.S. Department of Health Education and Welfare.

Klein, Malcolm W., and Lois Y. Crawford
  1967 Groups, gangs, and cohesiveness. *Journal of research in crime and delinquency* 3 (January):63-75.

Kobrin, Solomon
  1951 The conflict of values in delinquency areas. *American sociological review* 16 (October):653-661.

Kobrin, Solomon, Joseph Puntil, and Emil Peluso.
  1967 Criteria of status among street corner groups. *Journal of research in crime and delinquency* 4 (January):98-118.

Kvaraceus, William C.
  1945 *Juvenile delinquency and the school.* New York: World Book Co.
  1964 World-wide story. *The Unesco courier* 12 (May)

Lagache, D.
  1950 *Psycho-criminogeneses: Tenth general report.* Paris: 2nd International Congress of Criminology.

Land, Kenneth C.
  1969 Principles of path analysis. In Edgar F. Borgatta (ed.), *Sociological methodology*, p. 3-37. San Francisco: Jossey Bass, Inc.

Lemert, Edwin M.
  1951 *Social pathology*. New York: McGraw-Hill Book Co.
  1970 Juvenile justice. . . Quest and Realities. In Abraham S. Blumberg (ed.), *The scales of justice*, pp. 141-162. Chicago: Aldine Publishing Co.

Lofland, John
  1969 *Deviance and identity*. Englewood Cliffs, N.J.: Prentice-Hall.

Lohman, Joseph D.
  1957 *Juvenile delinquency*. Cook County, Illinois: Office of the Sheriff.

Martin, John M., Joseph P. Fitzpatrick, and Robert E. Gould
  1968 *The analysis of delinquent behavior: A structural approach*. New York: Random House.

Martin, Richard I., and Malcolm W. Klein
  1965 A comparative analysis of four measures of delinquency seriousness. Los Angeles: University of Southern California. Mimeographed.

Matza, David
  1964 *Delinquency and drift*. New York: John Wiley and Sons.

Matza, David, and Gresham M. Sykes
  1961 Juvenile delinquency and subterranean values. *American sociological review* 26 (October):712-719.

McEachern, A.W., and Riva Bauzer
  1967 Factors related to dispositions in juvenile police contacts. In Malcolm W. Klein (ed.), *Juvenile gangs in context*, p. 148-160. Englewood Cliffs, N.J.:Prentice-Hall.

McKay, Henry D.
  1949 The neighborhood and child conduct. *Annals of the American academy of political and social science* 261 (January).

Mead, George Herbert
  1928 The psychology of punitive justice. *American journal of sociology* 23:591.

Mensh, Ivan N.
  1963 Personality studies of mentally ill offenders. *The mentally ill offender: Variations in approaches, 2nd symposium*. Atascadero, Calif.: State Hospital:21-28.

Merton, Robert K.
  1957 *Social theory and social structure*. Glencoe: The Free Press.

Miller, Walter B.
  1958 Lower-class culture as a generating milieu of gang delinquency. *Journal of social issues* 14 (Summer):5-19.

Monahan, Thomas P.
  1957 Family status and the delinquent child: a reappraisal and some new findings. *Social forces* 35 (March):257.

Morris, Norval
  1966 Impediments to penal reform. *University of Chicago law review* 33 (Summer):627-656.

Murphy, Fred J., Mary M. Shirley, and Helen L. Witmer
  1946 The incidence of hidden delinquency. *American journal of orthopsychiatry* 16 (October):686-696.

Nye, F. Ivan, and James F. Short, Jr.
  1957 Scaling delinquency behavior. *American sociological review* 22 (June):326-331.
  1958 Reported behavior as a criterion of deviant behavior. *Social problems* 5 (Winter):207-213.

Nye, F. Ivan, James F. Short, Jr., and V. J. Olsen
  1958 Socio-economic status and delinquent behavior. *American journal of sociology* 63 (January):318-329.

Ohlin, Lloyd E.
  1970 *A situational approach to delinquency prevention.* Washington, D.C.: U.S. Government Printing Office.

Perlman, I. Richard
  1965 *Juvenile court statistics, 1964.* Children's Bureau Statistical Series, No. 83. Washington, D.C.: U.S. Government Printing Office.

Piliavin, Irving, and Scott Briar
  1964 Police encounters with juveniles. *The American journal of sociology* 70 (September):206-214.

Platt, Anthony
  1969 The rise of the child-saving movement: a study in social policy and correctional reform. *The annals of the American academy of political and social science*, 381 (January):21-38.

Polk, Kenneth
  1967 Urban social areas and delinquency. *Social problems* 14 (Winter):320-325.

Polk, Kenneth, and David S. Halferty
  1966 Adolescence, commitment and delinquency. *Journal of research in crime and delinquency* 4 (July):82-96.

Porterfield, Austin L.
  1946 *Youth in trouble.* Fort Worth: Leo Potishman Foundation.

President's Commission on Law Enforcement and Administration of Justice
  1967 *The challenge of crime in a free society.* Washington, D.C.:U.S. Government Printing Office.

1967 *Task force report: Corrections.* Washington, D.C.: U.S. Government Printing Office.

Quay, Herbert C., and Laurence Blumer
1963 Dimensions of delinquent behavior. *Journal of social psychology* 51:272-277.

Quinney, Richard
1970 *The social reality of crime.* Boston: Little, Brown and Co.

Rapoport, Anatol
1968 Foreword to Walter Buckley (ed.), *Modern systems research for the behavioral scientist.* Chicago: Aldine Publishing Co.

Reiss, Albert J. and A. Lewis Rhodes
1961 The distribution of juvenile delinquency in the social class structure. *American sociological review* 23 (October):730-732.
1963 Status deprivation and delinquent behavior. *The sociological quarterly* 4 (Spring):135-147.

Rivera, Ramon J., and James F. Short, Jr.
1967 Occupational goals: a comparative analysis. In Malcolm W. Klein (ed.), *Juvenile gangs in context: Theory, research, and action.* Englewood Cliffs: Prentice-Hall.

Robin, Gerald D.
1967 Gang member delinquency in Philadelphia. In Malcolm W. Klein and Barbara G. Myerhoff (eds.), *Juvenile gangs in context*, pp. 15-24. Englewood Cliffs, N.J.: Prentice-Hall.

Robinson, W.S.
1950 Ecological correlations and the behavior of individuals. *American sociological review* 15 (June):351-357.

Schrag, Clarence
1967 Elements of theoretical analysis in sociology. In Llewellyn Gross (ed.), *Sociological theory: Inquiries and paradigms.* New York: Harper and Row, Inc.

Schussler, Karl and Donald R. Cressey
1950 Personality characteristics of criminals. *American journal of sociology* 55 (March):476-484.

Schwartz, Richard D., and Jerome H. Skolnick
1962 Two studies of legal stigma. *Social problems* 10 (Fall):133-142.

Scott, Peter
1956 Gangs and delinquent groups in London. *The British journal of delinquency* 7 (July):4-26.

Sellin, Thorsten, and Marvin E. Wolfgang
1964 *The measurement of delinquency.* New York: John Wiley.

Shafer, Walter E., Carol Olexa, and Kenneth Polk
  1970 Programmed for social class: tracking in high school. *Transaction* 7 (October):39-46.

Shannon, Lyle W.
  1968 *Juvenile delinquency in Madison and Racine.* (mimeographed report). University of Iowa: Department of Sociology and Anthropology, 67-96.

Shaw, Clifford
  1929 *Delinquency areas.* Chicago: University of Chicago Press.
  1940 *The jack-roller: A delinquent boy's own story.* Chicago: University of Chicago Press.

Shaw, Clifford and Henry D. McKay
  1931 *Social factors in juvenile delinquency.* Report on the Causes of Crime. Washington, D.C.: U.S. Government Printing Office.
  1942 *Juvenile delinquency in urban areas.* Chicago: University of Chicago Press.

Short, James F., Jr.
  1960 The sociocultural context of delinquency. *Crime and delinquency* (October):365-375.
  1963 Street corner groups and patterns of delinquency: A progress report. *The American Catholic sociological review* 24 (Spring):13-32.
  1965 Social structure and group processes in explanation of gang delinquency. In Muzafer and Sherif (eds.), *Problems of youth*, p. 158-188. Chicago: Aldine Publishing Co.

Short, James F., and Ivan Nye
  1958 Reported behavior as a criterion of deviant behavior. *Social problems* 5 (Winter):207-213.

Short, James F., Jr., and Fred L. Strodtbeck
  1965 *Group process and gang delinquency.* Chicago: University of Chicago Press.

Shulman, Harry M.
  1949 The family and juvenile delinquency. *Annals of the American academy of political and social science* 26 (January):21-31.

Skolnick, Jerome H.
  1966 *Justice without trial.* New York: John Wiley and Sons.

Spergel, Irving
  1964 *Racketville, slumtown, haulburg: An exploratory study of delinquent subcultures.* Chicago: University of Chicago Press.

Strodtbeck, Fred L., and James F. Short, Jr.
  1964 Aleatory risks vs. short-run hedonism in explanation of gang action. *Social problems* 11 (Fall):127-140.

Tannenbaum, Frank
1938 *Crime and the community*. New York: Columbia University Press.

Terry, Robert M.
1967 The screening of juvenile offenders. *Journal of criminal law, criminology, and police science* 58 (June):173-181.

Thrasher, Frederic M.
1927 *The gang*. Chicago: University of Chicago Press.
1963 *The gang*. (revised edition) Chicago: University of Chicago Press.

Toby, Jackson
1957 The differential impact of family disorganization. *American sociological review* 22 (October):505-515.
1964 Is punishment necessary? *Journal of criminal law, criminology, and police science* 55 (September):332-337.

Wattenberg, William W., and J.J. Balistrieri
1950 Gang membership and juvenile delinquency. *American sociological review* 15 (December):744-752.

Westly, William A.
1953 Violence and the police. *The American journal of sociology* 49 (August):34-41.

Wheeler, Stanton S., and Leonard S. Cottrell, Jr.
1966 *Juvenile delinquency: Its prevention and control*. New York: Russell Sage Foundation.

Whyte, William F.
1955 *Street corner society*. Chicago: Chicago University Press.

Wilson, James Q.
1970 The police and the delinquent in two cities. In Peter G. Garabedian (ed.), *Becoming delinquent: Young offenders and the correctional system*. p. 111-117. Chicago: Aldine Publishing Co.

Zetterberg, Hans L.
1954 *On theory and verification in sociology*. Stockholm:,Almquist and Wiksell.
1963 *On theory and verification in sociology*. (A much revised edition). Totowa, New Jersey: Bedminster Press.
1965 *On theory and verification in sociology*. (Third enlarged edition). Totowa, New Jersey: Bedminster Press.

About the Authors

LaMar T. Empey received his Ph.D. in sociology from Washington State University. He is currently Chairman of the Sociology Department at the University of Southern California. He has been Director of the Youth Studies Center, University of Southern California; Director of the Provo Experiment; Director of the Silverlake Experiment; Visiting Professor of Criminology at the University of California, Berkeley. He has served as a consultant to the President's Committee on Law Enforcement and Administration of Justice, to the President's Committee on Juvenile Delinquency and Youth Crime and to other commissions of a similar nature. Professor Empey has contributed numerous articles to the scientific literature: His books include *The Silverlake Experiment* with Professor Lubeck as co-author; *Alternatives to Incarceration*; and (as co-author) *The Time Game: Two Views of a Prison*.

Steven G. Lubeck received his Ph.D. in sociology at the University of Southern California. He is presently an assistant professor at Washington State University and has served as a research associate at the Youth Studies Center, University of Southern California. Besides contributing articles to the scientific literature, Professor Lubeck is co-author with Professor Empey on the *Silverlake Experiment*.